Ed:

Research Handbook on Entrepreneurial Finance

Edited by

Javed G. Hussain
Birmingham City University, UK

Jonathan M. Scott
Teesside University, UK

Edward Elgar
PUBLISHING

Cheltenham, UK • Northampton, MA, USA

Published by
Edward Elgar Publishing Limited
The Lypiatts
15 Lansdown Road
Cheltenham
Glos GL50 2JA
UK

Edward Elgar Publishing, Inc.
William Pratt House
9 Dewey Court
Northampton
Massachusetts 01060
USA

A catalogue record for this book
is available from the British Library

Library of Congress Control Number: 2015950273

This book is available electronically in the **Elgar**online
Business subject collection
DOI 10.4337/9781783478798

ISBN 978 1 78347 878 1 (cased)
ISBN 978 1 78347 879 8 (eBook)

Typeset by Servis Filmsetting Ltd, Stockport, Cheshire
Printed and bound in Great Britain by TJ International Ltd, Padstow

Contents

Contributors

Michèle Akoorie is Professor in the Department of Strategy and Human Resource Management, Waikato Management School, University of Waikato, New Zealand.

Haya Al-Dajani is Associate Professor (Reader) in Entrepreneurship, Futures Entrepreneurship Centre, Plymouth Business School, Plymouth University, UK.

Robert Baldock is Senior Research Fellow at Centre for Enterprise and Economic Development Research (CEEDR), Middlesex University Business School, UK.

Zografia Bika is Senior Lecturer in Entrepreneurship and Small Business Management at Norwich Business School, University of East Anglia, UK.

Tiago Botelho is Lecturer in Business Strategy at Norwich Business School, University of East Anglia, UK; and PhD researcher at the Adam Smith Business School, University of Glasgow, UK.

Candida G. Brush is Vice Provost of Global Entrepreneurial Leadership, Franklin W. Olin Chair in Entrepreneurship, Babson College, Wellesley, MA, USA.

David Deakins is Honorary Researcher, Institute for Entrepreneurship and Economic Development, Lancaster University, UK; and former Director of New Zealand Centre for SME Research, Massey University, New Zealand.

Dilek Demirbaş is Professor in International Trade and Business, YBU Business School, Ankara, Turkey.

Safa Demirbaş is Ministerial Advisor for the Ministry of Customs and Trade, Ankara, Turkey.

Linda F. Edelman is Professor of Strategic Management at Bentley University, Waltham MA, USA.

Richard T. Harrison is Professor in Entrepreneurship and Innovation at the University of Edinburgh Business School, UK.

Sibylle Heilbrunn is Dean of Faculty of Social Sciences and Humanities at the Kinneret Academic College on the Sea of Galilee, Israel.

Javed G. Hussain is Professor of Entrepreneurial Finance at Birmingham City Business School, Birmingham City University, UK.

Nonna Kushnirovich is Head of the Economic Studies for Non-Economists at the School of Economics and Business Administration, Ruppin Academic Center, Israel.

Jun Li is Senior Lecturer of Entrepreneurship and Innovation at Essex Business School, University of Essex, UK.

Ciarán Mac an Bhaird is Lecturer of Finance at Fiontar (Enterprise), Dublin City University, Republic of Ireland.

Samia Mahmood is Senior Lecturer in Accounting and Finance at University of Wolverhampton Business School, University of Wolverhampton, UK.

Tatiana S. Manolova is Associate Professor of Management, Bentley University, Waltham, MA, USA.

Colin Mason is Professor of Entrepreneurship at the Adam Smith Business School, University of Glasgow, UK.

Harry Matlay is Editor of *Journal of Small Business and Enterprise Development*.

Miwako Nitani is Assistant Professor of Finance at Telfer School of Management, University of Ottawa, Canada.

David North is Professor of Regional Development at CEEDR, Middlesex University Business School, UK.

Indu Peiris is Lecturer at the Open Polytechnic, Wellington, New Zealand.

Allan Riding is Professor of Finance at Telfer School of Management, University of Ottawa, Canada.

Navjot Sandhu is Senior Lecturer in Finance at Birmingham City Business School, Birmingham City University, UK.

Jonathan M. Scott is Reader in Entrepreneurship and Head of the Centre for Strategy & Leadership, Teesside University, UK.

Paresha Sinha is Senior Lecturer in International Management at Waikato Management School, University of Waikato, New Zealand.

Madina Subalova is PhD researcher at Norwich Business School, University of East Anglia, UK.

Steve Talbot is Senior Lecturer in Economics and Enterprise at the School of Business and Enterprise, University of the West of Scotland, UK.

Geoff Whittam is Reader in the School for Business and Society at Glasgow Caledonian University, UK.

Foreword
David J. Storey

I am delighted to have been asked to contribute the Foreword to this book for three interconnected reasons. The first is because concerns over entrepreneurial finance are long-standing. They have been acknowledged, at least in the UK, since the last truly global recession of the 1930s, when the MacMillan Committee, reporting in 1931 (para 404) described:

> The great difficulty experienced by smaller and medium-sized business in raising the capital which they may from time to time require.

The fact that almost the same phrasing could be used 85 years later points to the continuing importance of the topic and our inability to solve the problem even when macro-economic conditions are benign.

It might seem self-evident that access to finance is critical to the success of new and small firms, but much of the current entrepreneurship literature could lead the unwary reader to assume the key to entrepreneurial success is the individual. By focussing so heavily upon their talent to identify and exploit opportunities the risk is that the key enabling role of finance is underplayed. This is a mistake since the key role of the financial sector in any economy is to support those entrepreneurs with talent and to avoid funding those without. But funding the good, and rejecting the bad, is considerably trickier than this simple statement implies. The core problem is that the small firm marketplace is one where information is difficult to acquire. To help assess the financial viability of public companies or governments there is an army of analysts, brokers and financial journalists whose task is to examine both public and private information relating to factors influencing performance. No such information is available about the hairdresser or window-cleaner who is about to start in business for the first time. If the individual has a bank account then their bank may be able to reach a judgement on whether they seem to be trustworthy and competent in their private financial management – but this will be only an imperfect guide as to how they will perform as a business owner. The challenge facing every government is to create a financial system which incentivizes the providers of finance to collect sufficient information to enable it to deliver the appropriate financial package to its customers.

The second reason why these essays are important is that these issues, albeit in different ways, are found in countries with very different levels of economic development. The Editors emphasize that a novelty of the book is the diversity of countries examined – from high income countries such as the US, Canada and the UK at one extreme to Pakistan and Kazakhstan at the other. Most helpfully, in their Introduction, they provide a table that captures that diversity – and one that should be mandatory in all editorial volumes!

The third focus that makes this book 'special' is the Global Financial Crisis. It is unlikely to be a coincidence that the access to finance for new and small firms becomes a matter of political concern during times of economic crisis. In part this is because denying such firms access to finance leads to business closures, unemployment and a loss of output in the economy. It also means that such firms will find it more difficult to lead the economy out of recession. And while that is true it remains the case that, even in developed economies, the SME finance market remains opaque.

The policy lesson, it seems to me, that emerges from these chapters is that the financial marketplaces where new and small firms thrive are the ones where the sources of finance are as diverse as the new and small firms themselves. Diversity is to be welcomed. These sources of finance have to include venture capital for the tiny proportion of technology-based firms that are found, even in developed countries. But for every technology-based venture there are thousands of new and small firms requiring more mundane sources to facilitate their cashflow and so give them a chance to survive. Factoring, invoice discounting, trade credit appear to be currently of less interest to the research community than, for example, crowdfunding, but they are critical to oiling the wheels of a financial system in which new and small firms can prosper. My casual observation is that diversity and choice characterize a well-functioning financial system and that diversity is well captured in these readings.

David J. Storey
Professor of Enterprise, University of Sussex

Acknowledgements

Entrepreneurship, entrepreneurial finance and small and medium-sized enterprises (SMEs) are the cornerstone of a functioning market economy that attempts to support both social and economic well-being and development. To this end, a great many people, the chapter contributors and the publisher have helped us greatly with all phases of producing this book.

We would like to acknowledge the support and encouragement of our families, friends, and colleagues and students at our respective institutions. Last but not least, it has been a privilege to work with Francine O'Sullivan, the commissioning editor, and Aisha Bushby, and the rest of their incredible team at Edward Elgar Publishing Ltd in assisting us with the production of this handbook.

Responsibility for all errors and omissions remain solely ours.

Javed G. Hussain   Jonathan M. Scott
Birmingham City University   Teesside University

1. Introduction: entrepreneurial finance in context in the twenty-first century
Jonathan M. Scott and Javed G. Hussain

Entrepreneurial finance has, and continues to be, a major avenue for entrepreneurship research and scholarly inquiry (Storey, 1994) because of the changing nature of the constituent empirical phenomena and theories, especially in light of the Global Financial Crisis (GFC) and newly emergent forms of innovative financing models such as microfinance and crowdfunding. Accordingly, this handbook draws comprehensively upon the current cutting edge theories, knowledge, research findings and analysis of the interaction between small and medium-sized enterprises (SMEs), entrepreneurs, and financial institutions globally. As well as including regional and international perspectives through research that deals with the business environment in the United Kingdom (UK), Europe, North America, the Middle East, Oceania, and Central, East and South Asia, it is augmented by deeper insights into the implications for practitioners (including SMEs, entrepreneurs and financial institutions) and policymakers. Its constituent chapters thus offer novel and unique contextualized theoretical and empirical insights and contributions (Welter, 2011; Zahra, 2007; Zahra et al., 2014).

In this introductory chapter we highlight the novel contributions of each chapter, as well as their method(s), key findings(s) and, finally, we conclude by offering some future directions for research into entrepreneurial finance across different distinctive spatial, sociocultural, political and economic development contexts. The handbook has been structured in such a way so as to provide four discrete 'bundles' of chapters with a differential focus upon various cutting-edge research topics and a mix of countries with both developed and emerging economies at different and distinctive stages of economic development (Porter, 1990; Porter et al., 2002; Amorós and Bosma, 2014).

Across the broad spectrum of research topics related to entrepreneurial finance that are covered in the handbook, rather than dividing this volume into sections, we have opted instead to group together – in four discrete bundles – sets of chapters from similar locations in terms of their broad level of economic development (that is, either developed or emerging economies). As a result of this rather innovative, though some would say idiosyncratic, approach to structuring the handbook, the volume commences with the first bundle that comprises three chapters focusing on various issues of entrepreneurial finance in Western developed economies. Hence Talbot, Mac an Bhaird and Whittam (Chapter 2) investigate credit unions as a potential source of start-up finance in the UK; Deakins (Chapter 3) conducts a general review of entrepreneurial finance in New Zealand; and Nitani and Riding (Chapter 4) consider internationalization and entrepreneurial finance in Canada.

Steve Talbot, Ciarán Mac an Bhaird and Geoff Whittam (Chapter 2) investigate recent policy proposals in the UK to utilize credit unions as a new source of finance for entrepreneurial new ventures by undertaking qualitative interviews with Chief Executive Officers (CEOs) of credit unions. Driven by new laws that would make such financial innovation possible and perhaps even feasible – if not necessarily desirable – Talbot et al. offer some reasons for the low levels of credit union lending to SMEs and, therefore, make some helpful suggestions for ways forward.

Next David Deakins (Chapter 3) draws on qualitative interviews of technology-based small firms to provide a case study of New Zealand as an example of a geographically peripheral country which has been rather isolated from the effects of the GFC, but has underdeveloped sources of equity capital and is, therefore, a fascinating laboratory for research into entrepreneurial finance.

A powerful mixed methods study in the context of Canada from Miwako Nitani and Allan Riding (Chapter 4) addresses how portfolio firms utilize post-investment venture capital (VC) to effect internationalization and how the value of this activity can be measured. Focusing on an intervention by an export credit agency, they make a number of novel empirical observations in connection with risk, contacts and intelligence and legitimacy (which they term 'accreditation').

The second of our four bundles then provides insights into entrepreneurial finance in two[1] emerging economies: capital structure and pecking order in Turkey by Demirbaş and Demirbaş (Chapter 5); and indigenous exports and networks for resource acquisition in the Sri Lankan tea industry by Peiris, Akoorie and Sinha (Chapter 6). Dilek Demirbaş and Safa Demirbaş (Chapter 5) undertook a literature review to examine the capital structure of SMEs in Turkey and, in so doing, they find that, in line with studies in more developed country contexts, Turkish SMEs also adopt the 'pecking order' of internal or family/friends sources of finance before seeking external finance.

Indu Peiris, Michèle Akoorie and Paresha Sinha (Chapter 6) conducted case studies of Sri Lankan tea exporters to identify how they have utilized their networks in order to acquire resources as part of their internationalization process. They highlight their key contributions to be related to their unique contextualization (the Sri Lankan tea sector); utilizing case studies – rather than the usual positivist approach – to explore the *process* of bootstrapping; confirming how bootstrapping contributes to performance; and identifying the temporal specificity of bootstrapping.

The third bundle comprises four chapters on entrepreneurial finance in developed countries with Mason, Harrison and Botelho (Chapter 7) examining business angel exits in the UK; Baldock and North (Chapter 8) investigating the finance gap for innovative SMEs and the role of UK government VC funds; Brush, Edelman and Manolova (Chapter 9) exploring investment readiness and entrepreneurial team diversity in the United States (US); and Heilbrunn and Kushnirovich (Chapter 10) studying the financing patterns of entrepreneurial minorities and migrants in Israel.

Colin Mason, Richard T. Harrison and Tiago Botelho (Chapter 7), drawing upon interview evidence and a review of secondary data, observe that business angels do not adopt an 'exit-centric approach' to their investments. Their main recommendation is that further research and policy intervention/support is required.

Robert Baldock and David North (Chapter 8) investigate the government's VC funds and the finance gap that exist for innovative SMEs. Their mixed method surveys of Hybrid Venture Capital Fund (HVCF) recipients (demand side) and fund managers (supply side) show, first, that the gap in equity finance may stunt innovative SMEs' growth. Indeed, while government can contribute to filling the gap, 'over-engineering' should be avoided. They conclude that exits should be planned for, and timely follow-on funding should be factored in, so that optimal growth and exit can be achieved.

Candida G. Brush, Linda F. Edelman and Tatiana S. Manolova (Chapter 9) studied investment readiness and entrepreneurial team diversity drawing upon a large quantitative survey of firms. Although diverse top management teams (TMTs) demonstrated a higher degree of investment readiness, TMT diversity alone was not responsible for increasing the possibility that the new start-up would even enter the 'administrative review stage' of the process by which angel investors select investees.

Sybille Heilbrunn and Nonna Kushnirovich (Chapter 10) examine financing patterns and social stratification among entrepreneurial minorities (for example, Arabs and Palestinians) and migrants (for example, Former Soviet Union and Ethiopian), utilizing a quantitative survey. As well as identifying a number of variations in financing patterns between minority and majority entrepreneurs, most significantly they found that social stratification 'encounters' entrepreneurship at different intersections, particularly in terms of educational and institutional barriers – and hence their social class – that thus impact upon their ability to obtain finance.

The fourth and final bundle of chapters on emerging economies comprises the final four chapters in the handbook, commencing with Li's (Chapter 11) consideration of the equity funding gap for technological entrepreneurs in China. Then Sandhu, Hussain and Matlay (Chapter 12) conduct a study of the role of informal lenders in financing small/marginal farmers in the Punjab region, India. In the penultimate chapter Subalova, Al-Dajani and Bika (Chapter 13) consider microfinance and diversity in Kazakhstan. Finally, Hussain, Mahmood and Scott (Chapter 14) examine microfinance, gender and poverty alleviation in the Punjab region of Pakistan.

Following the earlier chapters on venture capital and more informal sources of equity finance such as business angels, Jun Li (Chapter 11) utilizes interviews, case studies and documentary evidence review to investigate government-supported Venture Capital Guiding Funds (VCGFs) in China, providing fascinating evidence on the contextual drivers for public VC in China (primarily associated with a finance gap), the design of such publicly backed VC interventions and their overall impact. Although we know much about VC in the Western context, Li's chapter is hence contextually novel.

Navjot Sandhu, Javed G. Hussain and Harry Matlay (Chapter 12) use interviews to explore informal lending to small/marginal farmers in the Punjab, India. In so doing, they unveil some unique contextually novel insights, including particularly distinctive types of informal lenders such as the retail merchants (*arthiyas*), and focus upon the actual practice of lending (in terms of the process of decision-making), and how these are determined by cultural, human capital, reputational and other largely culturally determined contextual factors. Their main recommendation is a rather interventionist, and so perhaps controversial, one: to regulate informal lenders in India. Discuss.

Madina Subalova, Haya Al-Dajani and Zografia Bika (Chapter 13) investigate how microfinance contributes to firm growth in Kazakhstan, drawing upon interview evidence from both key stakeholders from microfinance institutions (MFIs) and entrepreneurs/SMEs who access MFI funding. They find differential capital structures, evaluative criteria and customer bases (in other words, investees in terms of the characteristics of entrepreneurs, for example, level of income, that they invest in) and offer unique theoretical and empirical contextualization by focusing upon this distinctive Central Asian, FSU emerging economy and the important role of MFIs in driving growth.

Finally, Javed G. Hussain, Samia Mahmood and Jonathan M. Scott (Chapter 14) examine how microloans can reduce both financial and human poverty for low-income women and their wider households in the context of the Punjab, Pakistan. Utilizing a binary logistic model to analyse their quantitative survey data, Hussain et al. reveal that financial poverty is, indeed, alleviated by microloans (especially where spouses act jointly as household heads) – whereas the impact on human poverty is much more tenuous and limited (with loan size being insignificant, but with human poverty being considerably more likely to be reduced for larger rather than smaller families).

ENTREPRENEURIAL FINANCE IN CONTEXT: CONCLUDING THOUGHTS AND FUTURE DIRECTIONS

These chapters investigate contextually a myriad of themes from the domain of entrepreneurial finance (Table 1.1) across diverse spatial and economic development contexts. Instead of providing a concluding chapter, we offer future research avenues here. Future research could explore the following key issues. First, now that we know more about why credit unions are 'reluctant' to lend to SMEs and in particular to smaller businesses because of the potential risk to their business models and various other issues (Talbot et al., Chapter 2), further research could explore how – and more importantly if – these perceptional barriers and the limitations of the credit unions' extant business models could be overcome in order to enable them to lend to SMEs. While it might well be the case that the barriers are actually insurmountable, nonetheless introducing credit unions as a novel source of lending to small firms is to be welcomed and perhaps should have its 'proof of concept' tested to breaking point to establish whether there is any way that it can be implemented (through, for example, learning from exemplars of good practice which have surmounted these barriers).

Second, to what extent can we learn from highly contextualized research of a 'unique environment' such as New Zealand (Deakins, Chapter 3) that is extremely positive as a place to 'Do Business' and has not been as ravaged by the GFC to anywhere near the extent as the US, UK and elsewhere have been? Future research could offer detailed, longitudinal comparative perspectives by comparing and contrasting particular entrepreneurial phenomena (theoretical concepts related, in this case, to entrepreneurial finance) in New Zealand to other locations with unique spatial and developmental contexts. Hence currently 'taken for granted' concepts and models could be stress-tested through focused micro-level research that could test their validity.

Table 1.1 Chapters: geography, themes, method(s) and key finding(s)

Ec Dev	Chapter: Authors	Geo	Theme	Method(s)	Key Finding(s)
D	2. Talbot, Mac an Bhaird and Whittam	UK	Credit unions Start-up finance	Qualitative interviews	Reluctance to lend to SMEs and other risks, for example, to business model reduces the level of lending by credit unions.
D	3. Deakins	NZ	Finance (general)	Qualitative interviews	Relatively sheltered from GFC but underdeveloped sources of equity capital.
D	4. Nitani and Riding	CA	Internationalization Export credit agency	Qualitative interviews and quantitative data analysis	Risks of SME internationalization are 'moderated' by investors, as well as providing the SME with contacts, intelligence – and legitimacy ('accreditation') with various key stakeholders.
E	5. Demirbaş and Demirbaş	TU	Financing Capital structure	Literature review	In line with studies in more developed country contexts, Turkish SMEs also adopt the 'pecking order' of internal or family/ friends sources of finance before seeking external finance.
E	6. Peiris, Akoorie and Sinha	SL	Internationalization Networks	Qualitative case studies	Explore the process of, and motivations for, the use of networks (social capital) in order to bootstrap. Highlight its contribution to performance and its temporal specificity.
D	7. Mason, Harrison and Botelho	UK	Business angels Exits	Interviews and review of secondary data	Angels do not adopt an 'exit-centric approach' to their investments. Further research and policy intervention/ support is required.

D	8. Baldock and North	UK	Government VC funds Finance gap Innovative SMEs	Mixed method surveys of HVCF recipients and fund managers	Gap in equity finance may stunt innovative SMEs' growth. Find that government can contribute to filling the gap; 'over-engineering' should be avoided; exits should be planned for, and timely follow-on funding should be factored in, so that optimal growth and exit can be achieved.
D	9. Brush, Edelman and Manolova	US	Investment readiness Entre. team diversity Angel investment	Quantitative survey	Although diverse top management teams (TMTs) more investment ready, TMT diversity alone was not responsible for increasing the possibility that the new start-up would even enter the 'administrative review stage' of the process by which angel investors select investees.
D	10. Heilbrunn and Kushnirovich	IS	Financing patterns Social stratification Minorities, migrants	Quantitative survey	Various variations in financing patterns between minority and majority entrepreneurs. Social stratification 'encounters' entrepreneurship at different intersections (for example, education and institutions) – and hence social class – that impact upon their ability to obtain finance.
E	11. Li	CN	Equity funding gap Tech entrepreneurship	Interviews, case studies and documentary evidence review	Provides evidence on contextual drivers for public VC in China, the design of publicly backed VC interventions and their overall impact.

Table 1.1 (continued)

Ec Dev	Chapter: Authors	Geo	Theme	Method(s)	Key Finding(s)
E	12. Sandhu, Hussain and Matlay	IN	Informal lenders Small/marginal farmers	Interview evidence	Distinctive types of informal lenders (for example, retail merchants (*arthiyas*)). Evidence on the practice of lending, and how influenced by largely culturally determined contextual factors.
E	13. Subalova, Al-Dajani and Bika	KA	Diversity Microfinance	Interview evidence	Differential capital structures, evaluative criteria and customer bases. Illustrate how MFIs contribute to firm growth.
E	14. Hussain, Mahmood and Scott	PA	Microfinance Gender Poverty alleviation	Quantitative survey using binary logistic model analysis	Financial poverty alleviated by microloans – esp. where spouses are jointly household heads. Impact on human poverty more tenuous and limited: loan size insignificant; human poverty more likely to be reduced for larger rather than smaller families.

Notes:
Ec Dev – level of economic development – D: Developed; E: Emerging.
In all cases, the developing economies are innovation-driven economies, using Porter's categorization (Porter, 1990; Porter et al., 2002). The emerging economies have been identified as a mix of efficiency-driven and factor-driven economies (Amorós and Bosma, 2014), but some are in transition from one phase to another.

8

Third, detailed policy-relevant research is clearly needed to investigate further the role that interventions such as the Export Development Corporation (and specifically its *Connect* program) as explored by Nitani and Riding (Chapter 4) can have in supporting SMEs to internationalize and, in particular, to enable them to obtain finance and other forms of capital (such as social capital – contacts) and legitimacy to enable this activity to succeed.

Fourth, can we distinguish genuinely unique aspects of entrepreneurial finance in SMEs in emerging economies? Hence, as Demirbaş and Demirbaş (Chapter 5) found that the pecking order hypothesis applied to Turkish SMEs just as to those from developed contexts, highly contextualized novel research studies are needed in such countries to explore at a more micro level the phenomena related to entrepreneurial finance and to identify unique and distinctive aspects that can be used to build rigorous new theories (Welter, 2011; Zahra, 2007; Zahra et al., 2014). In this sense, we call for more focused empirical research taking the approach of Chapters 6 (Peiris et al.), 12 (Sandhu et al.), 13 (Subalova et al.) and 14 (Hussain et al.) that adopt a contextualized, less Western-centric lens to approach the phenomena being investigated. Consequently, there are significant opportunities to conduct, respectively, future research in emerging economies on: the role of networks in internationalization; informal lending whether to farmers or other types of entrepreneurs or small-scale micro-enterprise founders; and the diversity of the microfinance sector in Central Asia and elsewhere. Similarly, marginalized, minority or migrant entrepreneurs within highly developed parts of, for example, the Middle East such as Israel (Heilbrunn and Kushnirovich, Chapter 10), ought to be subject to further detailed, contextualized research studies.

Fifth, and finally, in terms of the other chapters that focused on more developed countries, there is a clear need for further research that addresses key gaps in the extant literature in terms of business angel exit and the 'exit-centric' approach (Mason et al., Chapter 7), the finance gap facing innovative SMEs (Baldock and North, Chapter 8), the impact of investment readiness and entrepreneurial team diversity on angel investment (Brush et al., Chapter 9) and financing patterns and social stratification of minorities and migrants (Heilbrunn and Kushnirovich, Chapter 10). Indeed, while we might categorize China as an 'emerging' economy (and considering the crisis in its stock market in 2015 and its Government's command-and-control approach to achieve a correction), for all intents and purposes China is rapidly moving from the efficiency-driven to the innovation-driven (Porter, 1990; Porter et al., 2002) stage and we need further detailed research into VC – especially that which supports high-growth firms – in China (Li, Chapter 11) to illustrate how in this specific context entrepreneurial finance plays a major contributory role not only to its particular positive impacts upon, and outcomes for, SMEs and entrepreneurs, but also to economic development and growth more generally. All of these future studies would need to address the clear implications for policy and practice that are involved within each of these relevant and important themes of entrepreneurial finance in the twenty-first century.

NOTE

1. One might ask why we have opted here in our second bundle to have two chapters when we have three chapters in our first bundle and four in both our third and fourth bundles? Our reply is simply that we have opted to go for a 3-2-4-4 formation rather than a 3-3-4-3 formation. Decrypt that one.

REFERENCES

Amorós, J.E. and Bosma, N. (2014), *Global Entrepreneurship Monitor 2013 Global Report: Fifteen Years of Assessing Entrepreneurship Across the Globe*, London: Global Entrepreneurship Research Association, London Business School.

Porter, M.E. (1990), *The Competitive Advantage of Nations*, New York: Macmillan.

Porter, M.E., Sachs, J.D and McArthur, J.W (2002), 'Executive summary: competitiveness and stages of economic development', in K. Schwab, M.E. Porter, J.D. Sachs, P.K. Cornelius and J.W. McArthur (eds), *The Global Competitiveness Report 2001–2002*, New York: Oxford University Press, pp. 16–25.

Storey, D.J. (1994), *Understanding the Small Business Sector*, London: Routledge.

Welter, F. (2011), 'Contextualizing entrepreneurship – conceptual challenges and ways forward', *Entrepreneurship Theory and Practice*, **35** (1): 165–184.

Zahra, S. (2007), 'Contextualizing theory building in entrepreneurship research', *Journal of Business Venturing*, **22** (3): 443–452.

Zahra, S., Wright, M. and Abdelgawad, S. (2014), 'Contextualization and the advancement of entrepreneurship research', *International Small Business Journal*, **32** (5): 479–500.

2. SME lending: a new role for credit unions?

Steve Talbot, Ciarán Mac an Bhaird and Geoff Whittam

INTRODUCTION

Credit unions have a relatively long history, although the first modern day credit union was established in the United Kingdom (UK) in the mid-1960s (Birchall, 2013). The original purpose of credit unions was to provide banking facilities for the financially excluded and hence many credit unions can be found in economically disadvantaged areas of the UK (for example, Northern Ireland (French and McKillop, 2014)). Founded on the principle of mutualism, membership is limited by the requirements of a 'common bond', meaning that members either have to live within a certain geographic area or have other common association such as an occupation or a religious grouping. The idea is that a bond would 'strengthen the security of the union with members connected by more than financial ties' (Wright, 2013, p. 5). While the original rules of governance for credit unions specifically debarred credit unions from lending to corporations, recent changes in legislation facilitates lifting this restriction. In theory, this is a plausible policy initiative, as increased centralization of decision-making by financial institutions has exacerbated information asymmetries between small and medium-sized enterprises (SMEs) and lenders.

A further development within the credit union sector is the 'common bond' constraints being 'relaxed' to the effect that the potential geographical reach of a credit union has been extended from 'neighbourhoods' to city-wide and, in the case of occupational credit unions, country-wide. Additionally, there has been an expansion in some occupational credit unions so that they have become 'transnational' (Levitt, 2001).

Wider economic changes have affected credit union financial performance and have led to consolidation within the industry and the creation of 'super credit unions' which operate alongside the more traditional model (Bank of England, 2013). While many of the former are innovative, both in terms of their product offering and service delivery, 'traditional' credit unions continue to seek to maintain a service without providing a complete portfolio of innovative products and services. However, to date, there is little evidence that any credit union in the UK, whether 'super' or 'traditional', has advanced credit to businesses; that is, non-personal lending to firms. It must be noted that, while credit unions have always advanced personal credit, it may be that the individuals concerned were self-employed, or were in the process of starting a business, and at this stage 'personal' and 'business' finance tends to be closely connected (Avery et al., 1998). There is evidence, therefore, to support the contention that credit unions, by default rather than design, have exposure to business lending. This chapter examines the issues surrounding business lending by credit unions and addresses the question: what is preventing credit unions from lending to the small firm sector? Primary research from interviews conducted with chief executive officers of four of the largest credit unions in Great Britain was undertaken in an attempt to gain an understanding why there is an apparent reluctance by credit unions to lend to SMEs. Our sample represents 25 per cent of credit union membership and approximately 30 per cent of credit union assets and, as such, is a sensitive barometer of industry activity.[1] The chapter is organized as follows. First, an explanation of the role and function of credit unions is outlined. Second, the potential of credit unions to assist with reducing the 'finance gap' is provided. Third, the recent change in UK legislation is examined. Fourth, an analysis of primary research undertaken with representatives of four of the largest credit unions is undertaken, followed by the discussion and conclusions.

THE CREDIT UNION SECTOR

Credit unions are an essential component of the UK financial landscape providing an alternative means of saving and borrowing for many people who feel traditional banks do not serve their needs. Established in 1964, the modern UK credit unions have been a success in terms of membership, asset growth and geographic reach. While the modern credit union movement celebrates its fiftieth year, Birchall (2013) argues that the antecedents of credit unions (what he calls cooperative banking) has a history which can be traced back to 1798 with the establishment of a cooperative bank on the Solway Firth in the South West of Scotland. While the model established on the Solway Firth was successful and replicated across the rest of Great Britain, there were two weaknesses: first, on the issue of governance, it was managed by a trust, which led to the possibility of 'rogue owners'; and, second, they were purely and simply savings banks that could not lend. Birchall (2013) argues that we need to look at events in Germany pioneered separately by Schulze and Raiffelsen who established banks with saving and credit facilities, where the savers and borrowers became the owners. This was the birth of the mutual financial institution. Out of the two systems, it was Raiffelsen's that was proving to be the more successful. According to Birchall: 'The genius of Schulze and Raiffelsen was to solve persistent problems in banking for people on low incomes. Knowledge of the credit-worthiness of one's neighbours meant loans were safer. Unlimited liability meant members had a keen interest in monitoring each other. The homogeneous membership base meant peer pressure to repay' (Birchall, 2013, p. 8).

This citation from Birchall is significant because it highlights a fundamental principle of mutualism which underpins credit unions: the ownership and governance structure of a credit union is determined by its members. The mutual form of ownership depends on active participation of the membership, which requires participation in the running of the organization. Mutualism is established in individual unions by the 'member-customers' owning the union having the right to elect senior officers to ensure stewardship of the union (McKillop et al., 2011). Like shareholders, credit union members are assigned voting and ownership rights but, unlike shareholders, these cannot be traded with third parties. Ownership can only change when a member leaves the organization or new members join. It is often argued that thrift and self-help within specific communities is encouraged through 'the common bond', which would 'strengthen the security of the union with members connected by more than financial ties' (Wright, 2013, p. 5). Saving and borrowing is restricted to members, whose actions and freedom of movement are prescribed by the terms of the common bond.

This model is seen to contain certain efficiency gains for mutual organizations operating within the financial services sector due to the removal of potential costly and damaging conflicts of interest between shareholders and customers. Offsetting this benefit are traditionally lower profit margins within mutual organizations such as credit unions and building societies due to lower rates of interest for borrowers and lenders compared with the traditional commercial banking sector. The lower rates of interest and the narrower margins reflect the reduced level of risk associated with credit union lending. Restricting membership through the operation of the common bond, creating a membership where all members have something in common, assisted in establishing the credit worthiness of actual and potential members along with some degree of 'peer pressure' for repayment of loans. Nonetheless, credit unions are regulated by the government's financial watchdog, the Financial Services Authority.

THE CONTEMPORARY CREDIT UNION SECTOR IN GREAT BRITAIN

Recent developments within the credit union sector in Great Britain are evident from data presented in Table 2.1. The number of credit unions operating in Great Britain has significantly decreased between 2004 and 2012, while membership has doubled. This means that fewer credit unions are handling a greater membership, and the evolving structure of the sector appears to require them to become more mainstream in terms of services on offer. The regulatory framework allows credit unions a choice of 'credit union classification' as one means of enabling differentiation within the industry. The framework enables credit unions to seek one of two classifications: either Version 1 (restricted to smaller scale lending and with a 3 per cent capital–asset ratio requirement) or Version 2 (larger lending permissible including mortgage and SME lending but with a stricter 8 per cent capital–asset ratio requirement). This facility is important as it identifies the credit unions which are growth-oriented and have the potential at some future date to engage in non-traditional lending, for example to small businesses. Currently only 12 credit unions have sought and achieved Version 2 status and none of these engage in small business lending. This may be due to increased competition in the small loan market as new entrants enter and have a deterrent effect on the Version 2 credit union approach to small businesses. Thus stratification and consolidation are features of the credit union industry in Great Britain.

Consolidation of credit unions and restructuring of products appears to have resulted in flat inflation-adjusted profits over time and a declining loan to asset ratio (the latter is a key indicator of credit union health and interviews with credit union chief executives suggest this figure needs to be around 80 per cent if a credit union is to ensure long term survival). All of this suggests that further change to the credit union business model is necessary and further restructuring of the sector in the near term is likely. The more competitive credit unions are likely to have innovative products that are of mainstream interest to consumers. We find evidence of this innovative approach in the case studies discussed below. We also find that credit unions view the small loans market as one with a surplus of cash but with associated high risk with low returns.

A glimpse of the dynamics affecting the credit union business model helps to illustrate underlying forces driving industry consolidation and stratification. The crucial relationship between the loan to asset ratio and the ratio of income from members' loans to total income is a key dynamic which drives credit union activity in the short term and has a major influence on longer term strategy. Analysis of Table 2.1 and Figure 2.1

Table 2.1 Great Britain credit union statistics 2004–2012

	2004	2005	2006	2007	2008	2009	2010	2011	2012
Number of credit unions	565	544	521	504	477	454	439	405	390
Total number of staff employed	473	482	561	680	776	775	925	991	1,031
Total number of members	321,200	349,681	369,163	422,582	464,684	506,494	556,068	601,965	651,682
Profit (£,000) (Nominal data)	15,608	15,394	15,394	17,317	15,968	12,651	17,308	24,822	19,162
Total assets	231,993	249,468	270,506	299,543	324,543	372,969	418,191	487,747	538,930
Ave. loans as a % of total assets	75.30%	76.30%	75.20%	76.80%	77.20%	70%	69%	68%	65%

Source: Bank of England (2013).

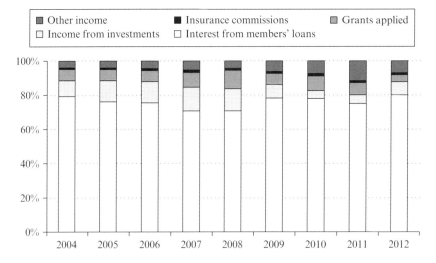

Source: Bank of England statistics.

Figure 2.1   Credit union income by category, 2004–2012

demonstrates that credit unions have experienced a declining loan to asset ratio and have become over-reliant on income from members' loans rather than expanding their investment portfolio, through for example small business lending. As Figure 2.1 illustrates, credit unions are heavily dependent on income from loans to members due to the precipitate fall in income from investments: that is, declining interest on government financial instruments. Credit unions are disproportionately affected by declining interest rates as a consequence of restrictions on the type of investment vehicles they can use, surplus cash must be placed on deposit in a bank or used to buy government bonds. The reduction in income is an unintended consequence of recent monetary policies around quantitative easing, restrictions on investment vehicles and an unwillingness to engage in alternative investments, for example business lending.

The internal and external dynamics of credit unions means that within the sector overall some credit unions will thrive, some will reach a steady state and others gradually fade away through merger or wind-up.

At the centre of this question is the issue of corporate governance and credit unions' approach to risk assessment. Credit unions are well placed to establish direct links between saver and investor (small business). The benefit of such direct linkage is found in the 2012 Kay Report into short termism in the UK financial sector. Kay (2012) noted that even with a successful system of financial intermediation there is a clear danger associated with information asymmetries and principal-agent problems. Kay (2012, p. 20) notes that 'information asymmetry and principal-agent conflict become steadily more serious as the modern corporate economy evolves'. One of the dangers identified by Kay (2012) is the impact of growing complexity in the financial sector on the relationship between savers and those looking to borrow funds: as lenders become more remote from borrowers, the potential for the interests of borrower and lender to diverge is increased. One of the contributors to the Kay Report stated that what was needed was a 'shortening of the investment chain in order to "tackle the issue of too many intermediaries between savers and the assets they own, and the cost of those layers"' (Kay, 2012, p. 8). This is an interesting statement and raises issues concerning the optimum depth of financial intermediation, suggesting that there may be an 'inverted U-shaped' relationship between financial intermediation and efficient allocation of funds. While the Kay Report refers to UK equities markets, there are valuable lessons for the provision of funding to the SME sector, specifically through minimizing potential agency problems that may arise between funders and borrowers. Furthermore, highlighting local economic benefits[2] may attract more savers and greater levels of savings.

REDUCING THE 'FINANCE GAP'?

As evidenced by the recent legislative change, credit unions are being encouraged by government to look beyond their traditional role as a savings club for their members and lend to the small firm sector. From a theoretic perspective, there is a sound argument for credit unions moving towards business lending. Levine (2005) makes a strong case for a link between the depth of financial systems and the rate of economic growth. While this link is widely seen as a 'stylized fact', there is still debate surrounding the direction of causality. That is, does economic growth bring forth a suitable financial system or does the creation of a sound financial system provide a necessary background for economic growth to take place? Again there is a significant literature attached to this issue. For example, Hassan et al. (2011) found strong linkages between financial development and economic growth in Organisation for Economic Co-operation and Development (OECD) countries and Odhiambo (2008) found that finance exerts positive influence on growth in Kenya. However, De Gregorio and Guidotti (1995) reported a negative relationship between financial development and growth in 12 Latin American countries. Great Britain was a developed economy when modern credit unions were first formed 50 years ago and, therefore, the issue of direction of causality may seem irrelevant. However, if we are looking at developing and growing a local economy when traditional lenders are in retreat, then the issue of local provision of credit bringing forth economic activity is clearly important. Patrick (1966) identifies the two main traditions under which the relationship between the financial sector and the real economy may be assessed. The first is in the Schumpeter tradition in which the financial system acts as an engine of growth, driving economic performance and is deemed supply leading whereby the financial sector acts as a means of targeting funds to productive investments (McKinnon, 1973; Shaw, 1973; Fry, 1978; Levine, 2005). The second is in the neoclassical tradition and views the financial sector as following the growth process and is deemed a demand-following phenomenon, whereby economic growth is determined by exogenous factors such as an infusion of new capital from government or foreign direct investment (Robinson, 1952; Thangavelu and Ang, 2004; Ang and McKibbin, 2007). Thus, while the literature is settled on the link between financial systems and the rate of economic growth (Levine, 2005), debate remains whether financial systems lead economic growth or are the follower of economic growth (Patrick, 1966; McKinnon, 1973; Shaw, 1973). Encouraging credit unions to move into business lending implies that a supply leading perspective is being adopted by policymakers.

The characteristics associated with credit unions would suggest that they are in an ideal position to lend to small firms and also to start-up ventures in order to stimulate economic growth at the local level. The case for credit union involvement can be argued because many of the key elements of the so-called 'finance gap' are associated with asymmetric information and moral hazard (Berger and Udell, 1998; Nofsinger and Wang, 2011; Denis, 2004). The issue of asymmetric information affects most markets and arises when one party to a potential transaction has more information than the other potential party. In relation to a commercial bank's involvement with a small firm or new start-up venture, the bank will typically have less information than the client. For example, most small firms and new ventures will not have an established trading record and the entrepreneur behind a new venture in particular will typically not have been known to the bank. In this scenario, if a bank is willing to lend, then the price of the loan will be at a premium because of the perceived higher level of risk involved. However, there is nothing sinister in this approach which demonstrates the market in operation, whereby risk assessment and pricing are key functions of banking.

However, it is possible for banks to be risk averse and to over-price the risk they are facing. Asymmetry of information and mis-pricing of risk has been exacerbated with the decline in relationship banking and increased centralization of functions within the banking sector. By centralizing operations, banks have sacrificed local decision-making by bank managers for potential efficiency gains. Erosion in the use and effectiveness of relationship lending adversely affects micro firms, which comprise over 92 per cent of SMEs in the UK. The reduction in relationship banking has the effect of increasing the level of asymmetry in the decision-making process and also increasing the risk of adverse selection (Baas and Schrooten, 2006). Weakening or removing the borrower–lender relationship increases bank reliance on systematized credit scoring platforms to the detriment of key parts of the small firm sector, as micro businesses and start-ups are likely to have limited track records (Henry and Craig, 2013). Recent work on bank lending-decisions focusing on credit scoring highlights the variability between lending officers within the same clearing bank, in terms of the application of their credit scoring framework (Wilson et al., 2007). Interestingly, Wilson et al. (2007) also showed the importance attached to the character of the business owner in business success, compared with other factors such as collateral and capitalization. The by-product of increased centralization within the commercial banking sector means that it is less likely that a commercial bank will be able to determine an individual entrepreneur's 'character' to a degree that would over-rule the centralized credit-scoring framework.

The reduction in relationship banking – added to the problems associated with information asymmetry – can lead to a corrosive dynamic: banks stringently considering loan applications leading to a higher failure rate among new ventures, leading banks to be even more stringent in assessing new loan applications. This creates a vicious circle resulting in new ventures being discouraged from applying for loans as they believe that banks do not lend to start-ups (Allinson et al., 2005). This problem is even more acute for start-ups in 'deprived' communities because of the role of post-codes in credit scoring potential loan applications. If postcodes are utilized as a means of accessing an application and a potential new start is located in an area with a poor credit rating, then the chances of the loan application being successful are somewhat diminished (Henry and Craig, 2013).

The precise impact of credit scoring on small firm lending is disputed, but the perception of a finance gap may reduce the willingness of SMEs to approach a financial institution. Allinson et al (2005, p. 3) commented: 'if people do not present themselves to a financial institution in the first place, because of self-selection and possibly underpinned by belief in a myth, then it may appear that the institutions' rates of granting loans are quite high – that they are meeting demand'. This can lead to businesses seeking to 'bootstrap' rather than securing more appropriate financial packages. The discouraged borrower effect (Kon and Storey, 2003) 'leaves a problem for anyone with a viable proposition but without family and friends with any resources to help' (Irwin and Scott, 2005, p.6), and is a key issue for some businesses at the start-up phase (Fraser, 2005).

Credit unions perform as financial intermediaries at the local level and in doing so are able to aid efficiency and growth in the local market as they are well placed to identify, assess and lend to promising firms led by local entrepreneurs (Greenwood and Jovanovic, 1990). In particular, community-based credit unions are reckoned to have access to local knowledge which, in turn, gives them a much better understanding of the risk profile of their customers (Birchall, 2013). More importantly, the potential borrower from the credit union will be known to the institution because of the mutual form of governance and also because the borrower will have had to have saved with the credit union for a period of time before taking out a loan. The borrower will, therefore, have the beginnings of a track record with the credit union unlike the typical new-start entrepreneur and a commercial bank. This type of knowledge is particularly valuable when lending to small firms that are without access to collateral, including tangible assets and receivables (Canales and Nada, 2012).

Information deficiency is costly to both the firm and to the local economy as alternative sources of finance involve leakage (income from interest) from the local area to large corporations. This is because firms lacking collateral are often compelled to access expensive sources of finance such as credit cards, bank overdrafts and trade credit from organizations outside the local area (DeYoung et al., 2004). Therefore, having the facility to substitute these sources with credit union short term loans is cheaper, more sustainable and facilitates more long term planning and leaves more cash to circulate locally. This is the experience of credit union lending to local firms in the United States (US) and Canada. Wilcox (2011) found that in the US, small business loans advanced by credit unions partially offset a reduction in loans from traditional banks. Credit unions, therefore, may have an important role in offsetting fluctuations in provision of credit by banking institutions.

Credit union lending to small firms should ensure that moral hazard is reduced, as firm owners become more prudent and avoid higher risk behaviour which would impact on the locally based lender through default on the loan. There appears to be a moral constraint of sorts attached to local borrowing and lending which lessens the danger to the survival of the community-owned bank (Baas and Schrooten, 2006; Department for Work and Pensions (DWP), 2011). In this way, social constraints are also introduced to economic decision-making.

While theoretic and practical cases can readily be made for credit union involvement in local economic development in general and for small firm lending in particular, recent changes to the credit union regulatory frame-work in the UK, along with increased competition from new entrants to the small-loan market, has led to consolidation within the sector, with the number of credit unions decreasing from 565 to approximately 390 in 2012 (Bank of England, 2013). McKillop et al. (2011) found that con-solidation within the sector has seen some credit unions cease trading and others merge as they seek the scale of operation and skill base necessary to compete in a rapidly changing environment. Consolidation within the credit union sector should be seen in the wider context of events within the banking sector, which became more concentrated post 2008 but has recently experience an influx of new entrants leading to a decline in the sector's concentration ratio.

METHODOLOGY

While the secondary research provided useful information regarding the establishment, development and recent changes to the legislative frame-work regarding the governance and operational activities of credit unions within the United Kingdom, interviews with four major credit unions enabled insights into decision-making processes at the individual credit union level. Two-stage interviews were conducted with a credit union 'industry group' which represented the largest credit unions in Great Britain in terms of assets (30 per cent) and membership (25 per cent). The initial interview involved a group discussion at a credit union office in Edinburgh. At this meeting six credit unions were represented (this group is consulted by government on industry matters). A series of subsequent telephone interviews were held with four of the group. In this way, we were able to get an understanding of the general concerns and issues at a group level while subsequently getting specific details on individual credit unions. Five of the six credit unions in the group are Version 2 credit unions. The smaller Version 1 credit unions would not be in a position to contemplate lending to SMEs and thus were not approached for a second interview. Hence we report only on the findings of interviews conducted with four Version 2 credit unions, these four being among the biggest by capitalization in the United Kingdom.

Each element of the two-stage interview process involved semi-structured interviews and lasted for between one hour and one hour fifteen minutes. Notes were taken of the contributions to the focus group and were subsequently written up and coded.

RESULTS

In many respects, this group constitutes the idealized credit union, able to compete fully with banks at the local level across many financial instruments. However, there is surprisingly little appetite to engage in SME lending, notwithstanding limited mortgage lending. Only one credit union, in northern England, is fully engaged in SME lending but this is indirectly through administering the government's start-up loans scheme. It advanced loans to 90 companies in 2013/14 and was planning to target a further 150 in 2014/15. This is an interesting hybrid lending model with the credit union acting as intermediary, using government rather than members' money. Interestingly, the credit union carries out the necessary risk assessment of business loan applicants before processing successful applications. In many respects, this enables the credit union to test their risk assessment capabilities with no risk to members' funds. The credit union is looking to build risk assessment capacity by recruiting a risk assessor to their staff, putting in place a key component should SME lending be offered at a later date.

Another northern England credit union advances credit to small businesses, but this is through personal lending rather than the firm. This 'informal' arrangement has been working for some time and is present in many credit unions. Interestingly, this credit union does not engage in the Department for Business, Innovation and Skills (BIS) scheme as it has insufficient risk assessment capability. However, the credit union uses an independent consultant who assists in this area and helps business loan applicants with business plans and the application process. At the time of the interview (November 2014), the credit union has processed 10 business loans for between £4k and £15k. Interestingly, the city's mayor has given a total of £1m to local credit unions to boost SME lending.

Another member of the group has one business loan to a local housing association, but no SME lending at present. The main concern of the group is the lack of risk assessment skills, and that any increase in risk is not outweighed by potential increases in revenue. In essence, the SME lending model is not an attractive proposition to this group or the majority of credit unions. Thus, while in theory credit unions are very well placed to assess local risk and identify viable SME projects, there is a distinct lack of appetite to do so. This appears to be the response of the credit union sector to the lending opportunities on offer.

While there has been reluctance by credit unions to engage in business lending, this has not been the case in other countries such as the Republic of Ireland. Furthermore, recent experience of credit unions in Ireland in lending to small firms provides a number of salutary lessons. While the credit union sector in Ireland is relatively more developed than the UK, with a greater market penetration (67 per cent in Ireland as opposed to 4 per cent in the UK), the economic environment is broadly similar. Small firms can be members of credit unions in Ireland, either as firms or through their owners. Under current legislation, credit unions in Ireland can lend to SMEs, and approximately 5 per cent of credit union loans are advanced to SMEs for business purposes (Irish League of Credit Unions (ILCU), 2014). This amounts to less than €250m, which is a small amount in relation to total outstanding bank debt to non-financial SMEs of approximately €25 billion (Intertrade Ireland, 2013). It is, nevertheless, an important source of microfinance for small firms.

DISCUSSION AND CONCLUSIONS

In this chapter it is argued that the modern day credit union sector is ideally placed to overcome the traditional hazards associated with lending to new ventures, namely information asymmetry and moral hazard. The mutual form of ownership, coupled with the operation of a common bond, suggests that the more available information generated through these relationships should ensure a reduction in the risk associated with lending to new ventures. However, in spite of new legislation, research conducted with four of the largest credit unions located in Great Britain reveals a reluctance to lend to SMEs or any new ventures to any meaningful degree. Indeed, the fourth is really acting as an intermediary facilitating the lending of government funds. The primary reason credit unions have not expanded lending to the small firm sector is that they perceive an unacceptable level of risk, or, alternatively, they believe they do not have sufficient in-house expertise to conduct risk assessment to advance intermediated debt to prospective new ventures.

A further explanation for the reluctance of credit unions in the UK to lend to SMEs is because of potential consequences for the business model. In order to facilitate lending to SMEs, additional fixed costs are incurred such as additional staff with risk-assessment skills and the ability to undertake due diligence of prospective new ventures. To absorb these additional costs, the credit union has to be of a certain scale, but in expanding, the credit union may well lose its original potential competitive advantage: namely its ability to reduce information asymmetry, adverse selection and moral hazard. Some credit unions have made use of relaxations to the 'common bond' criteria to expand, but the danger again is the potential dilution of the mutual model: members will become less active in the union and act like normal bank shareholders. Furthermore, by expanding and competing directly with the commercial banking sector, there is a temptation to utilize the model of established banks by adopting practices such as centralized credit scoring systems with the same results as experienced by this sector. Indeed, the government's Credit Union Expansion Project[3] is designed to facilitate such a move by creating a centralized 'back office' facility that all credit unions can buy into as an aid to their development. There may be a paradox here that cannot be resolved: in order to fill a void (the finance gap), credit unions have to surrender the features which make them distinctive.

Credit unions appear reluctant to play a full part in financing the small firm economy. They are proficient at attracting cash deposits, but reluctant to embrace the additional risk that is incurred by lending beyond their traditional client base. The result is that credit unions are cash rich but income poor (in other words, they are solely dependent on loan interest for their income). They are trapped in a financial model whose dynamic prevents them from developing their full potential as in Canada and the US, and partly closing the finance gap. As our research shows, at a local level credit unions in Great Britain have been slow to encroach into the traditional territory of banks by lending to the small firm sector, despite the opportunity presented by the legislative change in 2012. This reluctance to engage in business lending reveals much about credit unions and their attitude towards risk, their members, their understanding of corporate governance responsibilities and their role in the local economy. Our findings suggest that, at present credit unions are not prepared to produce the type of supply side response required of policymakers.

NOTES

1. We refer to credit unions in Great Britain (GB), rather than the UK due to Northern Ireland being an exceptional case in terms of how credit unions are organized and operated.
2. Although Birchall (2013, p. 2) notes that 'evidence for the power of financial cooperatives in local economic development and job creation is mostly indirect'.
3. The Department of Work and Pension's £38m Credit Union Expansion Project (CUEP) where a risk assessment tool and a banking platform will be made available to credit unions who join the scheme.

REFERENCES

Allinson G., Braidford P., Houston, M. and Stone, I. (2005), *Myths Surrounding Starting and Running a Business*, London: Small Business Service.

Ang, J.B. and McKibbin, W.J. (2007), 'Financial liberalization, financial sector development and growth: evidence from Malaysia', *Journal of Development Economics*, **84** (1): 215–233.

Avery, R.B., Bostic, R.W. and Samolyk, K.A. (1998), 'The role of personal wealth in small business finance', *Journal of Banking and Finance*, **22** (6–8): 1019–1061.

Baas, T. and Schrooten, M. (2006), 'Relationship banking and SMEs: a theoretical analysis', *Small Business Economics*, **27** (2): 127–137.

Bank of England (2013), 'Introduction to credit union statistics', accessed 30 August 2014 at http://www.bankofengland.co.uk/statistics/Documents/ms/articles/art1jul13.pdf.

Berger, A. and Udell, G. (1998), 'The economics of small business finance: the roles of private equity and debt markets in the financial growth cycle', *Journal of Banking and Finance*, **22** (1998): 613–673.

Birchall, J. (2013), *Resilience in a Downturn: The Power of Financial Cooperatives*, Geneva: International Labour Office.

Canales, R. and Nada, R. (2012), 'A darker side to decentralized banks: market power and credit rationing in SME lending', *Journal of Financial Economics*, **2** (August): 353–366.

De Gregorio, J. and Guidotti, P. (1995), 'Financial development and economic growth', *World Development*, **23** (3): 433–448.

Denis, D.J. (2004), 'Entrepreneurial finance: an overview of the issues and evidence', *Journal of Corporate Finance*, **10** (2): 301–326.

Department for Work and Pensions (2011), Credit Union Expansion Project, London: Department for Work and Pensions.

DeYoung, R., Hunter W. and Udell, G. (2004), 'The past, present and probable future of community banks', *Journal of Financial Services Research*, **25** (2/3): 85–133.

Fraser, S. (2005), *Finance for Small and Medium-Sized Enterprises*, Report on the 2004 UK Survey of SME Finances. Warwick: Centre for Small and Medium-Sized Enterprises, University of Warwick.

French, D. and McKillop, D. (2014), 'Financial literacy and over-indebtedness in low-income households', Working Paper no. 14-012, St Andrews: Centre for Responsible Banking and Finance, University of St. Andrews, accessed 27 July 2014 at http://ssrn.com/abstract=2505084.

Fry, M.J. (1978), 'Money and capital or financial deepening in economic development', *Journal of Money, Credit, and Banking*, **10** (4): 464–475.

Greenwood, J. and Jovanovic, B. (1990), 'Financial development, growth, and the distribution of income', *Journal of Political Economy*, **98** (5): 1076–1107.

Hassan, M.K., Sanchez, B. and Yu, J.S. (2011), 'Financial development and economic growth: new evidence from panel data', *The Quarterly Review of Economics and Finance*, **51** (1): 88–104.

Henry, N. and Craig, P. (2013), *Mind the Finance Gap: Evidencing demand for Community Finance*, London: Community Development Finance Association.

ILCU (2014), 'Presentation to the Joint Committee on Jobs, Enterprise and Innovation' by David Matthews, Dublin: 5 June 2014.

Intertrade Ireland (2013), *Access to finance for growth for SMEs on the island of Ireland*. Newry: Intertrade Ireland, accessed 27 July 2015 at http://www.intertradeireland.com/media/AccesstoFinancereportFINAL10.01.14.pdf.

Irwin, D. and Scott, J.M. (2005), 'The important role of micro-finance in supporting SMEs', Paper presented at the Institute for Small Business and Entrepreneurship Conference (ISBE), Blackpool, November.

Kay, J. (2012), *The Kay Report of UK Equity markets and Long-term Decision Making*, London: Department for Business Innovation and Skills (BIS).

Kon, Y. and Storey, D.J. (2003), 'A theory of discouraged borrowers', *Small Business Economics*, **21** (1): 37–49.

Levine, R. (2005), 'Finance and growth: theory and evidence', in P. Aghion and S. Durlauf (eds), *Handbook of Economic Growth*, Amsterdam: Elsevier Science, pp. 865–934.

Levitt, P. (2001), 'Transnational migration: taking stock and future directions', *Global Networks*, **1** (3): 195–216.

McKillop, D., Ward, A.M. and Wilson, J. (2011), 'Credit unions in Great Britain: recent trends and current prospects', *Public Money and Management*, **31** (1): 35–42.

McKinnon, R.I. (1973), *Money and Capital in Economic Development*, Washington, DC: Brookings Institution.

Nofsinger, J.R. and Wang, W. (2011), 'Determinants of start-up firm external financial worldwide', *Journal of Banking and Finance*, **35** (9): 2282–2294.

Odhiambo, M. (2008), 'Financial depth, savings and economic growth in Kenya: a dynamic causal linkage', *Economic Modelling*, **25** (4): 704–713.

Patrick, H.T. (1966), 'Financial development and economic growth in underdeveloped countries', *Economic Development and Cultural Change*, **14** (2): 174–189.

Robinson, J. (1952), *The Generalization of the General Theory, in The Rate of Interest and Other Essays*, London: Macmillan.

Shaw, E.S. (1973), *Financial Deepening in Economic Development*, New York: Oxford University Press.

Thangavelu, S.M. and Ang, J.B. (2004), 'Financial development and economic growth in Australia: an empirical analysis', *Empirical Economics*, **29** (2): 247–260.

Wilcox, J.A. (2011), *The increasing importance of credit unions in small business lending*, Report for the Small Business Association Office of Advocacy, Berkeley CA: Haas School of Business, U C Berkeley, Berkeley.

Wilson, F., Carter, S., Tagg, S., Shaw, E. and Lam, W. (2007), 'Bank officers' perception of business owners: the role of gender', *British Journal of Management*, **18** (2): 154–171.

Wright, J. (2013), *Credit Unions: A Solution to Poor Bank Lending?*, London: Citivas.

3. Entrepreneurial finance in New Zealand
David Deakins

INTRODUCTION: NEW ZEALAND – A UNIQUE ECONOMIC ENVIRONMENT

New Zealand is a unique economic, and hence entrepreneurial, environment. This is partly due to its geographical location, with New Zealand's entrepreneurs being remote and distant from major overseas markets, but also because it has a relatively small domestic economy with a population of 4.5 million[1] (Statistics New Zealand, 2014) and because it has a number of other unique features which are identified at the end of this paragraph. The importance of context for understanding entrepreneurial behavior has been identified by a number of researchers who point to the importance of embeddedness, networks and contacts for entrepreneurial behavior and consequential economic development (Zahra, 2007; McKeever et al., 2015). For example, embeddedness and networks are important for access to resources such as social capital and contribute to the richness of the environmental context. Likewise environmental context is important for understanding entrepreneurial finance, both the demand side behavior of entrepreneurs seeking external finance and the supply side behavior of investors and other actors such as financial institutions. Other factors that contribute to New Zealand's unique environment include:

- A resilient and expanding domestic economy.
- A relatively benign regulatory framework.
- Investment preferences of New Zealand's population and households.
- A large number of small businesses with comparatively few high growth and large firms.
- Strong preferential tendencies for internal over external finance of New Zealand's entrepreneurs.
- The institutional and financial infrastructure including New Zealand's major commercial banks.

In this introductory section we set out this context in more detail.

Historically, New Zealanders have a very strong preference for investment in property rather than in corporate bodies and this has restricted the flow of potential equity finance either directly to businesses or indirectly through investment vehicles and financial institutions. For example, the then Governor of the Reserve Bank, Allan Bollard commented that 'Kiwis like buying houses more than buying businesses' and that:

> It appears that holders of equity by New Zealand households are particularly low by OECD standards, with direct holdings of both domestic and foreign equities making up no more than about 4 percent of total assets. (Bollard, 2006)

The reasons for this strong preference by New Zealanders are complex and are probably culturally based, but traditionally New Zealanders have viewed property investments as a security for their retirement and a state superannuation scheme, the *KiwiSaver*, was only introduced in 2007 and is still a voluntary scheme allowing employees to opt out. Thus, although bank credit may be comparatively easy to obtain for New Zealand entrepreneurs, obtaining a supply side flow of equity investments from high net worth individuals (HNWIs) is limited and still at an immature stage.

The New Zealand economy has proved to be resilient in the post Global Financial Crisis (GFC) recession and currently continues to enjoy economic growth. For example, the New Zealand economy over the three years from 2012 to 2015 had grown about two-thirds faster than the average for other developed countries. New Zealand's central bank, the Reserve Bank, in its most recent annual report forecast the rate of gross domestic product (GDP) growth to be 3.5 percent in the year to March 2015 (Reserve Bank of New Zealand, 2014). This strong buoyant and resilient economic performance has meant that interest rates are relatively high internationally. For example, at the time of writing, the Official Cash Rate (OCR) is 3.5 percent (the OCR is equivalent to the Bank of England's base rate). This has meant that New Zealand has become an attractive home for overseas investments resulting in a substantial increase in the currency rate since the GFC with a current rate of New Zealand dollar (NZD) (the Kiwi) to 0.77 US dollars (USD).[2] This historically high Kiwi exchange rate is regarded as unsustainable by the Governor of the Reserve Bank.

New Zealand is consistently ranked in the top three economies for the ease of doing business in the World Bank's *Doing Business* reports. For example, it is ranked by the World Bank as one of the easiest economies in which to do business, New Zealand is ranked second behind only Singapore, and it is ranked first as the easiest economy in which to start a new business (World Bank, 2014). This reflects the fact that New Zealand has a relatively benign economic and financial regulatory environment and, significantly for this chapter, is ranked first for the ease of getting credit out of 189 economies that are included in the World Bank's rankings (World Bank, 2014). New Zealand does less well in areas such as resolving insolvency (28th) and trading across borders (27th). This relatively lower ranking in the latter category reflects the remoteness of the economy, despite the growth of multi-lateral and bi-lateral trade agreements that New Zealand has secured in the Asia-Pacific region following the ending of free access to the UK overseas market (when the UK joined the EU) and despite the growth of China as an overseas export destination for New Zealand's exports (Statistics New Zealand, 2012).

New Zealand is a small open economy that is dependent on international trade, but is also distant from larger overseas markets. The openness of her economy, coupled with this distance from major overseas markets, create challenges for New Zealand businesses that are unique for a small developed economy that is an Organisation for Economic Co-operation and Development (OECD) member. For example, comparisons are sometimes drawn between New Zealand and small peripheral, but developed economies in Europe such as Ireland, Denmark and Finland, yet none has the same challenge of remoteness. Despite the stalling of the World Trade Organization's Doha round of talks, reduction in trade barriers is still an important part of the agenda with the Doha Development Agenda (World Trade Organization, 2012) and increased globalization has seen a liberalization of trade and a reduction of tariffs in this century. This has opened up new markets for New Zealand businesses, but distance remains a challenge (Chetty and Campbell-Hunt, 2004).

It is recognized that for New Zealand businesses, distance has at least two dimensions. The first is physical distance with the lead time and cost involved in transport and freight, especially for businesses involved in the manufacturing sector. Second, is the concept of 'psychic distance' which operates through perceptions of business owners and managers. For example, Australia is New Zealand's closest overseas market physically, but psychologically businesses feel closer to their Antipodean neighbour than they do to other nations of different cultures and languages which may be perceived as having different business regulations. These challenges have been described as 'dimensions' of internationalization that are unique to New Zealand (Scott-Kennel, 2013).

New Zealand is a nation of small businesses. According to the Ministry of Business, Innovation and Employment (MBIE) small businesses, that employ less than 20 employees, account for 97 percent of all registered businesses (MBIE, 2014). The corollary is that there is a relatively small number of large and high growth or 'entrepreneurial' firms. There are a large number of small firms and a small number of large firms. For example, there were 320,000 enterprises with zero employees, compared to only 2,120 enterprises with 100 or more employees recorded (and estimated) in 2013 (MBIE, 2014). The predominance of the small enterprise sector, coupled with the economy's distance from major markets, means that a relatively small number of enterprises have overseas income. For example, the 2011 Statistics New Zealand Business Operations Survey indicated that only 18 percent of businesses surveyed had current overseas income (Statistics New Zealand, 2012). These factors limit the demand side numbers of high growth entrepreneurial firms with export potential that are seeking equity investments from HNWIs.

We will present evidence later in this chapter to support a view that an entrepreneurial preferential or 'pecking' order for finance, as outlined by Myers, is prevalent with New Zealand entrepreneurs (Myers, 2001); that is, for internal sources, credit and then a reluctance to dilute equity. This may be little different than has been demonstrated in other economies, but there remains a strong preferential order for internal sources, then credit and lastly equity, over the entrepreneurial life cycle (Berger and Udell, 1998). Although now over a decade ago, the last available survey on firms' financial preferences by Statistics New Zealand indicated that only 6 percent of firms actively sought equity (Statistics New Zealand, 2005a). Unfortunately, this survey of New Zealand businesses' financial preferences has not been repeated over the last decade. Thus, although the pecking order hypothesis is well known and has supporting evidence from elsewhere, we suggest that its strong existence in New Zealand entrepreneurs could be a further limiting factor in the demand for and active searching for HNWIs and for sources of equity investments.

The institutional financial infrastructure in New Zealand has remained stable throughout the post GFC economic environment. In terms of credit markets, the main commercial banks in New Zealand are largely Australian-owned, with out of the largest five main players, just one, Kiwibank, being New Zealand-owned, and the so-called 'big four' commercial banks are all Australian and dominate the personal and business banking markets. However, unlike their North American and European counterparts, they are very profitable and secure, since they did not engage in some of the sub-prime activity that contributed to the post GFC bail outs and spectacular financial crashes in North America and Europe. For example, a recent PricewaterhouseCoopers (PwC) report commented that the main five commercial banks in New Zealand are all listed in the world's fifty safest banks in *Global Finance Magazine*'s list for 2012 (PwC, 2013). Equity markets, however, remain underdeveloped and the funding escalator, as is known for example in Europe and North American venture and equity markets, has never been fully developed in New Zealand. In particular, early stage venture investment markets have remained immature (NZVIF, 2012).

In summary, New Zealand's economy remains something of an enigma in terms of entrepreneurial activity and entrepreneurial finance. There is a high rate of business start-up which is coupled with a benign regulatory environment, but few businesses go on to become 'high impact' entrepreneurial firms, there are strong and stable banking institutions and credit markets, but limited and immature venture and risk capital markets which are a combination of both limited demand for equity from entrepreneurs and restricted supply of equity from individual and corporate investors. Policy measures have been taken to try to stimulate equity markets and in particular to stimulate demand side growth performing, or entrepreneurial, firms through the encouragement of commercialization and technology transfer and we discuss some of these measures in more detail later in this chapter.

The rest of this chapter examines some of these issues, from demand and supply side perspectives, including policy measures, in more detail and presents evidence from research conducted by the author with technology-based entrepreneurial firms and key informants, before providing a concluding section.

ENTREPRENEURIAL FINANCE: A DEMAND SIDE PERSPECTIVE

As mentioned earlier in our introductory section, it has been over a decade since the last national survey in New Zealand, the *Business Finance Survey* (BFS), on the demand for and use of external finance by entrepreneurs and small firm owners (Statistics New Zealand, 2005a). The main conclusion of this survey was that; of those firms that sought external finance, the vast majority were able to obtain it. Further work conducted by the former Ministry of Economic Development which matched the BFS to the *Longitudinal Business Database* (LBD) to examine in more detail the issue of access to bank finance (Stevens, 2008) found that the entrepreneur/ small firm owner relationship with their bank manager was positively associated with the age of the firm and commented in a working paper as follows (Stevens, 2008, p. 26):

> We have considered access to finance, with a focus on bank finance, for a sample of firms between 1–500 employees across a number of dimensions. We have found that the length of firms' banking relationship increases with age and that more successful firms in terms of sales and (to a lesser extent) profitability tend to have longer banking relationships.

Further survey evidence on the dominance of the preference of New Zealand entrepreneurs for bank finance as virtually the sole form of external finance sought was provided by one of the annual surveys, called the *BusinesSMEeasure*, conducted by the New Zealand Centre for SME Research (NZSMERC) in 2010. This national survey of over 1800 New Zealand SMEs also examined whether preferences for finance had changed during the height of the recession since 2009. According to the Centre's report (Battisti and Deakins, 2011), in 2009 the most commonly used forms of finance which were used by at least half of the respondents were trade credit (69 percent), bank overdrafts (68 percent), personal credit cards (67 percent), business credit cards (63 percent), bank loans (60 percent) and personal savings (54 percent).

Table 3.1 provides data from the results of the NZSMERC survey. This shows that in 2010, entrepreneurs' response to the recession at the time was to rely more on internal sources and bootstrapping techniques rather than seek additional external sources of finance such as longer term

Table 3.1   Importance of the types of finance used by New Zealand SMEs in 2009 and 2010

Percent	2009				2010			
	Increased use	No change	Decreased use	Ever used	Increased use	No change	Decreased use	Ever used
Bank overdraft	25	33	10	68	28	32	9	69
Bank loans	18	29	13	60	16	35	13	64
Business credit cards	11	46	6	63	9	52	6	67
Personal credit cards	11	47	9	67	11	58	9	78
Leasing or hire purchase	7	31	8	45	6	37	8	51
Trade credit	10	57	3	69	16	56	6	77
Factoring, invoice discounting or stock finance	3	16	1	20	5	17	1	23
Grants or subsidized loans	2	6	1	8	1	6	1	8
Informal equity finance	8	11	1	20	8	11	2	19
Formal equity finance	1	5	1	6	1	6	1	7
Personal savings	22	29	4	54	24	33	3	60
Other types of finance	2	7	1	10	3	4	1	7

Source: Battisti and Deakins (2011).

bank credit and informal business angel venture finance. For example, the number of SMEs using personal credit cards increased from 67 percent in 2009 to 78 percent in 2010, making it the most widely used form of business finance, and the number of SMEs using trade credits increased from 69 percent to 77 percent. Entrepreneurs and small firm owners, rather than seek bank credit or informal venture finance and other sources of external finance, relied more on delving into their personal savings. The number doing so increased by 24 percent and the overall number of SMEs that had ever used personal savings rose from 54 to 60 percent.

Bank finance dominates the number of SMEs that used external sources of finance, but there was a remarkable increase in the number of SMEs that used bank overdrafts rather than bank loans, and the former increased by 28 percent in use from 2009 to 2010, compared to an increase of 16 percent for the number of SMEs using bank loans. This indicates, at least to some extent, that bank overdrafts have been the traditional credit instrument of corporate lending by New Zealand banks. A contributing factor is likely to be requirements for personal security for bank loans. We indicate later in qualitative evidence with technology-based entrepreneurs that this is a limiting factor in the use of bank loans.

Overall, the NZSMERC data confirms the earlier data from the BFS (Statistics New Zealand, 2005a) that there is a distinct preferential order for finance by New Zealand entrepreneurs. Characteristically, there is a heavy reliance on internal sources and the entrepreneur's own personal savings and, if external finance is used, this is likely to be bank overdrafts over bank loans. Lastly, although there is evidence of the use of informal sources of equity from individual investors, there remain only a small proportion of entrepreneurs that have ever used formal sources of equity. For example, in 2009 and 2010 this was only 6 and 7 percent respectively. The implications of this reliance upon internal sources for investment capital by New Zealand's entrepreneurs is that growth strategies are likely to be constrained with investments in projects either abandoned or shelved and the delaying of long term capital investment until it can be financed from internal sources. We turn now to examine qualitative evidence from research conducted by the author.

The qualitative evidence is drawn from a study conducted in 2011 with a sample of 20 technology-based small firms (TBSFs) and seven key informants (Deakins and North, 2013). Before discussing this evidence, it is worth noting that TBSFs are of interest in the New Zealand context which was described in our introduction. A number of official reports have investigated what appears to be a symptomatic failure; to develop, fund and retain the development of research and development (R&D) intensive, high value, TBSFs. This under development has often been seen as one of the factors behind New Zealand's relatively low rate of productivity per capita by international comparisons, for example, being some 25 percent lower than that of Australia's (Mai et al., 2010). A report on high value manufacturing for the former Ministry of Science and Innovation (MSI, 2011, p. 19) commented that:

> The New Zealand high value manufacturing and services sector is under-developed, and could contribute substantially more to the economy than it currently does, particularly through growth in high productivity advanced technology industries.

This context for TBSFs has meant that it has become a priority of policy to stimulate and encourage the growth of TBSFs and 'high impact' entrepreneurial firms. The current New Zealand government has introduced a range of measures, including R&D grants, technology vouchers and tax cuts, targeted at raising business levels of R&D (Key, 2010). At the center of these measures, the technology transfer vouchers and grants have been targeted at improving spin-out commercialization from New Zealand's higher education institutions (HEIs) and aimed at lifting the relatively low levels of business R&D spend. During 2011 the threshold levels were reduced making vouchers and grants available for smaller TBSFs. Further enhanced funding was announced with the establishment of *Callaghan Innovation* in February 2013. The relevance for entrepreneurial finance of the role of *Callaghan Innovation* is discussed later in this chapter when we consider alternative sources of finance.

This context and policy issues provided the background for undertaking the program of interviews. The TBSFs were recruited from the nation's two main urban centers: Auckland and Wellington together with a third location at Palmerston North. New Zealand has only three main urban centers, the third being Christchurch. As the interviews were completed in 2011, it was felt that TBSFs located in New Zealand's only other large urban area, Christchurch, will have been affected by the earthquakes of February and June that year which caused widespread disruption to local businesses. Information about the sample is relevant. The study involved a program of twenty in-depth, face to face qualitative interviews with the founders and chief executives of TBSFs drawn from different technology-based sectors (Table 3.2). A further seven interviews were conducted with key informants drawn from the three locations (Table 3.3). These interviews were conducted in the three month period of September to November 2011. The coverage of different stages in TBSFs development, or staged life cycle model (Berger and Udell, 1998), was ensured by including respondents from start-up, early stage, developing and more mature

Table 3.2 Technology-based small firms: size and sector profile data

TBSF	Sector	FTEs	Year Est.
#01	Bio-pharm	10	1996
#02	Software dvpt	5	2009
#03	IT systems	42	1996
#04	Electronics prdt	4	2008
#05	Software dvpt	4	2008
#06	Bio-pharm	3	2008
#07	Software and IT systems	12	1997
#08	Software dvpt	8	2009
#09	GPS application and prdt	5	2009
#10	Media and film prdn	17	1977
#11	Construction prdt	3	2001
#12	Software dvpt	21	2000
#13	Software dvpt	19	2002
#14	Admin and support prdt	1	2010
#15	Photographic and optical	2	2006
#16	Software simulation	31	1999
#17	Computer networking	2	2009
#18	Interactive software	3	2008
#19	IT systems	2	2009
#20	Interactive software	5	2004

Source: Modified from Deakins and North (2013).

Table 3.3 Key informants

Key informant	Respondent's role
#01	Regional Development Agency: economic development
#02	Incubator support
#03	Regional Development Agency: economic development
#04	Funder and Investor
#05	National Agency
#06	Funder and Investor
#07	Incubator support

Source: Modified from Deakins and North (2013).

firms and range of industry sectors was represented including bio-tech, IT and creative/media sectors (Table 3.2).

The qualitative findings from this study confirmed the heavy reliance on internal sources, bootstrapping and aversion to external finance that we have noted from the quantitative surveys, although a number of TBSFs had managed to raise additional private capital through their own contacts and networks. All TBSFs relied upon internal funding to some extent; however, thirteen (65 percent) either relied totally on internal funding (from the initial start-up) or relied upon a combination of internal funding, bootstrapping and private investors.[3] There was evidence that the entrepreneurs would prefer to fund internally, using bootstrapping techniques where possible, even if it meant a slower and perhaps more paced development:

> We have bootstrapped from the start; you have really got to know what you are doing with your cashflows and that is challenging . . . . Money earned was put back in the business to grow step by step. (TBSF # 13)

However, it would be incorrect to indicate that there was total aversion to raising external funding, but only a small number had raised venture capital (two companies) or had undertaken a search procedure for business angels. This was overlain by a strongly held perception that the informal and formal venture capital (VC) markets in New Zealand were perceived to be very limited and lack sufficient numbers of HNWIs with experience of investing in technology-based companies. For example, one respondent had sought VC funds in Australia and New Zealand and commented that

> We focus on highly worth individuals in Australia and New Zealand, that is the target market at the moment, because they are more likely to support a business in this part of the world. (However) the depth of capital markets is limited in New Zealand. The amount of risk capital is very low – and the pool for funding technology firms in New Zealand is incredibly low. (TBSF # 06)

A further illustrative comment was made by one respondent that had raised some VC funds, but also pointed to the difficulty of raising funding offshore for amounts less than NZ$5m:

> It is hard work to get funding in NZ, because there are not many places to go. It is difficult to get funding outside NZ because we are typically too small. For a lot of VC organizations (who are looking to invest $5+million) the company is too small. Other opportunities are offshore but that is also harder, because we are not US based. So we are restricted to where we can go. (TBSF # 16)

The interview evidence with TBSF entrepreneurs confirmed that there was a distinct reluctance to raise external debt finance. Only a small number had sought and raised finance from the commercial banks. There was a view that banks are not willing to value intellectual property (IP). One respondent from a mature company commented:

> Obtaining debt financing is nearly impossible and we can't even get a bank overdraft facility. (TBSF # 03)

Where bank finance had been secured, not surprisingly, it was property that had been used for collateral.

> The business was funded by a bank loan, as much money as possible, house as collateral. Nearly spent all that money (on product development), but made it back after the product launch. (TBSF # 15)

Overall, for raising both external equity and debt, technology-based entrepreneurs' perceptions of cost, time and difficulties, combined with the well-known reluctance to dilute ownership, meant that there was trade-off between avoidance of such external sources and acceptance of limiting their own company's business development. The following comment being representative:

> You might be wanting to grow faster than your capital will let you do so. You have to constrain your growth because you don't have the finance. (TBSF # 13)

The restricted nature of external equity markets was supported by views from the key informants:

> We have definitely got a funding gap over here. Public money needs to step up, especially in the tech-sector. Moreover, New Zealand struggles with a lack of skilled and experienced people who are able to take a leading role as lead investors. Problem is the early stage where there is still a high risk, not later stage. There is a need for more experience, the learning process yet to happen in New Zealand. (KI # 03)
>
> There is a particular gap in New Zealand with early stage TBSFs, Ministry of Economic Development[4] consider that this market has been sorted by the private sector and by business angels, but business angels need investor ready companies and there is a role that needs to be fulfilled through support. (KI # 04)
>
> There is a very thin pool of capital (in New Zealand), there is not the depth in investment funds as there is in the US or UK and we do not have the depth of larger companies, so less experienced in understanding how bigger companies look like. (KI #06)

There was also verification of the perspectives given on access to bank finance. It was recognized that in the post GFC era, raising bank finance required collateral in the form of property (rather than through securing intangible assets in IP).

> Before the recession two banks were interested in investing money with-out (private) property as collateral. It is less these days, you need at least to bring in tangible assets as collateral. (KI # 02)

This qualitative study confirms demand side limitations on external risk capital markets in New Zealand through preferences of New Zealand entrepreneurs and an over-reliance on internal funds and bootstrapping techniques. Although there is demand for external debt finance, there is a distrust of banks which produces a discouraged borrower effect in TBSF entrepreneurs and innovative companies (Deakins and North, 2013). This is substantiated by a subsequent further qualitative study with TBSF entrepreneurs in the agri-business sector (Deakins et al., 2015). This latter study involved a further 34 interviews with TBSF entrepreneurs and, although not specifically concerned with investigating financial preferences, concluded that, although there had been some supply side improvements (these are discussed later in this chapter):

> There is still evidence of an over-reliance on internal funds and evidence of a discouragement effect to apply for external funding.

The earlier study (Deakins and North, 2013, p. 97) concluded that there was an external equity finance gap:

> There was evidence of a distinct finance gap in the external equity market in New Zealand. For amounts below $1m these could be sought from networks of business angels, even though such sources were limited and restricted. If the funding sought was in the range $1m–$5m, this was likely to fall between the informal and formal venture markets.

Although we have not discussed finance gaps and market failure, the earlier Business Finance Survey indicated that the vast majority of firms that sought external finance were able to achieve it (Statistics New Zealand, 2005b, p. 4):

> The survey results indicate that the vast majority of finance requests made by New Zealand businesses result in finance being obtained. Ninety percent of finance requests made by businesses resulted in either some or all of the amount sought being received.

Of course, such surveys do not take into account entrepreneur preferences and the discouragement effects of the frustrations of New Zealand entrepreneurs with limited and narrow external equity markets, which were more clearly revealed by the much later qualitative studies reported here. However, before we reach conclusions about whether such finance gaps exist, and their extent, we need to consider the supply side perspective of entrepreneurial finance and review changes, if any, on the supply side.

ENTREPRENEURIAL FINANCE: A SUPPLY SIDE PERSPECTIVE

In this section we examine in more detail New Zealand's financial infrastructure and the supply of venture capital. We have indicated previously in our discussion of the New Zealand context that the economy has stable and secure banking institutions that are largely Australian owned, but fragmented and immature venture capital markets. As debt capital is clearly the most important source of external finance, we examine New Zealand's commercial banking system first, before venture capital markets and other alternative sources of external finance.

Debt Finance and New Zealand's Commercial Banks

Like other developed economies, New Zealand's banking system is highly concentrated with an oligopolistic market structure dominated by the four main commercial banks, which are Australian owned. For example, the big four have close to 90 percent of total banking sector assets and account for 95 percent of the residential mortgage market. An independent Working Paper by the International Monetary Fund (IMF) (Jang and Kataoka, 2013) not only confirmed the strength and security of the major four New Zealand banks, but commented that their published capital ratios underestimated their financial strength in the face of any corporate or bad debt shocks to the system and that they have capital well above the regulatory requirements with 'high quality' capital. Jang and Kataoka report that the top two banks, ANZ and BNZ, accounting for 76.7 percent by value of the corporate lending of these 'big four' commercial banks as of September 2011.

Despite the small size of the New Zealand economy, the commercial banks' profitability compares favorably with that of North American and European banks because there have not been any requirements to offset profits to meet bad debts. For example, recent reported profits for 2013–2014 show that ANZ is largest and most profitable with NZD1.68 billion profits, followed by Westpac at NZD864m, BNZ at NZD850m and ASB at NZD776m (interest.co.nz, 2014).

Despite the security of New Zealand banks, there are indications that their lending practices to entrepreneurs and small business owners have been considered to be conservative and reliant on security. For example, although now a dated paper, a former Ministry of Economic Development (MED) Working Paper on New Zealand banks' lending practices to SMEs considered that, at the time, the banks 'were yet to use credit scoring as a tool for assessing risk in the SME sector' (MED, 2003, p. 1), at a time when this practice had been widely adopted by commercial banks in other economies. Therefore, commercial banks' lending practices could be seen to be traditional and reliant upon the entrepreneur-bank manager relationship which would require time to develop and be dependent upon a company's financial track record. There is some evidence that the New Zealand banks have a reliance on traditional relationship banking, for example, a study by Khoo-Lattimore et al. (2010) on the New Zealand banks' customers and their banking relationships considered that New Zealand has a strong individualism culture and relatively sophisticated personal banking market which relies on personal trust and empathy (Khoo-Lattimore et al., 2010).

It is arguable, therefore, that obtaining entrepreneurial loan capital would be difficult for New Zealand entrepreneurs even during relatively strong economic growth conditions that existed before the post GFC environment without security and a well-established banking relationship. A scenario that is supported by the qualitative evidence reported earlier from TBSF entrepreneurs seeking risk and long term debt finance.

The relative stability and security of New Zealand's commercial banks has contributed to a stable debt finance supply for New Zealand's entrepreneurs. For example, there is no evidence that the New Zealand banks decreased lending to SMEs during the post GFC global economic recession as did happen, for example, in some Western economies such as the UK, where dramatic falls in lending to SMEs were reported (Fraser, 2009). By contrast, as reported earlier in our demand side discussion, lending to SMEs actually increased in 2010 which was during the height of the recession in New Zealand. However, rather ironically this has also meant that there has not been any stimulus for the emergence of alternative credit markets that have emerged elsewhere and more comment is made of this lack of 'innovation' in credit markets in our concluding section.

Equity Finance and New Zealand's Venture Capital Sector

New Zealand does not have a tradition of equity investments by HNWIs and, as indicated previously through the comments of a Governor of the Reserve Bank, New Zealanders have preferred historically to invest in property (Bollard, 2006). This has meant that the size of the informal angel investment market has been relatively small. A report for the former

Ministry of Economic Development in 2004 attempted to measure the size of the HNWI market in New Zealand. The report estimated that the market at the time was around NZ$500m and that the number of individual investors was between 1,000 and 20,000, but only a small proportion, less than 100, could be described as active angels. They found early development of syndicates with up to one-fifth of angels operating through syndicates. Only the *Icehouse*, a business incubator in Auckland, was mentioned as an example of a business accelerator and having a network of business angels (Infometrics, 2004). This immature informal angel market has continued to grow slowly and has been encouraged by attempts to stimulate networks through other business incubators in New Zealand and by the country's network of regional Economic Development Agencies (EDAs).[5] Three years later, by 2007 little had changed, an updated report on this market, undertaken by the former Ministry, found that the number of active angels had grown to 'currently at least 100' and that the majority were concentrated in Auckland with two-thirds of investments in the seed or start-up stage (MED, 2007).

By 2011, however, the early stage investment market had grown in New Zealand, but was still immature. A report by the New Zealand Venture Investment Fund (NZVIF) on early stage investments estimated that the median seed, start up and early expansion pre-money valuations were NZ$1.08m, NZ$2.4m and NZ$7.45m respectively (NZVIF, 2012) and the report indicated that 'significant progress' had been made in the last 10 years.

There has been some development in networks of informal business angels through the business angel networks (BANs) encouraged by New Zealand's EDAs. For example, by 2013, a study by the author with TBSFs in the agri-business sector, reported earlier in the chapter, found evidence of the emergence of specialized BANs which targeted specific sectors, such as fruit growing, stimulated in part by the work of local EDAs. Members of these locally based BANs were often former farmers or fruit growers now seeking to invest in similar technology-based small enterprises in the same sector (Deakins et al., 2015). Albeit that this development was still at 'an early stage' and could not be regarded as a significant change in the funding environment (Deakins et al., 2015). Nevertheless, there is greater informal business angel activity and the development of additional business accelerator programmes such as *LightningLab* now established in New Zealand's three main cities; Wellington, Auckland and Christchurch (LightningLab, 2014). In the New Zealand context, informal VC investors need to specialize (hence the sector specific BANs) or be prepared to spread risks through a larger number of smaller investments than might be the case in a larger economy in Western Europe or North America.

Growing developments, such as BANs based on business incubators, such as the aforementioned *Icehouse* in Auckland, represent attempts to bring together informal business angels willing to invest small amounts of equity (Icehouse, 2015).

A similar picture is apparent for later stage and development venture capital. Although New Zealand has a venture capital association, the NZVCA, it is difficult to judge the extent of any growth in formal venture capital activity. The NZVCA has grown activity and sponsored events through its core goal, its mission is to: 'develop a world-best private equity ('PE') and venture capital ('VC') environment for the benefit of investors and entrepreneurs in New Zealand' (NZVCA, 2014a). The NZVCA's annual monitor of equity and venture capital investments reported a 'significant increase' in activity in 2013 compared to 2012, with levels of activity similar to 2011 which was a 'record year' (NZVCA, 2014b). Figures 3.1 and 3.2 indicate the levels of private equity (PE) and venture capital (VC) investments and the recorded number of disclosed deals for the years 2011 to 2013 inclusive. It can be seen that there is a noticeable dip in activity in 2012, before recovery of investments and the number of deals in 2013. For 2013, total investment value was reported at NZ$456.3m with a total of 82 deals. This compares to a total invest-ment value of only NZ$111.4m and 62 deals in 2012 (NZVCA, 2014b). Historically, there can be years when activity and investment levels fall, even though the domestic economy can be performing strongly reflecting the rather shallow pool of investors, private equity and the levels of VC in a small economy such as is the case with New Zealand. Thus, historically there has been growth in private equity and venture capital markets, but they remain shallow, small and subject to large fluctuations in activity and investments from year to year.

Overall, there are limited sources of formal equity and venture capital. Indeed, the NZVCA's latest report (NZVCA, 2014b, p. 7) comments:

> Historical trends have highlighted a funding gap for early stage growth compa-nies seeking funds beyond the level of seed and start-up funding available from domestic VC and early stage funds.

This funding gap for entrepreneurial and growth companies persists despite the recent developments in angel networks and investors that have been mentioned earlier. It is a funding gap that has encouraged the New Zealand government to introduce a 'hybrid' seed and venture capital fund, the *New Zealand Seed Co-investment Fund*, and the main features are described in the next paragraph.

The New Zealand Seed Co-Investment Fund was established in 2005 and made its first investment in 2006. It provides a fund of NZ$40m of

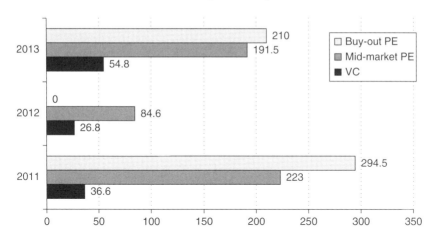

Figure 3.1   Private equity and venture capital investments (NZ$ million excluding divestments)

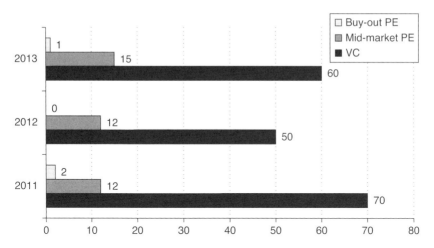

Source: NZVCA (2014b). *New Zealand Private Equity and Venture Capital Monitor 2013 full year review.*

Figure 3.2   Private equity and venture capital activity (number of deals excluding divestments)

matched seed funding, the aim being to further develop and support seed and early stage investment markets (NZVIF, 2014). Investments through the Fund are limited to a maximum investment of NZ$250,000 in any one company or group of companies; with the possibility of follow-on capital investments up to a maximum investment in any company of NZ$750,000. By August 2013, approximately NZ$140m had been invested (NZVIF, 2014). According to NZVIF, NZ$176m had been committed through the program in private equity (NZVIF, 2014).

However, despite the existence of the state supported Seed Co-Investment Fund, the development of business accelerator programs, the growing importance of business incubator-based informal VC networks and the growth of some angel syndicates, the formal private equity and VC sector, and hence the funding escalator, remains restricted in extent, fragmented, narrow and underdeveloped. For a potential high growth New Zealand-owned company, seeking staged VC investments, it is still likely to seek and source such funding overseas.

Alternative Sources of Entrepreneurial Finance

The New Zealand entrepreneur is faced with limited alternative sources of risk finance. There is state funded support assistance provided by the regional EDAs and their partners. Direct technology grants can be obtained for entrepreneurs and companies engaged in R&D and subsidized consultancy and training support, and is considered in more detail under the role of the national agency that administers assistance for R&D that has been mentioned previously: *Callaghan Innovation*. Otherwise, New Zealand has yet to benefit from Internet-based crowd-funding platforms that have become an important alternative market of both debt and equity finance in North America and Europe. A comment is added below about the first New Zealand crowdfunding platform, *PledgeMe*.

Callaghan Innovation[6] was established with over NZD$400m over four years on February 1, 2013 to work with New Zealand businesses and Crown Research Institutes and New Zealand scientists in universities to commercialize research and assist R&D with technology-based companies. It took over the management of technology grants and vouchers, previously administered by the former Ministry for Science and Innovation. Its importance is reflected by the employment of a team of about 400 researchers, scientists, engineers, technologists, business people investment managers and account managers. The level of current funding administered is more than NZ$140m a year in business R&D funding through the following grants and support:

- R&D Growth Grants, which are aimed at businesses experienced in research and development in New Zealand, to support an increase in investment.
- R&D Project Grants which are designed to support businesses with smaller research and development programs and those new to R&D.
- Research Student Grants as incentives for graduates to work with technology-based companies on commercialization projects.
- Business advice is also provided through its team of advisers and partner organizations. (Callaghan Innovation, 2014: http://www.cal laghaninnovation.govt.nz)

PledgeMe is New Zealand's sole crowdfunding Internet platform. Crowdfunding came late to New Zealand and *PledgeMe* has only been established for two years at the time of writing (2015). In that time the platform has raised funding for 700 projects claiming a success rate of 49 percent with a level of NZ$2.9m funds raised. However, none of the projects successfully funded so far are for equity funding and at present it remains a platform of potential for entrepreneurial equity finance rather than as an important addition to alternative sources (PledgeMe, 2014: http://www.pledgeme.co.nz).

There are a small number of microfinance schemes in New Zealand, which are limited to targeting poverty and social exclusion rather than the provision of small amounts of credit to potential entrepreneurs from disadvantaged backgrounds. This may be, at least partly, because the New Zealand government has focused resources on the encouragement of technology-based entrepreneurship and small funding schemes are not deemed a priority. Rather efforts have gone into ensuring the regulatory regime is relatively benign, making it easy to start and 'do' business. For example a scheme that targets the indigenous Māori community is *Nga Tangata Microfinance*, which focuses on making small loans to households in the Māori community in South Auckland and at alleviating poverty (Nga Tangata Microfinance Trust, 2014: http://www.ngatan gatamicrofinance.org.nz).

Overall, there is thus a conundrum and lack of innovation regarding entrepreneurial finance in New Zealand. There is perhaps a belief that successful entrepreneurs will be able to raise external finance from the emergent networks of business angels and other sources of private equity. This is explored in more detail in our concluding comments.

CONCLUDING COMMENTS

New Zealand is a unique environment for entrepreneurs; it is one of the easiest places for entrepreneurs to do business and the easiest economy in which to start a new business; it has stable and secure banking infrastructure which contains some of the highest ranked commercial banks for safe practices and its economy has shown resilience and positive growth rates during the post GFC environment. Yet, ironically, it can be almost stifling for growth orientated entrepreneurs seeking external finance, especially external equity finance either from HNWIs or formal VC companies.

New Zealand's relatively secure and stable financial credit institutions have not provided a financial environment that has benefited entrepreneurs that seek external finance. The lack of a state sponsored loan guarantee scheme has also meant that the commercial banks have not been able to transfer their high risk loans to any secure basis and will always require 100 percent guarantees for risk-based projects. We have suggested that this situation has also contributed to a discouraged borrower effect in this chapter and in other work (Deakins et al., 2015).

Private equity and venture capital markets are narrow and fragmented, even though there have been some promising recent developments. Most promisingly, the emergence of sector specific informal Business Angel Networks (BANs), encouraged by the regional EDAs, has been encouraging and has reflected the growing activity of HNWIs and business angels. The development of BANs has harnessed latent individual sources of risk capital through networks based on specific sectors such as subsectors of agri-business, for example, in fruit growing. In addition, returning 'cashed out' entrepreneurs (who may have left New Zealand to grow their business) may also prove to be an important source of investment for seed and early stage informal venture capital. However, later stage development capital and formal VC sources remains an issue with evidence that entrepreneurs are either forced to search for significant VC funding overseas or become takeover targets for MNCs. Government attempts to stimulate equity and VC markets through the Seed Co-investment Fund has had some effect, but this is primarily in early stage funding.

Direct government support has included technology grants and vouchers targeted at R&D and later stage growth and project development. Research by the author with TBSF entrepreneurs found that, while such grants have been welcomed as being valuable by respondents, nevertheless, they were not without criticism with a preference for R&D tax credits rather than direct grants and found entrepreneurs perceived bureaucracy, which had some discouragement effects on some firms that would have had eligible projects (Deakins et al., 2015). Rather ironically, we have noted earlier that New Zealand is recognized by the World Bank as one of the easiest nations in which 'to do business', it could be because of the minimization of regulation and ease of doing business in New Zealand more generally that requirements to complete paperwork for access to direct technology grants is seen as 'bureaucratic' by technology-based entrepreneurs.

The conundrum is that the relatively stable financial environment in New Zealand has not benefited growth orientated entrepreneurs who are looking for innovative sources of risk capital. For example, there has been little in the way of financial innovation in the supply of risk capital. New Zealand has, until very recently, nothing to compare to the crowdfunding platforms that have emerged in the US and the UK. Such growth orientated entrepreneurs, far from gaining advantages in being located in New Zealand, an economy relatively sheltered from the post GFC economic climate, can be considered to have been resource constrained in access to financial risk capital.

NOTES

1. Official population is 4,539,163 which continues to grow strongly due to net inward migration (http://www.stats.govt.nz).
2. Exchange rate at November 6, 2014.
3. Six firms were totally reliant on internal funding; four firms mentioned bootstrapping techniques, 11 firms relied upon a combination of internal funds and private investors, six firms using internal funds and government grants and only three firms were using either bank loans or overdrafts.
4. This refers to the former Ministry of Economic Development, this became the Ministry of Business, Innovation and Employment when it was merged in 2012 with the former Ministries of Labour and Science and Innovation.
5. New Zealand has network of 14 state-funded EDAs whose role is concerned with economic development and direct business support: http://www.edanz.org.nz.
6. The agency is named in honour of Sir Paul Callaghan, a world leading, pioneering New Zealand scientist who also became a successful technology-based entrepreneur. Sir Paul died from cancer in 2012.

REFERENCES

Battisti, M. and Deakins, D. (2011), *Managing Under Recession: Perspectives from New Zealand Small Firms: Report from BusinesSMEasure 2010*, Wellington: New Zealand Centre for SME Research, Massey University.

Berger, A.N. and Udell, G.F. (1998), 'The economics of small business finance: the roles of private equity and debt markets in the financial growth cycle', *Journal of Banking and Finance*, **22** (6): 613–673.

Bollard, A. (2006), Speech to PWC annual tax conference November 2006, Wellington: Governor Reserve Bank of New Zealand.

Callaghan Innovation (2014), retrieved from http://wwwcallaghaninnovation.govt.nz (accessed November 18, 2014).

Chetty, S. and Campbell-Hunt, C. (2004), 'A strategic approach to internationalization: a traditional versus a born global approach', *Journal of International Marketing*, **12** (1): 57–81.

Deakins, D. and North, D. (2013), 'The role of finance in the development of technology-based SMEs: evidence from New Zealand', *Journal of Entrepreneurship, Business and Economics*, **1** (1/2): 82–100.

Deakins, D., North, D., and Bensemann, J. (2015), 'Paradise Lost? The case of technology-based small firms in New Zealand in the post global financial crisis economic environment', *Venture Capital: An International Journal of Entrepreneurial Finance*, **17** (1–2): 129–150.

Fraser, S. (2009), 'Small firms in the credit crisis, evidence from the UK survey of SME finances', Coventry: Warwick Business School, University of Warwick.

Icehouse (2015), 'The Icehouse is where kiwi businesses grow', retrieved from http://www.theicehouse.co.nz (accessed February 25, 2015).

Infometrics (2004), *New Zealand's Angel Capital Market*, Report for the former Ministry of Economic Development, Wellington: Ministry of Economic Development.

Interest.co.nz (2014), 'Bank profits', retrieved from http://www.interest.co.nz (accessed November 13, 2014).

Jang, B.K. and Kataoka, M. (2013), 'New Zealand banks' vulnerabilities and capital adequacy', IMF Working Paper 13/7 January, Washington DC: IMF.

Key, J. (2010), 'Pre-Budget announcement', May 11, 2010, retrieved from http://www.beehive.govt.nz (accessed November 2012).

Khoo-Lattimore, C., Yang, L. and Ekiz, E.H. (2010), 'Banking the Kiwi way: examining the underpinnings of relationship quality in New Zealand banks', *Banking and Finance Letters*, **2** (4): 409–418. LightningLab (2014), retrieved from http://lightninglab.co.nz (accessed November 17, 2014).

Mai, B., Janssen, J., Lewis, G., and McLoughlin, S. (2010), 'Taking on the West Island: how does our productivity stack up?', Paper presented at Statistics New Zealand and New Zealand Treasury Paper prepared for New Zealand Association of Economists' Annual Conference, Auckland.

MBIE (2014), *The Small Business Sector Report 2014*, Wellington: Ministry of Business, Innovation and Employment.

McKeever, E., Jack, S., and Anderson, A. (2015), 'Embedded entrepreneurship in the creative re-construction of place', *Journal of Business Venturing*, **30** (1): 50–65.

Ministry of Economic Development (MED) (2003), 'Bank lending practices to small and medium sized enterprises', Wellington: Ministry of Economic Development.

Ministry of Economic Development (MED) (2007), 'Baseline Review of Angel Investment in New Zealand (Undertaken as Part of the Formation of the Seed Co-Investment Fund)', Wellington: Ministry of Economic Development.

Ministry of Science and Innovation (MSI) (2011), 'Powering innovation: improving access to and uptake of R&D in the high value manufacturing and services sector', report for the former Ministry of Science and Innovation, Wellington: Ministry of Science and Innovation.

Myers, S.C. (2001), 'Capital structure', *Journal of Economic Perspectives*, **15** (12): 81–102.

New Zealand Venture Capital Association (NCZVCA) (2014a), retrieved from http://www.nzvca.co.nz (accessed November 17, 2014).

New Zealand Venture Capital Association (NZVCA) (2014b), *New Zealand Private Equity and Venture Capital Monitor 2013 full year review*, Auckland: New Zealand Venture Capital Association.

New Zealand Venture Investment Fund (NZVIF) (2012), *The Valuation of Early-stage Investments in New Zealand*, Wellington: New Zealand Venture Investment Fund.

New Zealand Venture Investment Fund (NZVIF) (2014), 'New Zealand Seed Co-investment Fund', retrieved from http://www.nzvif.co.nz/seed-co-investment-overview.html (accessed October 30, 2014).

Nga Tangata Microfinance Trust (2014), retrieved from http://www.ngatangatamicrofi-nance.org.nz (accessed November 19, 2014).

PledgeMe (2014), retrieved from http://www.pledgeme.co.nz (accessed November 18, 2014).

PricewaterhouseCoopers (2013), *New Zealand's banks report lending growth, but profits are down: Banking perspectives*, February 2013, Wellington: PricewaterhouseCoopers.

Reserve Bank of New Zealand (2014), *Annual Report 2013–2014*, Wellington: Reserve Bank of New Zealand.

Scott-Kennel, J. (2013), 'Models of internationalisation: the New Zealand experience', *International Journal of Business and Globalisation*, **10** (2): 105–128.

Statistics New Zealand (2005a), *Business Finance Survey 2004*, Wellington: Statistics New Zealand.

Statistics New Zealand (2005b), *Business Finance Survey 2004 press release May 2, 2005*, Wellington: Statistics New Zealand.

Statistics New Zealand (2012), *Business Operations Survey: 2011*, Wellington: Statistics New Zealand.

Statistics New Zealand (2014), 'Employment outpaces strongest population growth in 10 years', Press Release, Wellington: Statistics New Zealand, retrieved from http://www.stats.govt.nz (accessed November 6, 2014).

Stevens, P. (2008), 'Just good friends? Relationship banking and access to finance in New Zealand firms', Wellington: former Ministry of Economic Development.

World Bank (2014), *Doing Business 2015: Going Beyond Efficiency: Economy Profile, New Zealand*, Washington DC: The International Bank for Reconstruction and Development / The World Bank.

World Trade Organization (2012), *Doha Development Agenda*, Geneva: World Trade Organisation, retrieved from http://www.wto.org/english/tratop_e/dda_e/dda_e.htm (accessed February 26, 2015).

Zahra, S. (2007), 'Contextualising theory building in entrepreneurship research', *Journal of Business Venturing*, **22** (3): 443–452.

4. Venture capital investment and internationalization: a case to consider
Miwako Nitani and Allan Riding

INTRODUCTION

This chapter reports on how an intentional program of post-investment activity on the part of a venture capital (VC) investor, a program that seeks to encourage internationalization of portfolio firms, can add incremental value. The chapter responds to the call voiced by Lockett et al. (2008, p. 56) for further research that 'trace[s] the changes in VC involvement in promoting export intensity over time in particular ventures' and is important for several reasons.

First, this chapter adds to our understanding of the specific processes through which a VC adds value, a topic described as a 'black box' for researchers (De Clercq and Manigart, 2007). Second, the chapter adds to our understanding of the role – or potential role – of venture capitalists in the internationalization process. According to Fernhaber and McDougall-Covin (2009), VCs, through their financial resources, knowledge, and reputation can induce portfolio firms to internationalize. This persuasion may be important because founders, left to their own devices, may be too conservative to do so (George et al., 2005). Third, the chapter contributes to our understanding of the internationalization process itself – especially the process through which new firms pursue internationalization. The internationalization of young small- and medium-sized enterprises (SMEs) has been discussed widely in the academic literature but consensus is lacking.[1] Finally, for business owners seeking international markets, the chapter may indicate a means of obtaining both financial and knowledge resources.

The chapter also holds implications for public policies and programs. As a matter of public policy, the Canadian government (like several other governments) has established an export credit agency (Export Development Corporation, EDC, a Canadian Crown Corporation[2]) that operates at arm's length from government with a mandate to facilitate and encourage Canadian exports. This chapter focuses on the impact of a strategic initiative, the *Connect* program, implemented by EDC as part of its larger role that includes being a VC investor. By marshaling its organization-wide expertise, networks and experience in international business, EDC has the potential to facilitate internationalization by adding otherwise unavailable knowledge and experience to firms in its VC portfolios. While most Canadian firms and VCs are aware of the imperative of internationalization, they typically lack the resources – such as lack of international contacts and knowledge of global markets – available to EDC. Accordingly, this chapter compares, with other investee firms, the valuations of portfolio firms that have been targeted by the EDC Equity group's *Connect* strategy.

Overall, this chapter seeks to gain a yet better understanding of the mechanisms through which VC involvement can lead to value creation and internationalization. The chapter begins with an overview of the Canadian context for this research. This is followed by a brief review of the research literature on SME internationalization with particular reference to the role of VC investors in the process. The chapter then describes the methodology and findings and closes with a discussion of implications, limitations and future research directions.

THE CANADIAN CONTEXT FOR THE RESEARCH

The context for this chapter is Canada, home to a relatively small – and widely dispersed – domestic product market. The rate of growth required for VCs to achieve their desired rate of return objectives, typically 30 to 40 percent per annum, can seldom be realized in the limited and geographically expansive Canadian marketplace: to attain VCs' required rates of return, therefore, Canadian firms need to internationalize.[3] In this respect, the Canadian setting differs from that in the US where, arguably, internationalization is not as important because of the large market within the country (even though much of the research on SME internationalization has been conducted in the US context). Canada is positioned on the US border and is connected to the US by highly developed road, rail, pipeline and telecom networks; the countries share a common language and both have highly developed legal systems. Moreover, trade is enabled through the North American Free Trade Agreement (NAFTA),[4] a long-standing free trade agreement involving Canada, the United States and Mexico. Accordingly, 90 percent of Canadian exporter firms export to the US market.

According to the Canadian Venture Capital Association (CVCA), the total investment in 2013 in 452 'classical' venture capital deals was $2 billion. However, with more than $29 billion invested by US VCs during 2013 the Canadian VC market is small, relative to the US, in absolute

terms.[5] In terms of venture capital stock on a per-unit-of-gross-domestic-product basis, Canada is home to a relatively large venture capital market, ranking sixth among 140 economies.[6] This work, therefore, also adds to the research literature by way of this different contextual setting.

The Canadian federal government participates in the venture capital market through the VC divisions of Export Development Canada (EDC) and Business Development Bank of Canada (BDC). Both are crown corporations that are direct investors in entrepreneurial firms and are also indirect investors as fund-of-funds providers for other VC firms. BDC holds a domestic mandate while EDC's mandate is to expand Canadian export capacity and to help Canadian companies respond to international business opportunities. With this goal, EDC seeks to invest in, and nurture, internationalizing high potential businesses.[7]

PREVIOUS RESEARCH

External capital is necessary for business growth in order to augment the base of productive fixed assets and to finance the need for the additional working capital that typically accompanies growth. However, Binks and Ennew (1996) argue that growth also adds to risk in the form of information asymmetry. Because of their risk, venture capital is regarded as a more appropriate source of financing for that important minority of enterprises that, through growth, provide a disproportionate share of job-creation and economic welfare (Brierley, 2001). Venture capital is also a particularly effective means of commercializing innovation (Kortum and Lerner, 2000).

As noted by, among others, Amit et al. (1998) returns to VC investment accrue from two sources: the investor's ability to 'pick winners' and the investor's ability to nurture early stage firms to a successful exit. Once a VC investment has been made, VCs' post-investment involvement typically involves activities that are either related to monitoring or to adding value (De Clercq and Manigart, 2007). Monitoring comprises the various means by which VCs protect themselves from moral hazard: potentially harmful actions on the part of entrepreneurs. Because VC investors hold a significant financial stake in investee firms, they also have incentives to do more than simply monitor performance: value-adding activities are those means by which VCs seek to enhance the potential returns from their investments.

Value-adding VC Activities

The early works of (among many others) MacMillan et al. (1989), Gorman and Sahlman (1989), Sapienza et al. (1994, 1996) and Rosenstein et al. (1993) provided initial insights into the nature of VCs' value added activities. De Clercq and Manigart (2007), in their review of the research literature on VC value-added activities, suggest considerable 'variation with respect to both what VCs do and the extent of their involvement' (De Clercq and Manigart, 2007, p. 193) and that the activities depend on both the characteristics of the VC portfolio companies and the attributes of the VC. Maula (2001) and Large and Muegge (2007) have sought to develop taxonomies of various forms of value-added activities employed by VCs.

Maula (2001), seeking to develop a parsimonious categorization of non-financial value-added activities, presents three themes to capture the broad scope of value-added VC activities:

- Facilitation of resource acquisition (for example, helping the owner-ship team obtain additional financing, networking with potential customers and suppliers, facilitating access to distribution and supply chains);
- Assistance with knowledge acquisition (for example, information about technology, markets and competitive intelligence); and,
- Providing credibility/accreditation.

In subsequent work, Maula et al. (2005) examined the impact of 'type of VC investor' on the relationship between value-adding inputs and out-comes. They found that investors differ in terms of the effectiveness of their respective value-added activities. They note (Maula et al., 2005, p. 4) that:

> [T]here has been little research to examine whether different types of venture capitalists differ in terms of their ability to deliver value-adding services.

Large and Muegge (2007) generated an eight-category typology of value-adding inputs in which they distinguish between externally and internally oriented activities. Externally oriented activities comprise *legitimation* and *outreach*. Legitimation refers to the passive process by which certain attributes (for example, credibility, reputation, validation and certifica-tion) accrue to the venture from its association with the VC. Outreach, according to Large and Muegge (2007), are those proactive activities that generate value for the venture by establishing direct connections to key external stakeholders. Internally oriented value-adding activities include recruiting (locating talented professional and managerial staff), men-toring, strategizing, helping with operational activities, consulting and working with the management team to maintain focus. Notwithstanding this taxonomy, Large and Muegge (2007, p. 21) observe that there seems to be 'little consensus regarding the definition and measurement of value-adding inputs and value-added outcomes, and little consensus regarding which of the VCs' value-adding inputs are most important'.

It is also not entirely clear whether so-called 'value-adding activities' actually do add value. De Clercq and Manigart (2007) point out that studies of VC value added inevitably include a survival bias in that survey respondents do not typically include failed portfolio firms. They suggest that this may account for divergent findings: where some researchers report positive impacts of VC non-financial value added, others do not.

This chapter focuses on value-added actions in the case of one particular venture capitalist: a publicly owned export credit agency that seeks to facilitate internationalization of portfolio firms. This prompts a review of previous research about the impacts of venture capital on internationalization.

The Role of Venture Capitalists in Internationalization

Previous research on the link between venture capital and internationalization is limited. In early research based in the US context, Carpenter et al. (2003) and George et al. (2005) contend that chief executive officers (CEOs) and senior management teams of young firms are reluctant to add the risks associated with internationalization to the risks already inherent in early stage growth-oriented enterprises. The researchers did report greater scope and scale of internationalization when board members with international experience complemented VC involvement. George et al. (2005) hypothesized that VC backing increases the likelihood of internationalization; however, and to some extent contrary to the findings of Carpenter et al. (2003), they found no empirical support for a relationship between VC ownership and international scope.

More recently, Fernhaber and McDougall-Covin (2009, p. 278) advanced three arguments as to why VC involvement could be related to internationalization. First, they postulated that: 'financial resources invested by VCs likely enable internationalization by allowing the new venture to exhibit higher levels of strategic aggressiveness'. Second, they reasoned that the nature of the VCs' knowledge can inhibit or encourage internationalization, where 'VCs lacking the knowledge resources to support internationalization might choose to discourage such a strategy' (Fernhaber and McDougall-Covin, 2009, p. 278). Third, they contend that the reputation of the VC matters in that it adds credibility: new ventures' inherently limited track records prompt potential external stakeholders to look to the reputation of firms with which a new venture might be associated in order to assess reputation. Based on a sample of 93 firms, the authors found that the international knowledge of a firm's VC was related to new venture internationalization, especially when the VC was reputable.

In research based on European data, Lockett et al. (2008) examined whether or not there is a positive relationship between VC involvement and export intensity. The analysis confirmed a positive association, finding that the impact of VCs on exporting performance was greatest at very early stages and then at the buyout stage (periods when both firms and investors are seeking rejuvenation). That is, the relationship between VC involvement and investee exporting was moderated by stage of investment.

Conversely, LiPuma (2006) reports that the absence of venture capital was positively correlated with increased internationalization and that differences in the nature of value added activity from differing sources of venture capital did not make a difference with respect to internationalization intensity. Moreover, Smolarski and Kut (2011) report that the type of VC financing affects internationalization: that staged financing and financing through a syndicate were positively associated with internationalization when used separately, but, curiously, were negatively associated with internationalization when used together. Why this is so remains unclear.

While these studies indicate that VCs may play a role with respect to internationalization, several questions and inconsistencies remain. First, the means by which VCs promote internationalization are unclear. Do VCs, in fact, modify the level of risk aversion of the management team or do they provide a means of reducing perceived risks? Do VCs influence the strategies undertaken by portfolio firms? Does internationalization in the context of VC involvement influence performance? These are among the directions for future research that had been posed by Fernhaber and McDougall-Covin (2009) and which this study seeks to address.

On SME Internationalization

Research on international entrepreneurship has been dominated for many years by the so-called 'stages theory'. It suggests that internationalization follows the gradual acquisition, integration and use of knowledge about foreign trade such that internationalization occurs over time and as the firm grows. As stated by Spence et al. (2011, p. 5), '[t]he premise is that smaller firms lack the efficiencies and economies of scale of larger SMEs as well as the management acumen required to survive in the international marketplace'. Likewise, Spence et al. (2011, p. 5) describe resource exchange theory – an alternative theoretical paradigm of internationalization 'that firm resources and competitive advantage are developed in a variety of ways that may depend on systemic differences between the entrepreneurial teams of exporters and non-exporters'. More recently, the advent of firms that internationalize early, for example, following or soon after inception, has challenged the traditional rationales. International new ventures (INVs) and 'born-globals' (BGs) comprise categories of firms for which internationalization occurs at very early stages. Spence et al. (2011) document that the frequency of firms that internationalize early seems unusual in the Canadian setting.

The Connect Program: The EDC Perspective

Like most VC investors, EDC provides various forms of non-financial value-added through direct involvement with investee firms. However, as Canada's export credit agency, EDC is distinct among Canadian VC investors by virtue of its familiarity with foreign markets. With its unique range of international expertise and the global scope of its contacts, EDC is well-positioned to select investee firms that are likely to internationalize and, therefore, more likely to grow. EDC marshals these resources by means of a strategic and intentional strategy known as the *Connect* program.

In keeping with EDC's broader mandate, EDC has a unique opportunity as an investor to offer incremental strategic value to its investment and business partners. It does so by leveraging its trade expertise from across the various departments within EDC, as well as its global networks and partnerships, to support foreign trade for Canadian active and potential exporters. The EDC equity team collaborates to form virtual *Connect* teams across EDC, which engage with strategic EDC customers to elicit intelligence. This knowledge is brought together by the Connect Team, which then works closely with EDC fund managers. In turn, the EDC equity team collaborates and disseminates the *Connect* intelligence with the general partners of the 45 investment funds in which EDC operates as a funder-of-funds as well as with selected firms in its own portfolio and selected firms within partner funds' portfolios. These interactions are carefully logged, which, at the time of the research, documented 446 interactions between the EDC equity team and firms in both the EDC portfolio and in the portfolios of EDC's fund partners.

According to EDC, the *Connect* strategy seeks to cultivate international sales and growth for Canadian SMEs and to increase access to international markets. To do so, *Connect* activities include: introducing Canadian SMEs to potential foreign clients and to companies that could be potential investors or partners; integrating Canadian portfolio companies into global supply chains; and exchanging market and business intelligence. The *Connect* initiative identifies trends and opportunities, and then assists portfolio companies by facilitating global business that capitalizes on those trends. These activities seek to support EDC's mandate by helping Canadian companies respond to international business opportunities. *Connect* activities include acquiring market intelligence, feedback and initial customer validation, finding partners and facilitating commercial relationships, plugging SMEs into roadmaps, sales channels and supply chains; assisting with movements into adjacent markets; and defining and implementing new business models.

The Connect Program: Clients' Perspectives

To obtain a wider perspective of EDC's *Connect* activities, the research team undertook a series of interviews with the CEOs of seven firms that had been recipients of *Connect* activity.[8] Because the seven firms had been identified by EDC, it is not surprising that all seven would be identified as international new ventures in that the primary owners all articulated that internationalization was a key goal at the founding of the firms. The findings from the interviews were consistent with several of the themes identified in the literature review. For example, previous research had reported that founders tend to be conservative and chary of internationalization because internationalization adds risk to an already-risky early stage venture. In the words of two CEOs,

> [G]oing beyond North America was a bigger hill to climb, especially for small companies . . . . You are talking tax structures, import restriction, currency exposure, high inflation . . . . It's fine if you are a GE going into the country. You've got the resource infrastructure, you got your tax guy who deals with the tax stuff, you got your legal team that deal with your legal stuff, but for a small company it takes up a [big] portion of our desks . . . travel costs, translation costs, aftermarket support . . . it's still a scary spot for us.
>
> It absolutely is risky: . . . IP issues, cultural issues, partnership issues. It is a massive time distraction – you can't just fly to China once and get a deal done.

In spite of this concern about risk, all seven of the CEOs of the firms interviewed understood the imperative of engaging in foreign trade. All of the founders perceived EDC's primary value added to the introductions and networking that it actively enabled. This networking included introductions to potential partners in foreign markets as well as to salient others within Canada and even within Canadian government. For example:

> EDC, which has a global mandate, [has] reduced the 'ghost in the closet' sort of concerns: that there are some massive risks out there, and you couldn't possibly

ever do business in some of these markets . . . . Instead, it's no, 'we [EDC] have relationships here, we do business here, we know these people, these are the things you do, and don't do', and I think it's increased the comfort . . . of our other shareholders and directors in the idea that we can successfully go international.

In addition, several firms noted that alignment with EDC brought credibility, for example:

[EDC] definitely brought faith, credibility as well as money. The backing of EDC, and [other investors] was great for the company . . . [to help] keep your staff on board too and they [the staff] all know what's going on.

Finally, the founders perceived EDC's role to be complementary to those which other VCs can provide, for example,

Our experience has been that they [EDC] have tried to add value in a way that the other shareholders haven't been able to. It's not available to them because of EDC's global reach and . . . that has manifested itself in different sorts of support and behaviour that we haven't gotten from our other shareholders. It's . . . complementary.

To investigate the extent to which these activities may have enhanced firm value, the following section outlines the data and methodology employed.

DATA, METHODOLOGY AND EMPIRICAL FINDINGS

Empirical analysis relies on data obtained from 426 entrepreneurial companies held directly within EDC's equity portfolio and indirectly among the portfolios of 41 of the VC funds in which EDC partners as a fund-of-funds. For 61 investee firms, information on current valuations was incomplete, thereby reducing the usable data to 365 firms. Among these 365 investee companies, EDC held an equity ownership position in 194 portfolio companies through direct and indirect investments and held no ownership share in 171 portfolio companies. Table 4.1 provides a categorization of the investee firms for which complete information were available.

To measure performance, the ratio of fair market value (FMV) to total VC investment was calculated for each of the 365 portfolio firms. Fair market values are usually calculated, as a matter of course, by fund managers so as to report valuations to limited partners and to management. While valuations within a given fund might be systematically high or low,

Table 4.1   Breakdown of portfolio firms

	Firms in which EDC had invested, directly or indirectly	Firms in which EDC had no investment	Total
Firms for which there is evidence of substantive *Connect* activity.	29	10	39
Firms for which there is no evidence of *Connect* activity.	165	161	326
Total	194	171	365

Table 4.2   Performance estimates, portfolio firms

Portfolio Firm Category	Mean FMV/Investment	N	Std. Error of Mean
1. EDC Ownership and *Connect*	1.32	29	0.16
2. No EDC ownership but *Connect*	1.29	10	0.22
3. EDC Ownership, no *Connect*	1.10	165	0.06
4. No EDC ownership, no *a*	0.69	161	0.07
Total	0.94	365	0.04

valuations are assumed to be independent across the funds. The ratio of FMV to total VC investment therefore provides a measure of total value add since initial investment.

Table 4.2 presents mean values of the ratio of FMV to total VC investment for each of the four groups in Table 4.1.

A one-way analysis of variance using Kruskal Wallis and the Jonckheere–Terpstra tests reveals that these differences were significant (p-value = 0.000). The impact of EDC's ability to select high potential firms may be gauged by comparing:

● Category 1 (both EDC investment and *Connect*) with category 2 (no EDC investment but *Connect* activity), and
● Category 3 (EDC investment, no *Connect*) with category 4 (no EDC investment, no *Connect*).

Among the 39 firms for which there was evidence of *Connect* activity (categories 1 and 2), the ratio of FMV to investment for firms in which

EDC had invested (category 1) was 1.32, a small and statistically insignificant (Mann–Whitney p-value = 0.516) premium over firms in category 2 (no EDC ownership).[9] Among the 325 firms for which there was no *Connect* activity (categories 3 and 4), the average ratio of FMV to VC investment was 0.69 for the 160 portfolio firms in which EDC held no ownership. For the 165 firms in which EDC held some level of ownership, the average ratio of FMV to VC investment was 1.10, significantly higher (Mann-Whitney U p-value = 0.000). These outcomes are consistent with the argument that EDC's Investment Team has generally invested in higher-potential portfolio firms. That is, some of the value-added was a consequence of good investment choices.

The impact of EDC's *Connect* strategy beyond the equity team's ability to 'pick winners' may be estimated by comparing:

- Category 1 (both EDC investment and *Connect*) with category 3 (EDC investment, no *Connect*), and,
- Category 2 (no EDC investment, but *Connect* activity) with category 4 (no EDC investment, no *Connect*).

Focusing on the 194 firms for which EDC holds an equity stake reveals an average ratio of FMV to investment of 1.32 for the 29 firms that received *Connect* activity (category 1) and 1.10 for the 165 EDC-held firms for which there is no evidence of *Connect* activity. This difference was not statistically significant (Mann–Whitney p-value = 0.138). For the 170 portfolio firms with no EDC ownership, the ratio of FMV to investment for the 10 that had received *Connect* assistance (category 2) was 1.29, compared with 0.69 for the firms in category 4 for which there is no record of *Connect* activity. This difference was statistically significant (Mann–Whitney p-value = 0.003) and also appears to be economically significant: a 70 percent premium. These results are consistent with the idea that EDC's *Connect* activities add value beyond the equity team's ability to 'pick winners'.

SUMMARY, CONCLUSIONS AND IMPLICATIONS

EDC, Canada's export credit agency, is positioned to help portfolio firms by facilitating internationalization and access to global markets. EDC does so by adding value to portfolio companies through direct involvement with investee firms by employing an array of *Connect* activities. In interpreting the findings, it is important to appreciate the geography of the Canadian context for the research. While Canada spans more than 7,300 kilometers from east to west, the most populous areas are a one-day truck drive from the largest consumer market in the world: the Northeastern United States. On the other hand, the size and proximity of the US may work against development of international trade beyond North America. Those ownership teams that do seek to engage in international trade would typically look South.

The research literature has long held that internationalization of SMEs proceeds through stages: that firms are founded with a purely local perspective, but grow regionally and expand internationally only after acquiring substantive knowledge, experience and a track record. Previous research has also found that, in general, founders are conservative and typically reluctant to take on the incremental risks of internationalization when the new firm is already a risky enterprise. This chapter finds that the presence of EDC, and its *Connect* strategy, allows founders to consider internationalization early and with fewer concerns: EDC has 'reduced the ghost in the closet'.

This chapter has noted that some SMEs intend to internationalize at inception, apparently contradicting the established paradigms and that the incidence of international new ventures was found to the higher than expected in Canada (Spence et al., 2011). It is a short step in logic to expect that the experience and expertise that EDC brings could, therefore, promote internationalization. This expectation was confirmed. Founders were unanimous in their appreciation for EDC's introductions and net-working and commented that EDC was especially helpful with respect to developing international trade opportunities. EDC was seen to be unique in terms of the scope and depth of its international experience and exper-tise. Within the Canadian venture capital landscape, the firms' owners reported that no other VC investors were similarly equipped to facilitate growth through internationalization.

The owners commented that EDC played an accreditation role, bring-ing additional credibility to the firms nationally, internationally as well as internally. The reputation of a VC can be an important means of miti-gating the low credibility of entrepreneurial firms in global markets. The presence of a reputable and internationally respected investor can alleviate information asymmetry, thereby enabling young firms to negotiate, and enter into, long-term relationships with suppliers, partners and customers at lower costs. EDC's international reputation appears to be a mediation tool in the internationalization process (Fernhaber and McDougall-Covin, 2009).

Analysis of VC portfolio data showed evidence that the EDC invest-ment team had selected high potential firms and that *Connect* activities were also associated with yet higher valuations: those firms for which substantive *Connect* activities had been reported were valued at a substantial and significant premium over those firms for which *Connect* activities had not been reported.

Overall, the evidence is consistent with the argument that *Connect* activities enhance the value of recipient firms. The findings confirm the expectations from the research literature to the effect that VCs, especially those public sector financial institutions tasked specifically with developing international trade, may be a particularly effective means of furthering international trade and supporting early internationalization of investee firms. These activities arguably add incremental value to portfolio firms and enhance their ability to compete internationally in three respects.

First, as a funder-of-funds, EDC makes smaller VC funds larger, possibly mitigating challenges typically faced by small VC funds (see Murray, 1999; Nitani and Riding, 2013). EDC's financial investments augment the overall supply of VC, augmenting that supplied by the private sector, without crowding out the private VC firms and without duplicating other initiatives. Qualitative findings suggest that EDC's *Connect* activities foster internationalization. To the extent that private sector or public VC fund managers may recognize the need for internationalization of portfolio firms, none can bring the array of contacts and intelligence that EDC can supply. Further, because EDC, as a funder-of-funds, works with more than 41 VC funds and other partners, EDC's *Connect* activities are contributing to a widespread consciousness of the internationalization aspects of VC investing.

Second, EDC's intelligence and networking are marshaled from within EDC and then promoted to its direct and indirect VC investments so as to encourage and facilitate internationalization of portfolio firms. These international connections are a useful catalyst to initiate international sales. Moreover, this work finds that the combination of EDC's capital investment and *Connect* support leads to yet greater enterprise values.

Third, this chapter finds, contrary to previous research based on US data, that owners of Canadian growth-oriented SMEs recognize early on that internationalization is necessary in order to achieve growth objectives. However, the owners interviewed for this work also acknowledged that internationalization entailed a range of additional risks beyond those inherent in starting a new venture. These owners appreciated that working with EDC moderated these risks. Moreover, owners were enthusiastic in support for the introductions and contacts that the *Connect* activities provided and they perceived EDC's ability to provide such networking to be unique among investors. Owners also valued the accreditation that being associated with EDC brought with respect to foreign clients and partners, domestic governments as well as to their own key employees.

Few other countries are in a position to lever the international knowledge accumulated within their export development agencies for their respective venture capital sectors. Accordingly, EDC's ability to apply its internationalization experience, contacts and connections to the Canadian VC sector is arguably a source of competitive advantage for Canada. Overall, this research confirms that EDC's venture capital investment approach is helping to address perceived impediments in a (small) VC market while acting in ways that are complementary to those of other participants. In doing so, the equity team is simultaneously helping to fulfill EDC's mandate and is contributing to national and regional goals of economic prosperity.

NOTES

1. See, for example, Jones et al. (2011) for a recent comprehensive review of this literature.
2. A crown corporation is a firm that is 100 percent owned by the federal government of Canada but that operates at arm's length and works in partnership with the private sector. EDC's mandate is to expand Canadian export capacity and to help Canadian companies respond to international business opportunities. EDC makes direct and indirect VC equity investments in domestic and foreign companies.
3. For example, the largest consumer and industry market in the world – the US Northeast – is a one-day truck drive from Toronto in Canada's industrial heartland. Yet Calgary and Vancouver – Western Canadian cities – are three days distant.
4. NAFTA, involving Mexico, the United States and Canada has been in effect since 1994 and follows from the Canada/US free trade agreement of 1988.
5. Data in this paragraph were extracted from www.cvca.ca/files/Resources/, accessed June 16, 2014.
6. See www.globalinnovationindex.org/gii/main/analysis/rankings.cfm#CGI.SCRIPT_NAME#, accessed June 16, 2014.
7. EDC, at the time of writing, held direct VC investments in 19 businesses and also acts as a fund of funds to 24 Canadian VC firms as well as to VC firms in China, Turkey, Israel and other countries. As such, EDC seeks to invest in, and nurture, high potential businesses. EDC's focus aligns with its internationalization mandate and, like most VC investors, EDC provides various forms of non-financial value-added.
8. Interviews were transcribed and analysed with the assistance of NVivo software.
9. Because the performance metric is a ratio (FMV/Investment), non-parametric test statistics were employed in post-hoc analysis.

REFERENCES

Amit, R., Brander, J., and Zott, C. (1998), 'Why do venture capital firms exist? Theory and Canadian evidence', *Journal of Business Venturing*, **13** (6): 441–466.
Binks, M. and Ennew, C. (1996), 'Growing firms and the credit constraint', *Small Business Economics*, **8** (1): 17–25.
Brierley, N. (2001), 'The financing of technology-based small firms: a review of the literature', *Bank of England Quarterly Bulletin*, **41** (1): 64–78.
Carpenter, M.A., Pollock, T.G., and Leary, M.M. (2003), 'Testing a model of reasoned

risk-taking: governance, the experience of principals and agents, and global strategy in high-technology IPO firms', *Strategic Management Journal*, **24** (9): 803–820.

De Clercq, D. and Manigart, S. (2007), 'The venture capital post-investment phase: Opening the black box of involvement', in H. Landstrom (ed.), *Handbook of Research on Venture Capital*, Cheltenham, UK and Northampton, MA, USA: Edward Elgar Publishing, pp. 193–218.

Fernhaber, S.A. and McDougall-Covin, P. (2009), 'Venture capitalists as catalysts to new venture internationalization: the impact of their knowledge and reputation resources', *Entrepreneurship Theory and Practice*, **33** (1): 277–295.

George, G., Wiklund, J., and Zahra, S.A. (2005), 'Ownership and the internationalization of small firms', *Journal of Management*, **31** (2): 210–233.

Gorman, M. and Sahlman, W.A. (1989), 'What do venture capitalists do?', *Journal of Business Venturing*, **4** (4): 231–248.

Jones, M.V., Coviello, N., and Tang, Y.K. (2011), 'International entrepreneurship research (1989–2009): A domain ontology and thematic analysis', *Journal of Business Venturing*, **26** (6): 632–659.

Kortum, S. and Lerner, J. (2000), 'Assessing the contribution of venture capital to innovation', *Rand Journal of Economics*, **31** (4): 674–692.

Large, D. and Muegge, S. (2007), 'Venture capitalists' non-financial value-added: an evaluation of the evidence and implications for research', *Venture Capital: an International Journal of Entrepreneurial Finance*, **10** (1): 21–53.

LiPuma, J. (2006), 'Independent venture capital, corporate venture capital, and the internationalisation intensity of technology-based portfolio firms', *International Entrepreneurship and Management Journal*, **2** (2): 245–260.

Lockett, A., Wright, M., Burrows, A., Scholes, L., and Paton, D. (2008), 'The export intensity of venture capital backed companies', *Small Business Economics*, **31** (1): 39–58.

MacMillan, I.C., Kulow, D., and Khoylian, R. (1989), 'Venture capitalists' involvement in their investments: extent and performance', *Journal of Business Venturing*, **4** (1): 27–47.

Maula, M. (2001), *Corporate Venture Capital and the Value-Added for Technology-based New Firms*. Doctoral dissertation, Helsinki University of Technology, Institute of Strategy and International Business, retrieved from http://lib.hut.fi/Diss/2001/isbn9512260816 (accessed July 28, 2015).

Maula, M., Autio, E., and Murray, G. (2005), 'Corporate venture capitalists and independent venture capitalists: what do they know, who do they know and should entrepreneurs care?', *Venture Capital: an International Journal of Entrepreneurial Finance*, **7** (1): 3–21.

Murray, G.C. (1999), 'Early-stage venture capital funds, scale economies and public support', *Venture Capital*, **1** (4): 351–384.

Nitani, M. and Riding, A. (2013), 'Fund size and the syndication of venture capital investments', *Venture Capital: an International Journal of Entrepreneurial Finance*, **15** (1): 53–75.

Rosenstein, J., Bruno, A.V., Bygrave, W.D., and Taylor, N.T. (1993), 'The CEO, venture capitalists, and the board', *Journal of Business Venturing*, **8** (2): 99–113.

Sapienza, H.J., Amason, A.C., and Manigart, S. (1994), 'The level and nature of venture capitalist involvement in their portfolio companies: a study of three European countries', *Managerial Finance*, **20** (1): 3–17.

Sapienza, H.J., Manigart, S., and Vermier, W. (1996), 'Venture capitalist governance and value added in four countries', *Journal of Business Venturing*, **11** (6): 439–469.

Smolarski, J. and Kut, C. (2011), 'The impact of venture capital financing method on SME performance and internationalization', *International Entrepreneurship and Management Journal*, **7** (1): 39–55.

Spence, M., Orser, B.J., and Riding, A.L. (2011), 'A comparative study of international and domestic new ventures', *Management International Review*, **51** (1): 3–21.

5. Small and medium-sized enterprises and their capital structure decisions in Turkey: a literature review

Dilek Demirbaş and Safa Demirbaş

INTRODUCTION

The capital structure mix of both small and large firms has implications for their operations and survival (Baker and Martin, 2011) as an optimal capital mix minimizes their cost of capital. All modern economies have a large number of small and medium-sized enterprises (SMEs); a similar trend is exhibited by the Turkish economy. SMEs in Turkey represent 99.85 per cent of the total businesses; 76 per cent of total employees; 63 per cent of turnover; 38 per cent of capital investment; 54 per cent of all investment; 38.9 per cent of total commercial research and development; 59.2 per cent of total export and 25.9 per cent of total credits (KOSGEB, 2014), and they play a significant role in the Turkish economy. Nevertheless, during the recent global crisis the Turkish economy shrank by 6.2 per cent annually since the fourth quarter of 2008 (Ministry of Industry and Trade, 2010), which adversely impacted on SMEs' performance and competitiveness and further exacerbated their access to external finance.

Kaygın et al. (2008) and Ekinci (2003) reported that SMEs' inability to secure finance from external sources affects their ability to acquire assets, inputs and operating efficiency that affects their other functions such as manufacturing, marketing and training needs. To overcome credit constraints in recent years, the Turkish government has initiated dedicated investment credit programs to support SMEs, but such schemes failed to mitigate the financial disadvantages encountered by Turkish SMEs and 30 per cent of firms reported that it was impossible to access external finance (Kaygın et al., 2008, p. 4632).

The main purpose of this chapter is to review the existing financial problems of SMEs in Turkey from the theoretical perspective in the capital structure literature. In particular, this chapter examines whether theories that have examined the financing structures of firms in the Western economies, and elsewhere in the emerging economies, are applicable to the Turkish case with its distinct financial institutions and cultural context. The chapter further investigates SMEs' financial difficulties in Turkey by evaluating the factors influencing SMEs' capital structure through theoretical and empirical studies. The key questions that this chapter examines are: what are the basic theoretical approaches that explain the capital structure phenomenon in the literature which are applicable to SMEs in both developed and emerging countries? Are factors such as firm size, profit and their capital structure significant for the Turkish economy and the firm? What determines the capital structure of Turkish SMEs? What strategies or policies may be advanced for Turkish SMEs to enable them to gain competitiveness in the domestic and international markets?

The chapter is organized as follows. First, it considers the literature on capital structure theories and SME related studies. Second, it examines factors affecting capital structure of Turkish SMEs in theory and practice. Third, it evaluates the causes and consequence of the finance gap for SMEs in Turkey. The chapter concludes by reporting conclusions drawn from the empirical literature on capital structure theory in general and for Turkey in particular.

BASIC CAPITAL STRUCTURE THEORIES AND SME RELATED STUDIES

Efficient capital structure has implications for firms' efficiency and productivity (Jahanzeb et al., 2013). For small and large firms, having an unbalanced capital structure causes financial distress and gives rise to bankruptcy. As decision-making is a cognitive process of selecting an alternative among many possible alternatives (Jahanzeb et al., 2012; Muneer and Rehman, 2012), capital structure requires complex decision-making tactics to meet the needs of individual firms (Jahanzeb et al., 2013). The debate relating to the capital structure of firms has been of central importance for academics and policymakers around the world and has given rise to several theories (Modigliani and Miller, 1958; Kraus and Litzenberger, 1973; Kim, 1978; Myers, 1984). These theories are labelled (Frank and Goyal, 2007; Copeland and Weston, 2005) 'point of view' theories, which have provided the conceptual framework and guidelines to formulate a well-defined mathematical model to be tested for further predictions. However, such theories tend to cater for large firms and are a poor fit for SMEs.

Basic Capital Structure Theories in General

Modigliani and Miller (1958) proposed that firms' value is independent of capital structure. Jensen and Uhl (2008) referred to it as the first real theory on capital structure. The contention is that choice of debt or equity does not change the firm value in the situation of a perfect market (Jahanzeb et al., 2013) under certain restrictive assumptions: (a) there are no government taxes; (b) transactions are costless; (c) no insolvency costs; (d) cost of borrowing for the company is the same as lender; (e) perfect information between lender and the borrower and (f) firm earnings, pre-tax and interest, are not affected by the level of debt (Chen, 2004).

There has been an ongoing debate among academics and practitioners as to whether the trade-off theory explains the firm's capital structure in terms of whether the benefits to be derived from the tax shield are sufficient to offset the accruing cost of debt, while the firm's value of asset and investments are held constant (Myers, 1984; Kraus and Litzenberger, 1973; Hul, 2014; Berens and Cuny, 1995). The benefits of borrowing are the tax shields in which interest as a payment is deductible from income tax payments; however, after a certain point, the cost of borrowing starts to rise as tax benefits are competed away and bankruptcy cost start to rise.

The pecking order theory (developed by Myers, 1984; Myers and Majluf, 1984) concludes that firms prefer to use retained savings (internal equity) to external loans because of information asymmetry about the firm value between the agent of the firm and the outside stakeholders (investors). Only when the internal financial resources are fully exploited do the firms seek external sources of financing. Managers prefer debt to equity finance to avoid losing control. The pecking order theory suggests that a firm prefers: first internally raised funds, such as cash reserves, then seeks external debt, and finally issues equity as a last resort. This order of finance is due to the fact that debtors are interested in security of funds and returns rather than in the value of the firm as they have the first claim on the assets of the firm (Myers, 2001).

Basic Capital Structure Theories in the Context of SMEs

In the capital finance literature, most research on the trade-off theory was performed on large firms due to the availability of data, but limited research has been conducted on small businesses, the dominant forms of business organization in any economy. This chapter examines to what extent SMEs encounter similar problems to those of large firms regarding their capital structure in the context of the trade-off theory. Sogorb-Mira (2005) suggested that SMEs and large firms use similar considerations with regard to capital structure theories as they all encounter the same trade-off between the tax shield benefits and debt distress costs but larger firms consider these issues much more seriously. However, SMEs have limited choice in accessing external capital and experience different challenges; therefore, the experiences of small firms differ.

One possible explanation of why SMEs might not follow the trade-off theory could be that owner-managers lack financial knowledge or expertise and due to the cost considerations they are unable to employ qualified experts. Therefore, SME owners' ignorance of the choice of sources of finance deprives them of potential benefits to be derived from the interest tax shield (Organisation for Economic Co-operation and Development (OECD), 2006) and they tend to operate at sub-optimal debt levels. Due to lack of collateral, size, reputation, information asymmetry and higher cost of borrowing, SMEs encounter finance constraint. Furthermore, family owned companies have a great deal of sentimental value and are often risk averse; any addition to debt gives rise to distress costs, consequently, they use lower than optimal debt in their capital structure (Jensen and Uhl, 2008; Cressy and Olofsson, 1997a, 1997b; Hamilton and Fox, 1998).

The pecking order theory's relevance for SMEs was generally accepted wisdom among academics and policymakers in the past; however, over the last few decades, academics (Howorth, 2001; Paul et al., 2007; Atherton, 2009; Ang, 1991; Holmes and Kent, 1991) have started to question this assertion due to hurdles, choices and the cost associated with external finance. The pecking order theory's relevance stems from the fact that SME owners do not wish to use external finance that will affect their ownership rights and, therefore they often rely on and prefer internal finance for debt (Lopez-Gracia and Sogorb-Mira, 2008), especially at the start-up and development phases (Dahlstrand and Cetindamar, 2000; Giudici and Paleari, 2000; Hyytinen and Pajarinen, 2002; Chen et al., 2013). Furthermore, due to information asymmetry, access to equity markets and costs such as legal and compliance makes it expensive for small firms to raise equity finance. When dealing with equity markets, large companies often employ experts as equity is both expensive and subject to price volatility which has been shown to be particularly severe for SMEs (Chittenden ct al., 1996; Ibbotson et al., 2001). Other sources of finance from private equity firms or business angels are not accessible due to the size of loan and the transaction costs which result from negotiating the complex contracts (Ou and Haynes, 2006). It is reported that financial constraints prevent SMEs from planning and acquiring long-term finance (Jensen and Uhl, 2008). Empirical evidence has suggested that there now exist a variety of pecking order theories due to varying financial and business environment facing firms (Atherton, 2009). The presence of the pecking order theory is particularly strong among SMEs operating in non-Anglo-Saxon countries (Sànchez-Vidal and Martìn-Ugedo, 2005) due to the underdeveloped financial environment that gives rise to the 'financing gap' (see also Holmes and Kent, 1991).

FACTORS AFFECTING THE CAPITAL STRUCTURES OF TURKISH SMES FROM THE THEORETICAL PERSPECTIVE

Size, value added and employment among Turkish SMEs' vary from sector to sector. Turkish SMEs' share of total production is similar to other countries and trade accounts for 40 per cent, followed by manufacturing at 13 per cent and the construction sector at 5 per cent (Ministry of Industry and Trade, 2010; Turkish Statistical Institute, 2011). This supports the argument that, for Turkey, the financial environment, government policies and support mechanisms compare favourably with other developed and developing economies.

The 'SME Financing Gap' Phenomenon and the Capital Structure of Firms

Holmes and Kent (1991) claim that access to capital markets is limited for SMEs, regardless of whether they are located within developed or developing economies – referred to as the 'financing gap'. Many organizations, including the OECD (2006), have examined the 'financing gap' and it too reports that a large number of SMEs are unable to raise adequate finance to operate efficiently and are unable to access external finance from banks, financial markets or other finance institutions. OECD (2006) also reported that the finance gap limits the growth of an economy, creates unemployment, reduces an economy's agility and gives rise to the cost of debt that affects optimality of the capital structure for firms.

Developed and emerging economies' experiences mirror the findings above. Hussain et al. (2006) examined and compared the financing preferences of SMEs in the UK and in China; they reported similar trends for both countries. For the SMEs' start-up finance, a large percentage of Chinese SMEs owner-managers suggested that they relied exclusively on their family and friends for unsecured finance. However, their reliance became less after two years, the respondents were able to access bank finance to an extent, and analysis after five years suggested family finance remained important. Whereas for the UK, after five years, most of the owner-managers reported that they had become bankable and acquired business loans from financial institutions.

The OECD's (2006) 'OECD SME Task Force Survey' of its members reported that finance constraints negatively impact on the growth of

SMEs. The major cause of the finance gap is due to the existence of asymmetric information among SMEs (Altı, 2006; Altı and Sulaeman, 2012; Leary and Roberts, 2005). At the start-up stage, the owner does not have a track record, and in most cases, financial education and knowledge to provide financial information for bank assessment, though the he or she may have considerable information and knowledge about the business itself (Beck, 2013). Moral hazard considerations impact significantly on the access to finance for SMEs. The bank's main consideration is to recover its capital and seek and support less risky propositions. However, on the other hand, the firm may wish to exploit its business potential by pursuing a high risk and return strategy that may expose banks to excessive risk. It has been recognized by OECD (2006) and other studies that once a loan is made to any organization its risk may change over time, a potential problem with all debt financing. However, the risk shift can be more severe when lending to SMEs as they often lack financial education and may give rise to cash flow management issues.

There appears to be a correlation between the growth of the economy and the bank finance used by SMEs. Japan appears to be in the lead and Turkey has merely 3.5 per cent of SMEs who have accessed bank finance (KOSGEB, 2012) that shows the financial environment is not favourable for SMEs as stated by Beck (2013).

Access to finance in Eastern Europe suggests that the finance gap exists in the region. Empirical evidence reported by Cornelli et al. (1998) and Egerer (1995) suggested that leverage in Eastern Europe is found to be low and that businesses have insufficient debt finance in their capital structure; this is due to either the cost of debt or its availability. Most empirical findings point to some sort of institutional factor as the source of this problem. Turkey has many similarities with Eastern Europe because of shortcomings in the institutional environment in the Turkish system and insufficient financing opportunities due to moral hazard considerations and asymmetric information between bank managers and SME owner-managers.

EXAMINING CAPITAL STRUCTURES OF TURKISH SMES FROM THE EMPIRICAL PERSPECTIVES

The Turkish SME literature suggests that a firm's capital structure is composed of variables, such as the firm size, asset tangibility, profitability and growth. These variables are used to test the trade-off and pecking order theories to make predictions of the impact of the variables on the firm's capital structure. An increase in the size of Turkish SMEs will decrease the probability of bankruptcy and will reduce information asymmetry problems (Çakova, 2011). Hence, both pecking order and trade-off theory predict that a firm's debt level increases in line with increases in its size. Moreover, collateral decreases cost of bankruptcy as the lender's risk is reduced, and has a positive effect on the cost of capital and the debt ratio. Pecking order theories suggest that firms use their profits to reduce debt levels while trade-off theory expects firms to have greater opportunity to take debt, up to a point and optimize their capital structure. It is also demonstrated that rapid and high growth opportunities are positively correlated with debt usage, results consistent with the pecking order theory. In contrast, trade-off theory anticipates that high financial distress, resulted from rapid and high growth opportunities leads firms to decrease their debt. Based on these findings, a number of empirical studies using the Turkish data are conducted to test capital structure theories (Çakova, 2011).

In the next section, capital structure theory related to empirical studies is evaluated to understand the financial difficulties encountered by SMEs in Turkey and to discuss policy implications.

To examine the capital structure of the Turkish SMEs, Korkmaz et al. (2007) carried out an empirical study among 37 firms over the seven year period from 1977 to 2004. To study what determinates the firm's capital structure, they employed proxy variables such as the firm size, risk (measured by the variability in net sales), profitability, tax shield and the firm growth rate (change in Gross Domestic Product). The results of the study found that the most important factors that influence SMEs capital structure were the firm's profitability, firm risk and non-debt tax shields. Korkmaz et al. (2007) also observed in this study that there is a relationship between the firm's assets and its leverage; an increase in a firm's assets leads to an increase in the firm's leverage. Korkmaz et al. (2009) tested the same model for 16 companies from the auto parts industry and confirmed the results of their 2007 research.

Yıldız et al. (2009) tested the predictions of trade-off theory and pecking order theory using data for small manufacturing firms during the period 1998–2006. They employed, total debt, short- and long-term debt scaled by equity and used as dependent variables in their regressions. They observed that there was a negative correlation between profitability of the firm and its leverage ratio. Moreover, asset tangibility is not correlated with total and long-term debt and has a significant negative effect on firm's short term debt. Furthermore, firm size is positively correlated with total and short-term debt, and asset growth is positively correlated with total and long-term debt. They also reported that the tax rate and non-debt tax shields are insignificant in explaining the capital structure of Turkish firms. According to Yıldız et al. (2009), this finding shows that taxes paid by companies are very low and they are omitted by firms in deciding their capital structures.

Acaravcı and Doğukanlı (2004) tested which factors affect the capital structure of small firms using the sample of firms from the manufacturing industry in Turkey. For this purpose, they analysed the data from 66 companies, for 12 years, for the period 1992–2003. The study examined the capital structure of the firms in relation to changes in Gross Domestic Product (used as a proxy for the growth rate), firm characteristics, the development of the financial environment, the growth of the banking sector and the government domestic debt level. The findings of the study suggested that the growth of total assets, the development of the banking sector, the rate of inflation and corporate tax revenue have a positive relationship with firm leverage.

Çakova (2011) analyses the factors of capital structure of SMEs from the manufacturing sector in Turkey. Çakova (2011) used data from 1998 to 2008 and had 4,003 firms with average annual observations of 44,029. This research used a two-way fixed effect model estimation to study the short and long term debt ratios of SMEs, and supported the assertion that the capital structure of SMEs can be explained using the pecking order theory. The results of this study also confirm that there is an inverse relationship between SMEs average debt ratios and economic conditions in Turkey. The study also found, taking into account the industry variations, that a firm's characteristics are important in explaining capital structure adapted by the Turkish SMEs.

Karadeniz et al. (2009) study showed that there is a negative relationship between the debt ratio and effective tax rates, tangibility of assets, return on assets of publicly listed Turkish small and medium-sized companies. However, variables such as 'free cash flow, non-debt tax shields, growth opportunities, net commercial credit position, and firm size' do not appear to be related to the debt ratio (Karadeniz et al., 2009); their findings suggest that the empirical results neither support the pecking order nor the trade-off theory. A major study carried out by Köksal and Orman (2014) for the period 1996–2009, using the data from Central Bank of the Republic of Turkey (CBRT), report the comparative tests of the trade-off and pecking order theories, for small, large and publicly traded firms for the Turkey. Köksal and Orman's (2014) findings report that the trade-off theory is in a better position to explain the capital structure of firms than the pecking order theory. The results of Köksal and Orman's (2014) study support the earlier studies findings and they reported that the trade-off theory is more suited to explain the capital structure of larger firms operating in economies that have a stable economic environment.

Using a similar methodology, Bayraktaroğlu et al. (2013) studies whether firm-specific capital structure determinants in Turkey support the capital structure theories. A survey was carried out in 2007, among 619 small and medium-sized companies to test their capital structure. Of the 163 SMEs that provided their personnel information, 45 firms were small and 118 medium-sized companies. The findings from the study were consistent with theoretical expectations; they confirm that pecking order hypothesis is applicable for the Turkish companies. Therefore, it can be concluded that Turkish companies follow pecking order hypothesis in their capital structure.

A study carried out by Booth et al. (2001) for ten developing countries (including Turkey) tested whether country-specific variables explain the capital structure of SMEs. They reported that general debt level of SMEs increases as the ratio of fixed asset to total asset rises, and it is the case for non-debt tax shields, growth rates and firm size. These findings are consistent with earlier studies discussed above. These findings suggest that financial institutions use asset profile and the age profile of the business to evaluate risk of the business. Their second finding is plausible – that financial advantage is negatively correlated with earnings, volatility and the probability of bankruptcy – as these variables make a limited contribution towards collateral and can encounter greater variability.

As observed in the empirical studies that tested capital structure theories, profitability, firm risk, and non-debt tax shields are the most important factors that influence SMEs capital structure in Turkey. Turkish SMEs, particularly small manufacturing firms, follow the pecking order hypothesis in their debt behaviour, when the economic environment is not stable.

In response, the Turkish government organization, KOSGEB has formulated policies for SMEs to enhance their competitiveness by enabling them to enhance their research and development and innovation capacities. Steps have also been taken to improve cooperation among SMEs themselves, support new entrepreneurial activities and enhance access to finance (KOSGEB, 2009). These outcomes would be achieved through improving the flow of information, financial education among SME owner-managers, and information problems through training of owners of SMEs. With these programs, KOSGEB has helped to increase the share of SME loans.

Despite the fact that KOSGEB actively engages with SMEs and develops plans to increase the competitiveness of Turkish SMEs to minimize their financial problems, Turkish SMEs continue to experience many obstacles in accessing finance. In Turkey, private equity and venture capital funds are relatively insignificant in comparison with the bank finance for SMEs. The emergence and rise of private equity can be traced back to 1993 when the regulation approved the formation of venture capital firms – revised in 2003. The equity based transaction was conducted in 1995 by a foreign investment firm. Since 1996, a number of Turkish private equity firms have been set up but their size and participation within the sector is limited. The insignificance of venture capital firms can be gleaned from their numbers. In 2014, there were only five venture capital investments trusts listed on the Istanbul Stock Exchange and had a market value of US$480m. However, due to the nature of loan size approved and legal issues, venture capital has limited relevance for a large number of SMEs.

There have been some bold government initiatives to mitigate the financial problems of SMEs in Turkey. To support SMEs, the Emerging Companies Market was established within the ISE after the financial crisis in 2009. To enable SMEs to tap into this fund, SMEs were exempted from the quantitative requirements of exchange trading. Furthermore to engage and support SMEs, Capital Markets Board of Turkey (CMB) and the Central Securities Depository of Turkey (ISE and CRA) reduced their fees. Furthermore, to support SMEs, the bond market was promoted through the revision of financial regulations to revive the market, which had a very positive outcome in that the corporate debt securities market expanded significantly since 2010 and it received support from the banks. There is now more willingness among the financial institutions to issue debt finance. In 2012, 98 financial institutions issued debt securities and instruments and their value exceeded US$2bn. Furthermore, 11 non-financial corporations also issued bonds worth US$490m (KOSGEB, 2012). Despite the mentioned initiatives and innovations, the financial problems of SMEs are still a major issue for the whole sector due to structural and institutional reluctance and rigidities.

Main Reasons to Seek Access to Finance for Turkish SMEs

It has been recognized that (Turkish Industrial Strategy Document, Munich Personal RePEc Archive (MPRA, 2013)) SMEs in Turkey have difficulties in acquiring access to finance due to four main reasons:

1. the credit limit given to the banking sector due to financial reorganization of 2001;
2. underdevelopment of the capital market;
3. the underdeveloped financial structure to support SMEs; and
4. administrative and legal obstacles to access finance.

These findings are supported by Kaya and Alpkan (2012) who reported that a lack of financial information, poor experience of business decision-making among owner-managers, the underdevelopment of financial systems and the environment, a lack of credit volume and the cost of credit are the main financial obstacles faced by SMEs in Turkey. However, Şeker and Correa (2010) indicate that SMEs in Turkey are more dependent on bank finance than other countries to fund their fixed assets. The bank funding for fixed assets in Turkey accounts for 47 per cent of all loans, backed-up with collateral, yet SMEs find it difficult to secure loans for operating cash flow and this is of particular concern during the periods of financial crises. Since the Turkish SMEs primarily depend on bank loans and the recent crisis revealed that bank financing is not a reliable source of financing, especially during periods of financial crises. In particular, after the financial crisis of 2008, that persuaded the banks to strengthen their capital requirement, which has created additional challenges for SMEs to secure bank loans. Therefore, there is the need for policymakers to produce conducive policies and environments to provide well-diversified funding sources for SMEs to promote growth and expansion of SMEs in Turkey. In response, the government and regulators have to promote policies for banks to improve access to loans and promote the equity markets to provide finance for SMEs. Yet there is no evidence that SMEs are able to access equity markets; even in well-developed economies equity markets such as private equity and venture capital investments fail to meet the needs of SMEs. ICSA (2013) reported that there are also a few securitized products backed specifically by SME loans. There is a move towards creating structure and developing capabilities of SMEs to secure formal external finance through education and training. In the Turkish equity market, government has promoted the specific segments for SMEs through relaxing the listing and disclosure requirements in comparison with the main markets. The other strategy adopted by the government is to provide incentives for SMEs to encourage them to list. One such initiative is to promote Over-The-Counter (OTC) markets to support the unlisted SMEs. The Turkish government has encouraged the market advisors to provide advice to SMEs to gain listing on the exchanges (Nurrachmi and Foughali, 2012).

The problem of access to finance is compounded when there is paucity of financial education and training among SMEs and consequently business owners fail to provide financial information to lenders. Müftüoğlu (2009) suggested training, mentoring, creating awareness initiatives for SMEs and training for bank lending managers to narrow the information gap, especially at the early stage where the business owners do not have enough finance knowledge, experience or necessary information about how the bank operates that gives rise to long term relational and operational problems (Kaya and Alpkan, 2012). Some of the other main problems are the cost of credit and collateral. The most important problem facing SMEs in Turkey is related to the high credit cost that adversely affects their survival. In addition, they do not have enough financial or physical asset security to negotiate competitive deals with the banks. Issuing of credit warranty is another hurdle or barrier for SMEs in Turkey. Because of the size of SMEs and their vulnerability in terms of management, the lending organizations see them as risky propositions. Hence providers of finance seek excessive collateral that works against the interests of SMEs. Another big issue for financial institutions is the pilferage of the loans specially approved for business activities; use of the loan other than business purposes increase the risk for the lenders (Kaya and Alpkan, 2012). Therefore, research conducted with SMEs supports the view that the initial capital is provided by the individual from their own savings and, second, that the debt finance from their family and friends and the bank loan is used as a last resort. It is suggested (Kaya and Alpkan, 2012) that in Turkey some SMEs are reluctant to use interest-bearing loans, due to their religious beliefs. Unlike Western economies, the Turkish government does not offer loan guarantee schemes to banks to support small businesses which lack collateral to secure finance. This leads enterprises to secure loans at higher interest rates in the absence of collateral or forgo the opportunity to enter self-employment. Finance constraints compound problems for SMEs. Lack of liquidity affect SMEs' purchases of stock on credit as they lack credit history, without which the provider of goods is not able to evaluate risk (Kaya and Alpkan, 2012). However, over time as the business develops a track record and a relationship – the access to purchase goods on credit improves, a pattern similar to that observed in the UK. Despite the track record and improvement in reputation, Özer and Yamak (2000) observed that institutional debt is still lacking for Turkish SMEs, and their finance profile is consistent with the pecking order theory. Entrepreneurs in Turkey are averse to external finance as they fear loss of control and hence rely on their savings and debt from close friends that often leaves small enterprises to be undercapitalized (Kaya and Alpkan, 2012; Ekinci, 2003).

CONCLUSION

The application, usability and role of the pecking order theory for SMEs have evolved over recent decades. Paul et al. (2007) suggest that the rationale for the applicability of the pecking order theory to SMEs is due, first, to the tendency of SME owner-managers to demonstrate a strong aversion to losing control over their business when new financiers are involved

(Berggren et al., 2000; Paul et al., 2007, Cosh and Hughes, 1994; Frank and Goyal, 2003, 2007). Consequently, the owner-managers of SMEs prefer retained savings as a source of finance to minimize the risk of losing control of their business (Newman et al., 2011). Secondly, due to poor management and financial control, SMEs tend to exhibit higher levels of asymmetric information when compared with the larger firms. This is due to the inability of SMEs to provide adequate financial and historical performance data to banks to use to make the lending decisions (Binks and Ennew, 1996; Reid, 1996; Hall et al., 2004), and small firms have to provide either collateral to secure external debt, use internal finance or borrow short-term or are more likely to rely upon internally generated retained profit that reduces their dependence on external finance. Therefore, the expectation, in line with the pecking order theory, is the more profitable the firm is, the less likely is the need for that firm to borrow externally, but is more likely to secure external debt. Several studies investigating the capital structure of SMEs have shown that there is a negative relationship between profitability and debt financing (Chittenden et al., 1996; Jordan et al., 1998; Michaelas et al., 1999: Hull, 2014; Karadeniz et al., 2011; Akkaya and Güler, 2008).

There is consistency in the findings of empirical research that investigated the capital structure of the Turkish SMEs and, indeed, successive studies have concluded that the pecking order theories are a better fit to explain the capital structure of Turkish SMEs (Çakova, 2011; Korkmaz et al., 2007, 2009; Yıldız et al., 2009; Acaravcı and Doğukanlı, 2004; Köksal and Orman, 2014). This suggests that the less profitable the SMEs are in Turkey, the more likely they are to seek external finance. Our chapter concludes that Turkish companies mainly follow the pecking order hypothesis in their capital structure for two principal reasons. First, because Turkish SMEs experience a 'finance gap', which prevents them from acquiring external finance at low cost. Second, they lack financial education and awareness about all the possibilities and aspects of external finance; thus the main long-term source of finance is retained earnings followed by bank loans. Turkish SMEs form the backbone of Turkish economic cohesion and social order, therefore it is imperative for the government and policy-makers to create and formulate progressive policies to support and encourage creation, and growth of SMEs by improving access to finance. Second, information asymmetry between insiders (owner-managers) and outsiders (lenders) gives rise to moral hazard that may be managed through financial education and the training of owner-managers of Turkish SMEs.

It is generally accepted that to facilitate external finance for SMEs, there is a need for a robust legal, institutional and regulatory environment. In such conditions the government or banks initiatives alone cannot ease the financial problems of SMEs. Therefore, Turkish national and local governments need to initiate long-term governmental policies and institutional reforms to enhance the legal, institutional and regulatory environment to enable SMEs to access external finance.

REFERENCES

Acaravcı, S. and Doğukanlı, H. (2004), 'Testing on manufacturing sector of determinants of capital structure in Turkey', *İktisatİşletmeveFinans*, **19** (225): 43–57.

Adedeji, A. (2002), 'A cross-sectional test of pecking order hypothesis against static trade off theory on UK Data', Working Paper, Birmingham: University of Birmingham.

Akkaya, G.C. and Güler, S. (2008), 'Capital structure, assets and profitability: an application on manufacturing firms', *İktisatİşletmeveFinans*, **23** (263): 41–52.

Altı, A. (2006), 'How persistent is the impact of market: timing on capital structure?', *The Journal of Finance*, **61** (4): 1681–1710.

Altı, A. and Sulaeman, J. (2012), 'When do high stock returns trigger equity issues?', *Journal of Financial Economics*, **103** (1): 61–87.

Ang, J.S. (1991), 'Small business uniqueness and the theory of financial management', *Journal of Small Business Finance*, **1** (1): 1–13.

Atherton A. (2009), 'Rational actors, knowledgeable agents: extending pecking order considerations of new venture financing to incorporate founder experience, knowledge and networks', *International Small Business Journal*, **27** (4): 470–495.

Baker, H.K. and Martin, G.S. (2011), *Capital Structure and Corporate Financing Decisions: Theory, Evidence, and Practice*, London: John Wiley and Sons.

Baker, M. and Wurgler, J. (2002), 'Market timing and capital structure', *The Journal of Finance*, **57** (1): 1–32.

Bayraktaroğlu, A., Ege, İ. and Yazıcı, N. (2013), 'A panel data analysis of capital structure determinants: empirical results from Turkish Capital Market', *International Journal of Economics and Finance*, **5** (4): 131–140.

Beck, T. (2013), 'Lessons from the literature – bank financing for SMEs', *National Institute of Economic Review*, **225** (1): 23–38.

Berens, J.L. and Cuny, C.J. (1995), 'The capital structure puzzle revisited', *Review of Financial Studies*, **8** (5): 1185–1208.

Berggren, B., Olofsson, C. and Silver, L. (2000), 'Control aversion and the search for external financing in Swedish SMEs', *Small Business Economics*, **15** (3): 233–242.

Binks, M.R. and Ennew, C.T. (1996), 'Growing firms and the credit constraint', *Small Business Economics*, **8** (1): 17–25.

Bistrova, J., Lace, N., and Peleckiene, V. (2011), 'The influence of capital structure on Baltic corporate performance', *Journal of Business Economics and Management*, **12** (4): 655–669.

Booth, L., Aivazian, V., Demirguc-Kunt, A., and Maksimovic, V. (2001), 'Capital structures in developing countries', *The Journal of Finance*, **56** (1): 87–130.

Çakova, U. (2011), 'Capital structure determinants of Turkish SMEs in manufacturing industry', unpublished Master's Thesis, Ankar, Turkey: Bilkent University.

Chen, D.H., Chen, C.D., Chen, J. and Huang, Y.F. (2013), 'Panel data analyses of the pecking order theory and the market timing theory of capital structure in Taiwan', *International Review of Economics and Finance*, **27** (C): 1–13.

Chen, J. (2004), 'Determinants of capital structure of Chinese-listed companies', *Journal of Business Research*, **57** (12): 1341–1351.

Chittenden, F., Hall, G., and Hutchinson, P. (1996), 'Small firm growth, access to capital markets and financial structure: review of issues and an empirical investigation', *Small Business Economics*, **8** (1): 59–67.

Copeland, T.E. and Weston, J.F. (2005), *Financial Theory and Corporate Policy* (4th edition), Reading MA: Addison-Wesley.

Cornelli, F., Portes, R., and Schaffer, M. (1998), 'The capital structure of firms in Central and Eastern Europe', in O. Bouin, F. Coricelli and F. Lemoine (eds), *Different Paths to a Market Economy: China and European Economies in Transition*, s.l.: CEPR/CEPII/OECD.

Cosh, A.D. and Hughes, A. (1994), 'Size, financial structure and profitability', in A. Hughes and D.J. Storey (eds), *Finance and the Small Firm*, London: Routledge, pp. 1–50.

Cressy, R. and Olofsson, C. (1997a), 'European SME financing: an overview', *Small Business Economics*, **9** (2): 87–96.

Cressy, R. and Olofsson, C. (1997b), 'The financial conditions for Swedish SMEs: survey and research agenda', *Small Business Economics*, **9** (2): 179–194.

Dahlstrand, A.L. and Cetindamar, D. (2000), 'The dynamics of innovation financing in Sweden', *Venture Capital*, **2** (3): 203–221.

Egerer, R. (1995), *Capital Markets, Financial Intermediaries, and Corporate Governance: An Empirical Assessment of the Top Ten Voucher Funds in the Czech Republic*, New York: World Bank.

Ekinci, M.B. (2003), 'Türkiye' de KOBİ' lerin Kurumsal Gelişimi ve Finansal Sorunları', İstanbul: AskonYayınları.

Fischer, E.O., Heinkel, R. and Zechner, J. (1989), 'Dynamic capital structure choice: theory and tests', *Journal of Finance*, **44** (1): 19–40.

Flannery, M.J. and Rangan, K.P. (2006), 'Partial adjustment toward target capital structures', *Journal of Financial Economics*, **79** (3): 469–506.

Frank, M.Z. and Goyal, V.K. (2003), 'Testing the pecking order theory of capital structure', *Journal of Financial Economics*, **67** (2): 217–248.

Frank, M.Z. and Goyal, V.K. (2007), 'Trade-off and pecking order theories of debt' in B. EspenEckbo (ed.), *Handbook of Corporate Finance: Empirical Corporate Finance*, Boulder, CO: Elsevier, pp. 135–202.

Giudici, G. and Paleari, S. (2000), 'The provision of finance to innovation: a survey conducted among Italian technology-based small firms', *Journal of Small Business Economics*, **14** (1): 37–53.

Hall, G., Hutchinson, P. and Michaelas, N. (2004), 'Determinants of the capital structures of European SMEs', *Journal of Business Finance and Accounting*, **31** (5–6): 711–728.

Hamilton, R.T. and Fox, M.A. (1998), 'The financing preferences of small firm owners', *International Journal of Entrepreneurial Behaviour and Research*, **4** (3): 239–248.

Holmes, S. and Kent, P. (1991), 'An empirical analysis of the financial structure of small and large Australian manufacturing enterprises', *The Journal of Small Business Finance*, **1** (2): 141–154.

Howorth, C. (2001), 'Small firms' demand for finance: a research note', *International Small Business Journal*, **19** (4): 78–86.

Hull, R. van 't. (2014), Determinants of the capital structure of Dutch SMEs, PhD Thesis, Twente University of Twente, Netherlands.

Hussain, J., Millman, C. and Matlay, H. (2006), 'SME financing in the UK and in China: a comparative perspective', *Journal of Small Business and Enterprise Development*, **13** (4): 584–599.

Hyytinen, A. and Pajarinen, M. (2002), 'Financing of technology intensive small business: some evidence from the ICT industry', *Discussion Paper*, **813**, Helsinki: The Research Institute of the Finnish Economy.

Ibbotson, R.G., Sindelar, J.L. and Ritter, J. (2001), 'Initial public offerings', *Journal of Applied Corporate Finance*, **6** (2): 37–45.

ICSA (2013), *Financing of SMEs through Capital Markets in Emerging Market Countries*, London: ICSA Emerging Markets Committee.

Jahanzeb, A., Muneer, S. and Rehman, S.U. (2012), 'Implication of behavioral finance in investment decision-making process', *Information Management and Business Review*, **4** (10): 532–536.

Jahanzeb, A., Rehman, S.U., Bajuri, N.H., Karamiand, M. and Ahmadimousaabad, A.

(2013), 'Trade-off theory, pecking order theory and market timing theory: a comprehensive review of capital structure theories', *International Journal of Management and Commerce Innovations*, **1** (1): 11–18.

Jensen, N.S and Uhl, F.T. (2008), *Capital Structure in European SMEs. An Analysis of Final and Country Specific Variables in Determining Leverage*, Aarhus: Aarhus School of Business.

Jordan, J., Lowe, J. and Taylor, P. (1998), 'Strategy and financial policy in UK small firms', *Journal of Business Finance and Accounting*, **25** (1–2): 1–27.

Karadeniz, E., Kandır, S.Y., Balcılar, M. and Onal, Y.B. (2009), 'Determinants of capital structure: evidence from Turkish lodging companies', *International Journal of Contemporary Hospitality Management*, **21** (5): 594–609.

Karadeniz, E., Kandır, S.Y., İskenderoğlu, Ö. and Önal, Y.B. (2011), 'Firm size and capital structure decisions: evidence from Turkish lodging companies', *International Journal of Economics and Financial Issues*, **1** (1): 1–11.

Kaya, S. and Alpkan, L. (2012), 'Problems and solution proposals for SMEs in Turkey', *Emerging Markets Journal*, **2** (2): 30–45.

Kaygın, B., Tankut, A.N. and Çaylı, M. (2008), 'The structural analysis of small and medium size furniture enterprises in Turkey based on production, capacity use and working environment', *African Journal of Biotechnology*, **7** (24): 4628–4634.

Kim, E.H. (1978), 'A mean-variance theory of optimal capital structure and corporate debt capacity', *Journal of Finance*, **33** (1): 45–63.

Köksal, B. and Orman, C. (2014), 'Determinants of capital structure: evidence from a major developing economy', Working Paper, **14/26**, Ankara: Central Bank of the Republic of Turkey.

Korkmaz, T., Albayrak, A.S. and Karataş, A. (2007), 'The analysis of the capital structure of the SMEs registered in the ISE: 1997–2004', *İktisatİşletmeveFinans*, **22** (253), 79–96.

Korkmaz, T., Başaran, Ü. and Gökbulut, R.D. (2009), 'The determinant factors of the capital structure of the automotive and auto parts companies registered in the ISE: panel data analysis', *İktisatİşletmeveFinans*, **24** (277): 29–60.

KOSGEB (2012), *Enhancing the Competitiveness of SMEs in Turkey*. Submitted to the 28th Session of the COMCEC, Ankara: KOSGEB.

KOSGEB (2014), *Financing of SMEs by KOSGEB*. SME Development Centers, Ankara: KOSGEB.

Kraus, A. and Litzenberger, R.H. (1973), 'A state-preference model of optimal financial leverage', *Journal of Finance*, **28** (4): 911–922.

Leary, M.T. and Roberts, M.R. (2005), 'Do irms rebalance their capital structures?', *Journal of Finance*, **60** (6): 2575–2616.

Lopez-Gracia, J. and Sogorb-Mira, F. (2008), 'Testing trade-off and pecking order theories financing SMEs', *Small Business Economics*, **31** (8): 117–136.

Michaelas, N., Chittenden, F. and P. Poutziouris (1999), 'Financial policy and capital structure choice in UK SMEs: Empirical evidence from company panel data', *Small Business Economics*, **12** (2): 113–130.

Ministry of Industry and Trade (2010), *Turkish Industrial Strategy Document 2011–2014*, Ankara: Ministry of Industry and Trade.

Modigliani, F. and Miller, M.H. (1958), 'The cost of capital, corporation finance and the theory of investment', *American Economic Review*, **48** (3): 261–297.

Müftüoğlu, T. (2009), 'SME support policies in Turkey after 1990: review, evaluation and suggestions', Paris: Agence Française de Développement, mimeo.

Muneer, S. and Rehman, S.U. (2012), 'Materialization of behavioral finance and behavioral portfolio theory: a brief review', *Journal of Economics and Behavioral Studies*, **4** (8): 431–435.

Munich Personal RePEc Archive (MPRA) (2013), *The Development of SMEs in Turkey*, Munich: Munich Personal RePEc Archive.

Myers, S.C. (1984), 'The capital structure puzzle', *Journal of Finance*, **39** (3): 575–592.

Myers, S.C. (2001), 'Capital structure', *Journal of Economic Perspective*, **15** (2): 81–102.

Myers, S.C. and Majluf, N. (1984), 'Corporate financing and investment decisions when firms have information that investors do not have', *Journal of Financial Economics*, **13** (4): 187–221.

Newman, A., Gunessee, S., and Hilton, B. (2011), 'Applicability of financial theories of capital structure to the Chinese cultural context: a study of privately owned SMEs', *International Small Business Journal*, **30** (1): 65–83.

Nurrachmi, R. and Foughali, K.A. (2012), 'The development of SMEs in Turkey', *MPRA Paper*, No. 46817, Munich: Munich Personal RePEc Archive.

OECD (2006), *The SME Financing Gap – Theory and Evidence*, Volume 1, Paris: OECD Publishing.

Ou, C. and Haynes, G.W. (2006), 'Acquisition of additional equity capital by small firms: findings from the National Survey of Small Business Finances', *Small Business Economics*, **27** (2–3): 157–168.

Özer, B. and Yamak, S. (2000), 'Self-sustaining pattern of finance in small business: evidence from Turkey', *International Journal of Hospitality Management*, **19** (3): 261–273.

Paul, S., Whittam, G. and J. Wyper, J. (2007), 'The pecking order hypothesis: does it apply to start-up firms?', *Journal of Small Business and Enterprise Development*, **14** (1): 8–21.

Reid, G.C. (1996), 'Financial structure and the growing small firm: theoretical underpinning and current evidence', *Small Business Economics*, **8** (1): 1–7.

Sànchez-Vidal, J. and Martin-Ugedo, J.F. (2005), 'Financing preference of Spanish firms: the pecking order theory in the context of small and medium-sized enterprises: a note evidence on the pecking order theory', *Review of Quantitative Finance and Accounting*, **25** (1): 341–355.

Şeker, M. and Correa, P.G. (2010), 'Obstacles to growth for small and medium enterprises in Turkey', WPS 5323, New York NY: World Bank.

Sogorb-Mira, F. (2005), 'How SME uniqueness affects capital structure: evidence from a 1994–1998 Spanish data panel', *Small Business Economics*, **25** (5): 447–457.

Turkish Statistical Institute (2011), *SME Statistics*, Ankara: Turkish Statistical Institute.

Yıldız, M.E., Yalama, A., and Sevil, G. (2009), 'Testing capital structure theory using panel data regression analysis: an empirical evidence from Istanbul Stock Exchange manufacturing firms', *İktisatİşletmeveFinans*, **24** (278): 25–45.

6. Resourcing indigenous export ventures through networks: insights from the Sri Lankan tea industry

Indu Peiris, Michèle Akoorie and Paresha Sinha

INTRODUCTION

Entrepreneurial actions need to be financed either through external means or internally by the entrepreneur (Shane, 2003). Not all entrepreneurs have inherited wealth at their disposal at the initiation of a new venture. Hence, the entrepreneur must find external sources to fulfil their resource (financial, physical and human) requirements, the absence of which can be a major constraint to a venture start-up and growth (Casson, 2003; Penrose, 1966). Access to resources is fundamental to opportunity exploitation, as someone who has identified a good opportunity needs access to resources to exploit it (Chrisman et al., 1998). Likewise, small firms that suffer from resource restrictions or means of accessing capital have inadequate capacity to grow due to limited availability of opportunities (Gilbert et al., 2006; Thakur, 1999). Access to capital and human resources can be considered a central factor in the success of a new venture (Bhidé, 2000).

The purpose of this chapter is to fill some of these gaps and investigate the underlying factors that led to successful exploitation of external social capital (in other words, the relationships developed by entrepreneurs with actors not employed by the firm as opposed to their internal social capital developed with their employees) in accessing bootstrapping resources. In essence, we try to answer why/how entrepreneurs use social capital as a bootstrapping strategy and what brings the entrepreneurs and external networks together to create new resource configurations.

Our chapter is structured as follows: first we review the literature related to bootstrapping and social capital. Then, we describe how we conducted the study. In the findings section we present propositions which explain how entrepreneurs initiated their ventures with limited external debt and equity financing, and used social capital to bootstrap resources. Finally, we discuss the study's implications and future directions for research.

LITERATURE REVIEW

Bootstrapping

New businesses face challenges due to the liability of newness coupled with the liability of smallness (Witt, 2004). However, the literature also provides evidence that entrepreneurs frequently pursue new opportunities despite severe and persistent resource constraints (Baker and Nelson, 2005). Entrepreneurs who are unable to raise adequate amounts of capital from traditional sources may attempt to raise additional capital from alternative sources (Van Auken and Neeley, 1996; Winborg and Landström, 2001). Arguably, these entrepreneurs 'bootstrap' their ventures in order to grow (Harrison et al., 2004).

A commonly used definition in the literature for bootstrapping is 'access to resources not owned or controlled by the entrepreneur' (Harrison et al., 2004, p. 307). Winborg and Landström (2001, p. 235) also define bootstrapping as 'methods for meeting the need for resources without relying on long-term external finance from debt holders and/or new owners'. However, the literature does not specifically distinguish between bootstrapping and financial bootstrapping and use these words interchangeably. In this chapter, we will use the term bootstrapping.

Bootstrapping involves acquiring finance without recourse to banks or raising equity from traditional sources (Freear et al., 1995) and securing resources at little or no cost (Winborg and Landström, 2001; Winborg, 2009). It is also viewed as an alternative resource management approach directed at avoiding market-based resource transactions (Grichnik et al., 2014). Based on these directions and following previous definitions by Freear et al. (1995), Van Auken and Neeley (1996) and Winborg and Landström (2001), we define bootstrapping in this study as 'the use of methods to meet the needs of resources after personal savings, debt and equity from traditional sources (financial institutes) are either exhausted or these resources are not available'.

Such methods can involve sharing resources/employees, advance payments from customers, delayed payments to suppliers, subsidies, emotional support and loans from friends and family (Carter and Van Auken, 2005; Jones and Jayawarna, 2010; Van Auken and Neeley, 1996; Vanacker et al., 2011; Winborg and Landström, 2001). In their study of 900 Swedish small business managers, Winborg and Landström (2001) identified 32 bootstrapping methods. Their study highlighted that there are three financial bootstrapping orientations: internally oriented (using resources found inside the business), socially oriented (use of personal relations as the means of absorbing and borrowing resources at no financial cost) and quasi-market modes of resource acquisition (use of governmental institutions for securing resources).

Previous research indicates that as many as 85–95 per cent of small firms utilize some form of bootstrapping (Harrison and Mason, 1997; Winborg, 2009). After studying a sample of 211 entrepreneurs in the UK, Jones and Jayawarna (2010) found a direct positive relationship between bootstrapping and firm performance. Similarly, a longitudinal study by Vanacker et al. (2011) of 214 new ventures identified that some bootstrapping strategies such as the use of temporary personnel and speeding up cash collection from customers have an impact on firm growth.

However, despite its wide use in practice, there has been relatively little research on bootstrapping in general and it is not clear if the results of these studies can be generalized (Carter and Van Auken, 2005; Harrison et al., 2004). Recent empirical studies have dealt with European countries such as Sweden, Germany, Belgium (Grichnik et al., 2014; Jonsson and Lindbergh, 2013; Vanacker et al., 2011; Winborg, 2009), UK (Jayawarna et al., 2011; Jones and Jayawarna, 2010) and USA (Ebben and Johnson, 2006; Ebben, 2009).

Apart from empirical validations of the concept, we have yet to uncover the many different facets of bootstrapping. For example, although we know about the relative use of different bootstrapping methods or techniques, the underlying motives for using such techniques has received little attention (Carter and Van Auken, 2005; Winborg, 2009). Furthermore, our knowledge about the process dynamics of resource acquisition related to bootstrapping is limited. Therefore, we need to explore more rigorously the nature and the causes of the processes through which entrepreneurs acquire bootstrapped resources (Grichnik et al., 2014; Harrison et al., 2004).

Bootstrapping may seem to be the preferred method of financing in the absence of internal or external funding (Ebben, 2009). Even though it may be easier to access bootstrap sources, they are also scarce resources. For example, deferring payments to suppliers, borrowing equipment from other businesses, obtaining payment in advance from customers, and obtaining loans from relatives and friends, have capacity limitations and depends on having strong relationships developed by entrepreneurial individuals with these parties. However, the influence of social capital for bootstrapping behaviour has attracted only limited attention to-date (Grichnik et al., 2014). Little is known about the impact that the dynamics of entrepreneurs' social capital have on bootstrapping in entrepreneurial ventures (Jonsson and Lindbergh, 2013). In this study we focus primarily on the socially oriented bootstrapping methods used by the entrepreneurs.

Social Capital and Social Networks

The central proposition of social capital theory is that networks of relationships constitute a valuable resource for the conduct of social affairs where people gain privileged access to information and opportunities (Nahapiet and Ghoshal, 1998). Social capital (SC) can be defined as the 'sum of the actual and potential resources embedded within, available through and derived from the network of relationships possessed by an individual or social unit' (Nahapiet and Ghoshal, 1998, p. 243). In short, an entrepreneur's set of relationships and the resources that can be acquired through them constitute his/her social capital (Adler and Kwon, 2002).

A network structure involves the pattern of interconnected relationships among the various actors that comprise a network (McFadyen and Cannella, 2004). An entrepreneur's social network begins with family and friends. In social network terms such linkages are described as 'strong ties'. Granovetter (1973) distinguishes a strong tie from a weak tie based on the number of interactions, and emotional intensity. The literature reasons that entrepreneurs initially rely on strong tie networks and when the venture develops they tend to deal more with their weak tie networks, formed by more distant business contacts (Hanlon and Saunders, 2007). The literature also indicates that strong ties are characterized by high levels of affective trust (Lewis and Weigert, 1985) and emotional support and financial resources not solely on the economic grounds but rather to support the entrepreneur personally (Brush et al., 2001; Chua et al., 2008).

Weak ties are comprised of suppliers, competitors and professional business contacts, who can provide information, expertise and tangible resources (Grichnik et al., 2014; Seghers et al., 2012). These ties are based on cognition-based trust that is, an entrepreneur chooses who he/she will trust based on the circumstances, and based on seemingly 'good reasons' (Lewis and Weigert, 1985). Taken together, both the weak and strong ties facilitate the acquisition of key resources, avoiding market transactions and thus enabling entrepreneurs to use bootstrapping. This depends on firm's stage of development.

Even though social capital is an asset in which other resources can be invested, it can be used for different purposes and can act as a substitute or a complement to other resources. Social capital needs to be maintained, but it does not depreciate with proper use; rather it grows and develops with appropriate use (Adler and Kwon, 2002; Coleman, 1988). In essence, social capital is about the value of connections that are capable of a multitude of outcomes such as power, leadership, mobility, individual performance, individual creativity, entrepreneurship, and team performance (Borgatti and Foster, 2003). Overall, the literature provides ample support for the notion that social capital is the antecedent to knowledge creation through the mechanism of combinations and exchanges. It also acts as a promoter of resource mobilization (Davidsson and Honig, 2003; De Carolis and Saparito, 2006; Manolova et al., 2010; Nahapiet and Ghoshal, 1998; Prashantham and Dhanaraj, 2010; Vaghely and Julien, 2010).

According to McFadyen and Cannella (2004), the relationship between social capital and the amount of knowledge created is not simply linear. They also state that social capital is costly to create and maintain, and at some level it may even create diminishing returns to the number and strength of exchange relations. In a similar vein, Jones and Jayawarna (2010) suggest that the strategic value of social capital depends on the entrepreneur's ability to use network relationships effectively. So far our knowledge about the dynamics between social capital and bootstrapping is limited. Hence there is a need for an in-depth inquiry into this phenomenon (Harrison et al., 2004).

CONTEXT

History of the Tea Industry in Sri Lanka

The tea industry in Sri Lanka dates back to over 150 years. The country was made the British Crown Colony of Ceylon in 1802. From the late 1860s, sterling companies (owned and managed by the British) based in London dominated the tea industry. At the time of Sri Lanka's independence in 1948 two-thirds of the tea sector was still owned by British companies, while the marketing of tea was totally in their hands. Even after independence, the structure of the tea plantation industry remained largely unaffected, and power was simply transferred to the native elite who were eager to maintain ties with the British. However, this started to change after 1950 when the government introduced the concept of the nationalization of the tea industry. Political independence caused widespread uncertainties in the market and led the British to sell their shares in the plantation companies. Ceylonese individuals were quick to seize the opportunity of purchasing the shares of sterling companies and by 1958 British ownership in sterling companies had dropped to 37 per cent (Fernando, 2000).

However, the legacy of the vertically integrated British companies made a lasting impression in the tea industry. The most important aspect of all was the transfer of knowledge to Ceylonese managers. Companies like George Stuart & Co. (est. 1835), Mackwood & Co. (est. 1841), Forbes & Walker (est. 1881), Harrison & Crossfield Ltd. (est. 1892), Lipton Ltd.

(est. 1892), James Finlay & Co. (est. 1893), Bartleet & Co. (est. 1904), A.F. Jones & Co. (est. 1918) and Brooke Bond Ceylon Ltd. (est. 1919) had started as small trading firms. Later they became multinationals that brought in a wealth of resources to the tea industry by way of plantation management (some of these companies integrated backwards into plantations), brokering, tea tasting, exporting, and marketing of tea to developed countries. The invaluable knowledge and the vast networks built up by these companies were later exploited by the local managers who started their own exporting firms in the late 1970s after many years working under British multinationals.

Transfer of Knowledge

The transfer of knowledge that built the industry over a century happened gradually and rather hesitantly. The management structure of the British trading companies consisted of boards of directors or a dominant shareholding family. The local directors were expatriates who had served long periods of time overseas and accumulated considerable region-specific experience. They were a close-knit group who collectively held a formidable tacit knowledge about products and regions, and had extensive personal contacts with directors of other firms and government officials. The British trading companies gave considerable attention to the selection of their future expatriate managers. The recruitment process, which usually happened in England, focused primarily on the personal recommendations, or acquaintance and relations with the past and present directors. The potential employees were extensively questioned on their family backgrounds, and family's social position. 'The general profile of a recruit was of a respectable, privately educated young man preferably with some sporting achievements at school' (Jones, 2000, p. 207).

The expatriate directors developed extensive bureaucratic rules, regulations, and routines to formalize flows of information and decision-making (Jones, 2000). These rigid structures and recruitment processes that prevailed until the late 1970s offered little or no career advancement opportunities for local managers.

A different kind of control was exercised by multinationals that organized the tea distribution and marketing. Even today, large multinationals such as Unilever (which owns Lipton, the top selling tea brand in the world and also PG Tips and Brooke Bond), Tetley (est. 1837 in England, now owned by Tata Global Beverages), and Twinings (est. 1706 in England), dominate the world's branded tea market. They form the interface between the tea trading houses and the consumers. Until the late 1980s, tea blending, branding, marketing, and distribution came under the exclusive control of these multinationals. Tea producing countries became mere exporters of bulk tea. For example, even today Unilever is the third largest bulk exporter of Sri Lankan tea (Colombo Tea Traders Association, 2009).

Sri Lankan exporters started value adding in the early seventies but it was in the late 1980s that single origin Ceylon tea entered the era of branding. This was the result of the entrepreneurial opportunity exploitation by several Sri Lankan entrepreneurs who created ventures which subsequently began competing with the tea multinationals. Coinciding with brand development, these tea-exporting firms started using sophisticated packaging methods. Sri Lankan exporters were able to customize and provide specialized services to premium end tea markets. These innovative strategies allowed them to fetch higher export revenue per kilogram than their competitors and reduce their dependence on the multinational packers. In the following section, we discuss the methods we used to explain how these entrepreneurs obtained resources for the exploitation of the entrepreneurial opportunity that they had identified.

METHOD

Rationale for a Qualitative Approach

The aim of this study is to create empirically grounded propositions explaining how entrepreneurs developed their social capital using bootstrapping resource acquisition during the early stages of the firm's life cycle. To do this, we take a subjectivist approach in developing our core ontological assumptions, because we expect to obtain phenomenological insights through projections of human imagination and experiences. As such a qualitative approach is more suited to investigate our research agenda, where richness and depth of insight is gained which is beyond the aggregative methodology of the positivist paradigm (Hindle, 2004). The research questions are broader and exploratory in nature, and entrepreneur research is a practice-based discipline (Gherardi, 2006).

Thus, the methodological choice in the research has to reflect both the nature and objective of the study. Case study methodology was considered well suited to achieve this aim (Yin, 2003), because it allows us to capture the dynamics of social capital, a novel context that focuses on traditional industry and developing country perspectives in more detail and in ways not possible through quantitative research (Harrison et al., 2004). Eisenhardt (1989, 1991) advocated case studies for theory-deficient areas. Therefore, the authors believed that using an interpretivist type methodology such as case study can extensively capture the resourcing side of entrepreneurial ventures (Neergaard and Parm Ulhøi, 2007). As noted by Eisenhardt and Graebner (2007), multiple cases create more robust theory because the propositions are more deeply grounded in varied empirical evidence.

We used purposive sampling (Eisenhardt, 1989; Eisenhardt and Graebner, 2007) to identify information-rich cases for this study. This purposive sample represents respondents who built their businesses from scratch and who were well established in the tea industry and well known for their entrepreneurial endeavours. Then we sought information from the Chamber of Commerce, National Chamber of Exporters, and Board of Investment to identify entrepreneurs in the tea industry in Sri Lanka. We selected six cases from the privately held (founder entrepreneur driven) tea exporting firms.

Firms were identified using the Colombo Tea Traders Association (CTTA) Annual Reports (Colombo Tea Traders Association, 2009). The sample consisted of medium (two) to large (four) firms. Sri Lanka does not have a nationally accepted definition to differentiate SMEs from their larger counterparts (Task Force for Small Medium Enterprise Sector Development Program, 2002). The most often used criteria when measuring size by employment is: micro <5 employees, small 5–29, medium 30–149 and large >150 employees (Task Force for Small Medium Enterprise Sector Development Program, 2002). This study adopted the above definition and focused mainly on the mature organizations, since to date the major focus has been on new ventures (Jones and Jayawarna, 2010; Vanacker et al., 2011; Winborg, 2009).

Data for this study was triangulated using four major sources; semi-structured interviews; review of publicly available secondary data sources (including newspaper articles, trade magazines, media releases, and government and non-governmental published reports); and field observations (through market and factory visits). The key informants were the founders of these tea-exporting companies.

These interviews were conducted in English, as English is widely used for official and commercial purposes in Sri Lanka. Tea has been an export commodity for over a century. The strong British influence in the tea industry still governs the trade and English is the first language of choice when conducting business, even today.

To ensure reliability, all interviews were transcribed verbatim (Eisenhardt, 1989) and the respondents were provided with the transcripts to ensure authenticity of the captured data. A summary of case firms is given in Table 6.1.

By following Yin's (2003) guidelines for case analysis using case

Table 6.1 Summary of case firms

Case	Size (Empl.)	Prior Industry experience		Year Started	Generation	Growth	Interviewee	Number of Interviews	Total hours
		Other	Same						
C01	<350	–	13	1982	1st	High	Managing Director (Founder)	2	3.5
C02	<160	–	21	1994	1st and 2nd	Medium	Director (Family member)	2	4
C03	<700	–	17	1994	1st	High	Managing Director (Founder)	2	2
C04	<150	2	12	2000	1st	High	Managing Director (Founder)	2	4.5
C05	<300	–	14	2000	1st	High	Managing Director (Founder)	1	5
							Senior Director (Partner)	2	–
C06	<50	10	2	2002	1st	Low	Managing Director (Founder)	2	2
								13	21

descriptions, comprehensive individual case descriptions were written using the general analytic strategy approach. This descriptive framework covered three areas, namely venture formation, growth and survival; these were used to identify underlying social capital factors that influenced the internationalization paths of these firms. Next, we used cross-case synthesis to compare and contrast the findings of the individual cases.

Data collection and data analysis were carried out concurrently and iteratively. First, the data was structured in chronological order (Ghauri, 2004). Entrepreneurial activities and internationalization are time-bound processes; therefore, chronological order helped to identify the critical incidents and key actors, and to segregate them into identifiable time gaps to track the phenomenon over time. The second stage sorted the data into meaningful categories (coded using NVivo 9.0) according to concepts and themes (Miles and Huberman, 1994) that were closer to venture formation, growth and survival phases of the entrepreneurial process. Analysis included word frequencies, graphs, and tables. This initial analysis helped us identify common themes and build a perceptual model comprising linkages to social capital and bootstrapping.

FINDINGS AND DISCUSSION

Bootstrapping Techniques

In the early 1980s the Sri Lankan tea industry started building its own identity through a few budding indigenous entrepreneurs who had years of multinational experience behind them and extensive knowledge about the tea industry and its consumers. Local managers who worked for multinational tea traders saw the market potential but the bureaucracy in these firms prevented them from reaching the top positions of these companies. They started building their own social and market networks and started thinking about venturing out on their own.

> I always had this thing [to start his own venture] in my mind when I joined BB I could see that to become a managing director of BB I would have to wait a long time. I left BB after just under 10 years as the tea manager and joined Shaw Wallace. I was made a director within one year. By the end of three years I decided to leave. When you turn the place around senior directors don't like it. All the clients were coming direct to me, then I changed it and I left with a few key people and started my company. (C01 – Managing Director)

However, the institutional environment that was built upon the colonial foundations did not give way to their wishes that easily. Government support and bank financing favoured the resource-rich multinational companies. Since the tea trade involved foreign transactions and negotiating documents through banks, they played a dominant role in the industry. A highly successful entrepreneur described the difficulties in accessing funds that he encountered in the early 1980s:

> [The] biggest challenge was finding funding. We are talking 27 years ago you have to go behind the banks with a begging bowl. And they would keep the bowl without giving us the funds. Today we don't have any issues with that. Remembering that, I try never to go to a bank. (C01 – Managing Director)

Bank financing is not a popular option among new ventures even now. Often bank financing was off limits, and entrepreneurs had to find alternative funding sources.

> The banks used to say that we do not know you. I did not have any known people in my setup so it was very difficult. I had to mortgage my house to get the first facility. Even that was not from a bank. (C03 – Managing Director)

In this study we found order and payment guarantees from potential customers (pre-venture formation) were instrumental in forming new ventures in the tea industry. Almost all the entrepreneurs left their work and started on their own, knowing that they will be able to get some support from these potential customers. Potential suppliers provided materials on credit terms and provided them with the flexibility of managing their resources. Family and friends provided funding, advice and market information. Former colleagues offered their support by joining the new venture and working with little job security and income. Finally, an interesting observation came through from a few case discussions about re-investment of their own earnings. Due to the difficulty in obtaining external finances, entrepreneurs developed a defence mechanism by re-investing their income in long-term deposits and assets. The excerpt from one of the interviewees below explains this situation vividly:

> We now have no mortgages on anything. This system [voluntary deposits] went on and we started doing this voluntarily not as a condition on our own, we are still doing it. (C03 – Managing Director)

Table 6.2 provides a summary of the main bootstrapping techniques commonly employed by all the case companies.

There is no doubt that bootstrapping is crucial to the success of entrepreneurial ventures (Jones and Jayawarna, 2010; Van Auken, 2005; Winborg, 2009). It also seems that the use of bootstrapping is not a question of last

Table 6.2 Bootstrapping techniques

Bootstrapping source		Case evidence	Typical activities
Formal networks	Customers	'It's the contacts that which I have made during my time really helped me, actually some of my clients sent me money when I was short of money.' (C04 – Managing Director) 'I knew them *(clients he dealt with when he was employed)* but there was no guarantee of buying from me, but if the things were okay they were willing to buy from me.' (C03 – Managing Director) 'My background has created the opportunity for me to start. I mean the work experience. . . . When I started all the customers came with me.' (C05 – Managing Director)	• Advance payments • Confirmed orders • Client fellowship
	Suppliers	'Sometimes we have to do the shipment before the money comes. Of course when you work for a big company like Brooke Bond, you are well connected you are known in the market. Especially if you had a good reputation and trusted reputation as an honest person then everybody gives you credit.' (C01 – Managing Director) 'There was a crowd of people who backed me, like guys not only in the company but in the tea trade as well. Because they helped a lot.' (C04 – Managing Director)	• Delivery on credit • Trade recommendation • Market information
Informal networks	Social networks	'I used to get credit from the brokers without any quota for any big amounts of that era. And when you pay them once money comes from the shipment.' (C01 – Managing Director) 'I had to mortgage my house to get loans . . . I had [to] work [for my own] provident fund, about 700,000 rupees at that time. I did not even have a vehicle. My wife had some cash and we bought a van for 400,000 rupees. This was the only cash we had.' (C03 – Managing Director) 'I was 34 years old and did not have much money, but the banks backed me. I also had a partner who backed me up with initial finances.' (C04 – Managing Director) 'I joined CBL in 1996 I worked for them for almost eight years. From there I developed my entrepreneurial skills.' (C06 – Managing Director)	• Funding • Cheap labour • Market information • Guidance and advice

resort, rather a resource that every entrepreneur will exploit irrespective of the context, industry, size or stage of a firm's life cycle.

While our study supports some of the techniques identified by Winborg and Landström (2001), in order to bring clarity into the existing research, we propose two network classifications based on their links to the firm. Formal networks have direct links with the venture activities, such as customers, suppliers, and institutions, and informal networks exhibit indirect/ potential links with the venture activities, such as family and friends, former colleagues and business contacts. This classification helps us to understand the network dynamics from a different perspective. Unlike strong and weak ties, which are based on subjective measures, we can clearly distinguish the relationship between formal and informal ties using their linkages to the venture.

Also, we can study the changing dynamics of formal and informal ties less ambiguously. For example, informal links can eventually be turned into formal links, that is, business contacts entering into partnerships and family members joining a firm as employees. Here we use value creation based measures instead of using interaction times and emotional intensity to identify the tie strength. Formal ties are capable of creating higher value creation possibilities for a firm (directly responsible for top and bottom line performance); whereas informal ties act on the periphery, and come into effect when the conditions are ripe to create value for the firm.

We contend that it is not prudent to classify family and friends as strong ties, and business contacts as weak ties. For example, our findings revealed that commonly associated definitions of strong and weak ties were not associated with bootstrapping in any identifiable patterns. Tie strength depends on its ability to create value for the firm and was also contingent on historical affiliation, reputation, and reciprocity.

In the next section, we examine the entrepreneur's ability to access bootstrapped resources which are embedded in networks.

Social Capital and Bootstrapping: Accessing the Power of Networks

Our findings emphasized the value-adding capability of social capital when accessing bootstrapped resources. Cassar (2004) states that obtaining debt and equity for a new venture heavily depends on the reputation, experience, and collateral processed by the nascent entrepreneurs. In our study we found three factors that influenced the ability to access resources embedded in networks. These are: time spent, reputation and experience, and reciprocal services.

Time spent (historical dimensions)

The resource constraints experienced at the individual level, and at the firm level, were mitigated by the support of resourceful networks (not the number of networks). C02, C03, C04 and C06 started their ventures because of the support they received from their network contacts which were developed from previous work experiences in multinational companies. As such, C02 and C04 depended entirely on their network partners to carry out their operational activities and the continuation of their ventures.

> Actually when my dad was there (Harrison and Crossfields), he was pretty much in charge of everything there. So when he moved he took the XXX account with him. They knew him from that time. That connection goes back that long. (C02–Senior Director)

Entrepreneurs developed both informal and formal networks intentionally over a long period of time. Often time was not measured in literal terms; rather it was about keeping in touch through good and bad times. For the entrepreneurs the longer they knew someone, the more they knew about them, and it became easier to access their resources.

Reputation

With historical affiliation (time spent) comes experience and also one's reputation. Formal and informal networks valued entrepreneurs' experience, superior knowledge about their products, markets and solutions to customer problems. Another aspect was the entrepreneur's reputation. Being a trustworthy individual had a significant bearing on their relationships. Trust between the entrepreneur and his/her network partner was a key reason to engage in cooperative behaviour that led to knowledge and resource sharing. Of the four relational dimensions of social capital (trust, norms, obligations, and identification) (Nahapiet and Ghoshal, 1998), we found trust to be the most significant dimension of social capital.

> [E]specially if you had a good reputation from there and trusted reputation as an honest person then everybody gives you credit. (C01 – Managing Director)
> It is not easy to build up a relationship. I maintain my integrity and I maintain my standards, as an honest person. (C03 – Managing Director)

According to Rousseau et al. (1998), relational trust derives from repeated interactions over time between trusted and trustee. Information available to the trusted person from within the relationship itself forms the basis of relational trust. Relational trust limits the opportunistic behaviour between parties and drives the transaction cost down. As such, knowledge and trustworthiness complement each other and contributes towards building one's reputation. All the firms in this study were engaged in non-contractual relationships, knowledge and resource sharing with many of their customers, suppliers and distributors; such relationships were based purely on the trustworthiness of their partners.

Our study found that relational trust and knowledge were co-dependent with reciprocal services or in other words *perceived strategic exchange of value*, that is, the network partners belief that the partnership has potential to add value (socially, psychologically, and physically) to the firm's activities in the present or at some time in the future. The entrepreneur in C01 explained what happens when either of these two factors is absent in a network partnership:

> In some markets like China, Hungary and Poland, mainly due to dishonesty [discontinuing the distributorship], when your business grows with trust we help them to build the business by giving them credit and they can misuse that. (C01 – Managing Director)

Perceived strategic exchange of value
This involves the *perception* of network partners that, by being in a partnership, there are benefits which are either tangible (physical resources) or intangible (knowledge, information and psychological). This creates potential for developing value-creating opportunities. As this study finds, there was an element of *reciprocity*, but more importantly, it was the perceived expectation of embedded value in a relationship that mattered. For example, with all the case entrepreneurs, relational trust built up between the two parties over time. When the entrepreneurs started their own ventures, these customers followed them and started giving business to these newly founded ventures. These customers took a risk but had confidence in the capabilities of these entrepreneurs to provide better value (in terms of pricing, quality of the product, and service) for them.

The discussion in this section leads to the following three propositions:

P1: *Formal and informal networks are the foundation of effective bootstrapping techniques.*

P2: *Access to network resources (social capital) is time dependent and developed with conscious effort, through building reputation (knowledge and trustworthiness), and strategic value reciprocity.*

P3: *Network resources (social capital) decay as a result of diminishing knowledge, reputation and strategic value reciprocity.*

CONCLUSION

Entrepreneurship scholars highlight the importance of bootstrapping as a way of responding to the resource constraints that nascent ventures face (Grichnik et al., 2014). The entrepreneurship literature has increasingly emphasized the relevance of entrepreneur's social capital in financing and acquisition of information that improves access to new international opportunities and resources (Jonsson and Lindbergh, 2013; Lindstrand et al., 2011; Manolova et al., 2010; Prashantham and Dhanaraj, 2010).

Despite the recognized importance of entrepreneur's social capital to a firm's resource acquisition, little is known about the influence and development of entrepreneurs' social capital with respect to bootstrapping. As such, we know that access to debt and equity is extremely difficult for nascent entrepreneurs because in the eyes of the banks and financiers they do not have a track record, are considered inexperienced and often do not have security for loans (Cassar, 2004). Typically, entrepreneurs turn to their personal savings, followed by family and social networks to compensate for the lack of financial and non-financial resources. In short, entrepreneurs use various bootstrapping strategies to fill this gap. However, there is limited research examining the way in which nascent entrepreneurs use their social networks to engage in bootstrapping activities.

In this study we fill some of the gaps in the entrepreneurial bootstrapping literature and investigated the underlying factors that led to successful exploitation of external social capital in accessing bootstrap resources. In essence, we tried to answer the question of how entrepreneurs use social capital as a bootstrapping strategy and what brought the entrepreneurs and external networks together to create new resource configurations. The conclusions that can be drawn from this study are as follows:

First, our study findings emerged from a novel research context. It provided insights from entrepreneur-led firms coming from a mature industry with a historical influence (the tea industry in Sri Lanka). Formerly regarded as a low value commodity industry, single origin and region specific tea Sri Lankan tea has attained something of a cult status among the tea-drinking cognoscenti. Previous research on entrepreneurship has almost exclusively focused on technology-based start-up ventures in developed countries (Ebben, 2009; Van Auken, 2005). However, our findings indicate that in certain parts of the world such as Sri Lanka, the involvement of venture capital firms is almost negligible even today. Banks play a key role in funding, brokering and managing the financial resources of firms but when banks turned nascent entrepreneurs away they used bootstrapping and networks to access the capital and resources they needed.

Second, we used case study methods to explore our research questions.

To our knowledge except for one recent study (Jonsson and Lindbergh, 2013), all the other studies looked at the bootstrapping phenomenon using quantitative methods. By using case studies, we were able to examine the stages of the entrepreneurial journey and the cause and effect of relationship building though the eyes of founding entrepreneurs. This gave us first-hand insights into how and why social capital was developed and used and the reasons behind its growth and decay.

Third, we affirm the findings of the previous research (Jones and Jayawarna, 2010; Van Auken, 2005; Winborg, 2009) who state that bootstrapping is crucial to business success. Bootstrapping is a deliberate and a natural choice for all the entrepreneurs. Winborg (2009) found three important motives behind financial bootstrapping: lower costs, lack of capital and helping and getting help from others. While we support his findings, we suggest that ease of access, historical affiliation (time spent) reputation and reciprocal behaviour also helps explain the intensity of bootstrapping behaviour in entrepreneurs in the Sri Lankan tea industry.

Finally, our study revealed that access to network bootstrapping resources (social capital) is time dependent and developed with conscious effort by entrepreneurs. Entrepreneurs form existing and future network relationships through building their reputation (knowledge and trustworthiness), and reciprocal behaviour. As such, reputation and reciprocal behaviour are the fundamental elements that are needed to access network (either formal or informal) related bootstrapped resources.

Our study took a qualitative approach to uncover the dynamics of network related bootstrapping; hence we looked at a small sample from a single industry. Therefore, unique factors that exist in this industry will limit the generalizability of the findings of this study. Future research can verify the findings across a larger number of industries and using multiple countries.

REFERENCES

Adler, P.S. and Kwon, S.W. (2002), 'Social capital: prospects for a new concept', *Academy of Management Review*, **27** (1): 17–40.
Baker, T. and Nelson, R.E. (2005), 'Creating something from nothing: resource construction through entrepreneurial bricolage', *Administrative Science Quarterly*, **50** (3): 329–366.
Bhidé, A. (2000), *The Origin and Evolution of New Businesses*, Oxford: Oxford University Press.
Borgatti, S.P. and Foster, P.C. (2003), 'The network paradigm in organizational research: a review and typology', *Journal of Management*, **29** (6): 991–1013.
Brush, C., Greene, P. and Hart, M. (2001), 'From initial idea to unique advantage: the entrepreneurial challenge of constructing a resource base', *The Academy of Management Executive*, **15** (1): 64–78.

Carter, R. and Van Auken, H. (2005), 'Bootstrap financing and owners' perceptions of their business constraints and opportunities', *Entrepreneurship and Regional Development*, **17** (2): 129–144.

Cassar, G. (2004), 'The financing of business start-ups', *Journal of Business Venturing*, **19** (2): 261–283.

Casson, M. (2003), *The Entrepreneur: An Economic Theory*, Cheltenham, UK and Northampton, MA, USA: Edward Elgar Publishing.

Chrisman, J.J., Bauerschmidt, A. and Hofer, C.W. (1998), 'The determinants of new venture performance: an extended model', *Entrepreneurship Theory and Practice*, **23** (1): 5–30.

Chua, R., Ingram, P. and Morris, M. (2008), 'From the head and the heart: locating cognition-and affect-based trust in managers' professional networks', *Academy of Management Journal*, **51** (3): 436–452.

Coleman, J.S. (1988), 'Social capital in the creation of human capital', *The American Journal of Sociology*, **94** (1): 95–120.

Colombo Tea Traders Association (2009), *Annual report and accounts*, Colombo: Sri Lanka: Colombo Tea Traders Association.

Davidsson, P. and Honig, B. (2003), 'The role of social and human capital among nascent entrepreneurs', *Journal of Business Venturing*, **18** (3): 301–331.

De Carolis, D.M. and Saparito, P. (2006), 'Social capital, cognition, and entrepreneurial opportunities: a theoretical framework', *Entrepreneurship Theory and Practice*, **30** (1): 41–56.

Ebben, J. (2009), 'Bootstrapping and the financial condition of small firms', *International Journal of Entrepreneurial Behaviour and Research*, **15** (4): 346–363.

Ebben, J. and Johnson, A. (2006), 'Bootstrapping in small firms: an empirical analysis of change over time', *Journal of Business Venturing*, **21** (6): 851–865.

Eisenhardt, K.M. (1989), 'Building theory from case study research', *Academy of Management Review*, **14** (4): 532–550.

Eisenhardt, K.M. (1991), 'Better stories and better constructs: the case for rigor and comparative logic', *Academy of Management Review*, **16** (3): 620–627.

Eisenhardt, K.M. and Graebner, M.E. (2007), 'Theory building from cases: opportunities and challenges', *The Academy of Management Journal*, **50** (1): 25–32.

Fernando, M. (2000), *The Story of Ceylon Tea*, Colombo, Sri Lanka: Mlesna (Ceylon) Limited.

Freear, J., Sohl, J.E. and Wetzel, W.E. (1995), 'Who bankrolls software entrepreneurs?', in W.D. Bygrave, B.J. Bird, S. Birley, N.C. Churchill, M.G. Hay, R.H. Keeley and W.E. Wetzel, Jr. (eds), *Frontiers of Entrepreneurship Research*, Wellesley, MA: Babson College, pp. 394–406.

Ghauri, P.N. (2004), 'Designing and conducting case studies in international business research', in R. Piekkari and C. Welch (eds), *Handbook of Qualitative Research Methods for International Business*, Cheltenham, UK and Northampton, MA, USA: Edward Elgar Publishing, pp. 109–124.

Gherardi, S. (2006), 'Practice-based theorizing on learning and knowing in organizations', *Organization*, **7** (2): 211–223.

Gilbert, B., McDougall, P.P. and Audretsch, D. (2006), 'New venture growth: a review and extension', *Journal of Management*, **32** (6): 926–950.

Granovetter, M.S. (1973), 'The strength of weak ties', *American Journal of Sociology*, **78** (6): 1360–1380.

Grichnik, D., Brinckmann, J., Singh, L. and Manigart, S. (2014), 'Beyond environmental scarcity: human and social capital as driving forces of bootstrapping activities', *Journal of Business Venturing*, **29** (2): 310–326.

Hanlon, D. and Saunders, C. (2007), 'Marshaling resources to form small new ventures: toward a more holistic understanding of entrepreneurial support', *Entrepreneurship Theory and Practice*, **31** (4): 619–641.

Harrison, R.T. and Mason, C.M. (1997), 'Entrepreneurial growth strategies and venture performance in the software industry', Paper presented at Babson College Entrepreneurship Research Conference, Wellesley, MA.

Harrison, R.T., Mason, C.M. and Girling, P. (2004), 'Financial bootstrapping and venture development in the software industry', *Entrepreneurship and Regional Development*, **16** (4): 307–333.
Hindle, K. (2004), 'Choosing qualitative methods for entrepreneurial cognition research: a canonical development approach', *Entrepreneurship Theory and Practice*, **28** (6): 575–607.
Jayawarna, D., Jones, O. and Macpherson, A. (2011), 'New business creation and regional development: enhancing resource acquisition in areas of social deprivation', *Entrepreneurship and Regional Development*, **23** (9/10): 735–761.
Jones, G. (2000), *Merchants to Multinationals*, Oxford: Oxford University Press.
Jones, O. and Jayawarna, D. (2010), 'Resourcing new businesses: social networks, bootstrapping and firm performance', *Venture Capital*, **12** (2): 127–152.
Jonsson, S. and Lindbergh, J. (2013), 'The development of social capital and financing of entrepreneurial firms: from financial bootstrapping to bank funding', *Entrepreneurship: Theory and Practice*, **37** (4): 661–686.
Lewis, J. and Weigert, A. (1985), 'Trust as a social reality', *Social Forces*, **63** (4): 967–985.
Lindstrand, A., Melén, S., and Nordman, E. (2011), 'Turning social capital into business: a study of the internationalization of biotech SMEs', *International Business Review*, **20** (2): 194–212.
Manolova, T., Manev, I. and Gyoshev, B. (2010), 'In good company: the role of personal and inter-firm networks for new-venture internationalization in a transition economy', *Journal of World Business*, **45** (3): 257–265.
McFadyen, M. and Cannella, A. (2004), 'Social capital and knowledge creation: diminishing returns of the number and strength of exchange relationships', *Academy of Management Journal*, **47** (5): 735–746.
Miles, M. B. and Huberman, A.M. (1994), *Qualitative Data Analysis: An Expanded Source Book*, Thousand Oaks, CA: Sage Publications.
Nahapiet, J. and Ghoshal, S. (1998), 'Social capital, intellectual capital and the organizational advantage', *Academy of Management Review*, **23** (2): 242–266.
Neergaard, H. and Parm Ulhøi, J. (2007), 'Introduction: methodological variety in entrepreneurship research', in H. Neergaard and J. Parm Ulhøi (eds), *Handbook of Qualitative Research in Entrepreneurship*, Cheltenham, UK and Northampton, MA, USA: Edward Elgar Publishing, pp. 1–15.
Penrose, E.T. (1966), *The Theory of the Growth of the Firm*, Oxford, UK: Blackwell.
Prashantham, S. and Dhanaraj, C. (2010), 'The dynamic influence of social capital on the international growth of new ventures', *Journal of Management Studies*, **47** (6): 967–994.
Rousseau, D.M., Sitkin, S.B., Burt, R.S. and Camerer, C. (1998), 'Not so different after all: a cross-discipline view of trust', *Academy of Management Review*, **23** (3): 393–404.
Seghers, A., Manigart, S. and Vanacker, T. (2012), 'The impact of human and social capital on entrepreneurs' knowledge of finance alternatives', *Journal of Small Business Management*, **50** (1): 63–86.
Shane, S. (2003), *A General Theory of Entrepreneurship: The Individual–Opportunity Nexus*, Cheltenham, UK and Northampton, MA, USA: Edward Elgar Publishing.
Task Force for Small Medium Enterprise Sector Development Program (2002), *National Strategy for Small Medium Enterprise Sector Development in Sri Lanka*, Colombo, Sri Lanka: Ministry of Enterprise Development.
Thakur, S. (1999), 'Size of investment, opportunity choice and human resources in new venture growth: some typologies', *Journal of Business Venturing*, **14** (3): 283–309.
Vaghely, I. and Julien, P-A. (2010), 'Are opportunities recognized or constructed? An information perspective on entrepreneurial opportunity identification', *Journal of Business Venturing*, **25** (1): 73–86.
Van Auken, H. (2005), 'Differences in the usage of bootstrap financing among technology-based versus nontechnology-based firms', *Journal of Small Business Management*, **43** (1): 93–103.
Van Auken, H. and Neeley, L. (1996), 'Evidence of bootstrap financing among small start-up firms', *The Journal of Entrepreneurial Finance*, **5** (3): 235–249.

Vanacker, T., Manigart, S., Meuleman, M. and Sels, L. (2011), 'A longitudinal study on the relationship between financial bootstrapping and new venture growth', *Entrepreneurship and Regional Development*, **23** (9/10): 681–705.

Winborg, J. (2009), 'Use of financial bootstrapping in new businesses: a question of last resort?', *Venture Capital*, **11** (1): 71–83.

Winborg, J. and Landström, H. (2001), 'Financial bootstrapping in small businesses: examining small business managers' resource acquisition behaviors', *Journal of Business Venturing*, **16** (3): 235–254.

Witt, P. (2004), 'Entrepreneurs' networks and the success of start-ups', *Entrepreneurship and Regional Development*, **16** (5): 391–412.

Yin, R.K. (2003), *Case Study Research: Design and Methods*, Thousand Oaks, CA: Sage Publications.

7. Business angel exits: strategies and processes
Colin Mason, Richard T. Harrison and Tiago Botelho

INTRODUCTION

The core of the entrepreneurial process is the creation of financial value. Yet, compared to the emphasis that has been given to the processes of opportunity recognition and start-up, scholars have devoted remarkably little attention to the exit process, and specifically to the harvest event where some or all of the financial value that has been created is realized. Where the harvest event has been considered – primarily in the venture capital (VC) literature – it has typically been in the context of an Initial Public Offering (IPO) where the focus is on pricing issues (for example, Megginson and Weiss, 1991; Brav and Gompers, 1997; Gompers, 1996), or in the context of the entrepreneur's exit rather than the investor's exit (DeTienne, 2010; DeTienne and Cardon, 2012; Wennberg et al., 2010; Wennberg and DeTienne, 2014).

Our focus in this chapter is on business angels – high net worth individuals (often successful cashed-out entrepreneurs) who invest their own money directly in emerging entrepreneurial businesses. As the main source of risk capital for such companies, they play a critical role in the entrepreneurial ecosystem. The business angel literature reflects in microcosm the criticism that has been levelled against the wider literature. Its emphasis is on the investment decision-making process (Mason and Harrison, 1996; Mason and Rogers, 1997; Feeney et al., 1999; Mason and Stark, 2004; Clark, 2008; Maxwell et al., 2011; Brush et al., 2012), and on the types of investments that business angels have made (Mason and Harrison, 2010, 2011). In contrast, both the outcomes of the investments and, for those that delivered positive returns, the process of achieving the exit, have been largely ignored. This reflects the priorities of business angels themselves, with studies of business angels in both the United States (US) and Europe presenting a picture in which they give very little thought to future exit routes, do not have clear exit plans at the time of investing and are relaxed about the timing of the exit (Wetzel, 1981; Gaston, 1989; Harrison and Mason, 1992; Landström, 1993; Mason and Harrison, 1994; Lumme et al., 1998). Indeed, in one study, 'potential exit routes' was ranked 24th (out of 27) investment criteria by angels (Van Osnabrugge and Robinson, 2002). There is also no evidence in studies of the post-investment involvement of angels in their investee business that preparing the business for an exit is one of their value-added contributions. Indeed, this activity was not mentioned in any of the studies reviewed by Politis (2008). This attitude is reflected in the view, as expressed by a former angel group gatekeeper,[1] that 'good investments will always find exits'. Another explanation for the apparent low priority given to exits is that the tax incentives that are now available in many countries encourage business angels to focus their attention on making the investment rather than on the return.

Business angels are a major focus of government support across the globe (Mason, 2009; Organisation for Economic Co-operation and Development (OECD), 2011). However, these interventions – notably tax incentives to reduce the cost of investing and support for networks to help investors and entrepreneurs connect with one another – have had the objective of increasing the number of investments made. Little attention has been given to the outcomes of the investments. Yet, the positive economic benefits – for example in terms of employment, generating exports, adding to the tax base, and improving economic efficiency through innovation and better resource allocation – only come from the 'winners'. The twin processes of entrepreneur and investor recycling (Mason and Harrison, 2006) – the re-investment of money and expertise in new businesses – also requires 'winners'. Businesses which subsequently fail have, at best, a fleeting impact on economic development. Meanwhile, while the 'living dead' – businesses that generate enough profits to survive but do not have the necessary attributes to attract a buyer – also have limited economic impact and may absorb the attention of investors and further funding that would both be better devoted to their more promising investments. Accordingly, influencing the outcomes of investments should be of concern to policymakers.

Putting exits onto the agenda of researchers, the practitioner community and government is, therefore, well overdue. The UK angel community has been singled out for particular criticism because of 'the tendency to see angel investing as something that people do for a whole host of reasons other than making a profit. Britain has a long tradition of characterizing angel investing as tax efficient, as benefiting from government subsidies, as an opportunity to provide mentorship or help local businesses and so forth, but unlike other types of equity investments, angel investing is very rarely talked about as a way to make capital appreciate over time' (Lynn, 2010).

The structure of this chapter is as follows. In the next section we review the returns to angel investing and highlight their skewed nature. Next we examine the current low level of exit activity and identify the failure of investors to adopt an exit-centric approach to investing. Finally, we elaborate on the practices associated with this approach to investing. Some preliminary evidence is offered which suggests that an exit-centric approach is associated with successful exits.

RETURNS TO ANGEL INVESTING

Despite different time-periods and geographical contexts, the small number of studies on returns to angel investing are remarkably consistent, finding that around half of all investments fail to generate a return while a minority of investments generate more than ten times cash return (Lumme et al., 1998; Mason and Harrison, 2002; Wiltbank and Boeker, 2007; Wiltbank, 2009; Vo, 2013). For example, this small minority of successful investments generate the majority (c. 80 per cent) of the cash generated by the entire sample of investments in Wiltbank's (2009) sample.

These studies are controversial. Shane (2009) argues that the returns achieved by the typical angel are overstated. Most of these studies use biased samples, typically the members of specific successful angel groups. There is likely to be survivor bias, with angels who are no longer active investors, perhaps because of poor returns, not included. There is also likely to be a response bias, with those angels with successful investments more likely to respond. It is further argued that the unpaid time that angels devote to evaluating investment opportunities and supporting their investee companies is not accounted for; taking account of the opportunity cost of this time would reduce returns. But it can also be argued that financial returns are understated: financial return is measured crudely as the return on capital, cash-on-cash, and, therefore, does not take account of any ongoing financial remuneration (for example, director's fee, consulting fee; salary; dividend income).

The typical exit route for angels is via a trade sale. IPOs are rare. The holding period for successful investments is four to five years. Failed investments, in contrast, emerge after about two years, confirming the investment cliché that 'lemons ripen before plums'. Mason and Harrison (2002) find that the moderately performing investments actually have the longest holding period because of the limited opportunities to exit. Often these investments are sold back to the management team, typically for a nominal price.

The most successful investments are associated with the amount of due diligence undertaken by the investor and the familiarity of the investor with the sector (Wiltbank and Boecker, 2007; Wiltbank, 2009). Making a follow-on investment is associated with less successful investments (Wiltbank and Boecker, 2007; Wiltbank, 2009), whereas deals which involve multiple investors have higher returns (Mason and Harrison, 2002). The involvement of venture capital funds in the investment is associated with both more failures and a greater number of larger exits (Wiltbank and Boeker, 2007). Peters (2009) attributes this to the investment approach of venture capital funds, which seek to maximize the returns of the portfolio and, therefore, put more emphasis than angel investors do on 'hitting a home run' and are more ruthless with their 'living dead' investments. The impact on returns of the angel investor's hands-on involvement in the business is less clear cut (Wiltbank, 2009). Mason and Harrison (2002, 2004) find that the highest performing investments are management buyouts – which represent a small minority of all angel investments. They also find no difference in the returns from technology and non-technology-based firms. Finally, Vo (2013) notes that there is a positive relationship between distance and angel investment performance, with more distant investments generating higher returns. This is consistent with the hurdle effect, where investors impose a higher return requirement on distant investments to compensate for the costs associated with information disadvantages compared with local investors. Distant investors are also more likely to have different, and hence complementary, networks (Harrison et al., 2010).

Business angels typically make several investments, hence the returns from individual investments are less important than the overall return to their portfolio. A focus on individual investments does not tell us how the successful and unsuccessful investments are distributed across the population of angel investors. A study of angel investors in Finland (Lumme et al., 1998) grouped angels into two categories: successful investors (only profitable exits) and unsuccessful investors (no profitable exits). Successful investors were more likely to have worked in senior management positions in large companies, whereas unsuccessful investors were more likely to have held senior positions in small companies. Successful investors seemed to be motivated to a greater extent than unsuccessful investors by the buzz that they get from being a business angel, whereas altruism was a more important motivational consideration for unsuccessful investors. Successful investors received a higher number of investment opportunities and invested in a smaller proportion of them than unsuccessful investors and invested smaller amounts per deal, suggesting that they are more discriminating in their investments. A further difference is that unsuccessful investors were more likely to rely on friends for their investment opportunities and to have invested in friends' businesses. Unsuccessful investors also rated their value added contributions to their investee businesses more highly than successful investors did. They also gave greater emphasis to value added contributions that have been suggested as being of lesser importance.

Angels are increasingly investing as part of structured angel groups (Sohl, 2007; 2012; Gregson et al., 2013; Mason et al., 2013), motivated at least in part to achieve greater diversification, thereby reducing risk. Roach (2010) calculates the portfolio returns of one angel group to be higher than for other equivalent investment benchmarks. However, this is a theoretical return as no members participated in every investment that the group made.

Shane (2009, p. 162) offers a summary of the available evidence: 'the returns on investments made by angels are not very high'. He goes further – albeit with less evidence – claiming that 'the typical angel investment does not perform as well as the typical investment in other asset classes' (Shane, 2009, p. 161). Nevertheless, many angel investments are successful, generating significant returns. Although these are most likely when the angel does a significant amount of due diligence prior to investing and is investing in an industry in which he or she is familiar, some successful investments simply result from luck.

TRENDS IN EXITS

Achieving an exit is now also increasingly challenging. One experienced angel has observed that 'the overall impression when talking to Angels around the world is that they have become frustrated with the lack of successful exits or liquidity events, resulting in them not receiving the return on their investments they hoped for' (Gray, 2011). Those exits which do occur are taking longer to achieve. John Waddell, manager of Archangels in Edinburgh Scotland, which claims to be the oldest functioning angel group in the world, has observed that 'in 2005 the average time between investing and exiting for early stage companies was about three years; it is now 10 years or more . . . . There has been an exit drought' (Waddell, 2013: col. 3697). The same problem has been highlighted by the National Angel Capital Association (NACO) of Canada in its most recent investment report (NACO, 2014, p. 44). 'A main challenge for a number of angel groups is the length of time to exit. Long investment time horizons restrict the Angels' ability to reinvest in new companies'. The resulting investor fatigue depresses investment activity.

A survey undertaken by the authors of one Northern Ireland and 18 Scotland based business angel groups confirms the small number of exits that they have achieved (Figure 7.1). These groups have collectively made

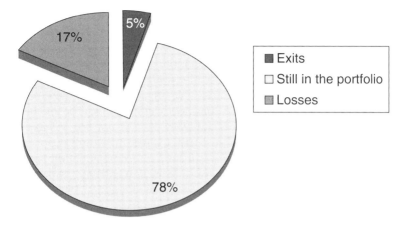

Source: Mason et al. (2013).

Figure 7.1   Outcomes of investments by Scottish business angel groups

37 exits which represents just 4 per cent of their investments. The majority of groups – 12 of the 17 that provided data – have not made any exits. To some extent this reflects the young age of many of the groups. Indeed, four of the five groups that have achieved exits were formed at least eight years ago, with the three longest established groups accounting for 92 per cent of total exits. Nevertheless, the vast majority of groups that were founded between five and eight years ago have not made any exits – contrasting with earlier studies of exits by UK business angels which reported median holding periods to exit of four years (Mason and Harrison, 2002) and six years (Wiltbank, 2009). However, it could be argued that we no longer know what represents the 'norm' and, accordingly, we risk interpreting these data with unrealistic expectations.

Equally notable is the low number of failed investments (Figure 7.1) which account for 17 per cent of total investments. The three oldest groups account for 82 per cent of all losses. Previous studies have reported that the median failed investment emerges after two or three years (Mason and Harrison, 2002; Wiltbank, 2009). In view of the recessionary conditions that have prevailed since 2008, it would be surprising if general business failure rates have been lower in recent years, so this might suggest that angel groups are managing their unsuccessful investments badly. This is largely confirmed in our survey, with two-thirds of the groups reporting that they had no formal strategy for dealing with the 'living dead' in their portfolios, creating the risk that these investments absorb unproductive time and further funding.

The low rate of exits is attributed by Gray (2011) to the failure of the angel community to build the exit into their investment appraisal. There are two widely held views among the angel community that discourage an exit-centric approach to investing. First is the belief that 'good investments will always find exits'. This view has been articulated by the prominent UK entrepreneur, venture capitalist and angel investor Luke Johnson (2012) who has stated that 'if the business works you will be spoilt with choice of exit'. Angels who hold this view would not see any need to consider exit possibilities at the investment stage nor would they seek to pursue an exit strategy after the investment had been made. Second is the belief is that it is inappropriate to discuss exits with entrepreneurs prior to investing or to actively pursue exits post-investment as somehow this puts the entrepreneur and the investor on an unequal basis. Johnson (2012) has argued that it is off-putting to the entrepreneur who is passionate about their business to be asked about the exit in their first conversation with a prospective investor. This approach to investing has been claimed to reduce the prospects of achieving a successful exit. First, it increases the risk that investments will be made in companies for which there are no prospective acquirers. Second, those exits which do occur will be opportunistic and, therefore, less likely than if a strategic approach to the exit was adopted.

A more detailed study (Mason and Botelho, 2016) of the investment decision-making of so-called 'gatekeepers' – in other words, the managers of angel groups – suggested that they were attuned to the need to consider the exit at an early stage in the investment decision-making process, especially the likelihood of an exit, likely buyers and likely returns. However, in most cases this did not translate into a proactive approach to seeking an exit, nor to a process for dealing with the 'living dead' in their portfolio. Most were of the view that building value in their investee businesses would secure an exit. Indeed, when presented with a real investment opportunity to consider, the exit attracted the lowest share of comments of nine categories. Just three of the 21 gatekeepers interviewed took an exit-centric approach to investing.[2] In each case, these were fairly recently established groups which had yet to make their first investment. A similar lack of exit-centricity was found among individual business angels who were also asked to review the same investment opportunity. Here again, the exit attracted the lowest proportion of comments. Only one of the 30 angels in the study took an exit-centric approach to investing.[3]

In summary, achieving exits is becoming increasingly challenging for the angel community. This may not have mattered in the past. Then angel activity was more of a hobby activity, angels were making fewer investments and investing less money and personal reasons for investing were more important, notably the excitement of being involved in a new venture or investing in 'hot buttons' (Wetzel, 1981), from which psychic income was derived. In addition, in the past the existence of a stronger funding escalator meant that there was greater likelihood that an angel-backed business would go on to attract follow-on funding from a venture capital fund (Freear and Wetzel, 1990) which, in turn, would manage the exit. However, the emergence of managed angel groups and various fee-based intermediaries offering 'packaged' investment opportunities might be expected to have increased the emphasis on the need for an exit. Angel groups operate more professionally, with a more formal process of assessing opportunities. There is a more arms-length relationship with investee businesses and hence less likelihood of developing an emotional attachment to investments (Ibrahim, 2008). For both reasons, there is less opportunity to derive psychic income. Moreover, angel groups are investing more frequently, making bigger investments, are less reliant on venture capital funds for follow-on investment and hence are more likely to fund a business to an exit. They also need exits both to provide their members with the liquidity to make new investments and to attract new investors. Fee-based intermediaries need to demonstrate that the investment opportunities they offer their members are capable of generating good financial returns. The following section reviews exit-centric investment strategies.

EXIT-CENTRIC APPROACHES TO INVESTING: EMERGING THEMES

Our discussion draws on our ongoing relationships with various angel associations, regular involvement in angel conferences in the US, UK, Canada, Europe and Australia, discussions with some of the prominent thought leaders in the field and a review of written materials by various practitioners and commentators. From these sources, four emerging themes in angel investment practices can be identified. These are presented separately, although it will quickly become apparent that there are strong interrelationships.

Start with the Exit

The conventional view of the investment process is one which comprises a series of stages that are undertaken sequentially (see Mason, 2006 for an overview). First, the angel generates a deal flow. This can be done with varying levels of pro-activity. Professional contacts and friends are the main sources. Opportunities are then subjected to an initial screening where the emphasis is on investor fit, the market potential and the characteristics of the entrepreneur (Mason and Rogers, 1997). Between 70 per cent and 90 per cent of the deal flow is rejected at this stage (Riding et al., 1993). The remaining opportunities are then subjected to a detailed investigation and due diligence. The main emphasis here is on people factors, specifically the personal qualities of the management team (for example, trustworthiness, capability for hard work, coachability) and a judgement of their capability to exploit the opportunity successfully (Feeney et al., 1999). In those cases where the angel wants to make an investment, a due diligence process would be undertaken to verify all material facts (Mason and Harrison, 1996). If nothing negative emerges from that stage, the angel will then seek to negotiate the terms and conditions of an investment. Central to this process is the valuation of the business. In some cases, this process ends in failure with both sides unable to agree. Legal documents are then drawn up and signed. In contrast to venture capital funds, because the size of investments made by business angels typically does not support high legal costs, and they are investing their own money, the legal documentation will be short and may take the form of a standard investment contract (Kelly and Hay, 2003). The money is then passed over. The post-investment stage may take several years. It may include one or more further funding rounds, possibly including additional investors. Here the angel will monitor the performance of their investment. Most will also seek to add value to their investments by giving advice and mentoring to the management team and various hands on contributions (Paul et al., 2003; Madill et al., 2005; Politis, 2008). Angels hope for a successful exit in which they achieve a significant multiple on their original investment when the business is acquired by another business or, in exceptional circumstances, achieves an IPO. However, in this approach to investing the exit is only considered towards the end of the process and is not proactively sought.

An exit-centric approach to investing puts the exit at the core of the investment process. As an illustration, the Ohio Techangels (2012) documentation states that they will only invest 'in companies that are scalable, led by a solid management team, and can articulate a well-designed capital access plan and *liquidity event*' (emphasis added) – specifically 'a clear path to a $30m–$50m exit via sale to a targeted strategic bidder within five years'. In the tradition of Covey (1989) this approach therefore starts with the desired outcome – an exit. Each of the preceding stages in the investment process is undertaken from the perspective of facilitating the exit.

At the initial screening stage, one of the first considerations in an exit-centric investment approach would be to establish how much money is anticipated to be required to reach an exit. Angels might hesitate if they think that substantial follow-on investment will need to be raised from venture capital funds because of the risk of dilution that it creates and the control implications. According to Peters (2009), involving venture capitalists in a business also has significant implications for the time to exit (longer) and the probabilities of success (lower). Venture capitalists will determine when the company is sold, if necessary using their preferred shares and the terms and conditions in their investment agreement (Peters, 2009; Smith, 2005) to block exits that would provide a good return to the entrepreneurs and angels (because they are paid less for their shares) but are not sufficiently high to enhance its overall fund performance. But the effect of delaying an exit in an attempt to achieve a 'home run' is to increase the risk of failure. As Wiltbank and Boeker (2007) show, the effect of venture capitalists investing in businesses backed by angels is to increase the proportion of failures and reduce the proportion of 1x to 5x returns, but also to increase the likelihood of a 5x–10x return (Peters, 2009). However, some angels argue that there is merit in bringing a venture capital investor into a deal prior to an exit because of their expertise in achieving exits (Amis and Stevenson, 2001).

Angel investors then need to discuss the necessity of an eventual exit with the entrepreneurial team in the context of their ambitions and aspirations and the realism of their expectations. Ohio Techangels have an alignment question which they put to the Chief Executive Officer (CEO) of every company that they consider investing in: 'if we invest in your company we'll work really hard with you so that it can be sold in three to five years and generate cash proceeds for you personally of $3m–$5m, after taxes. Is that an adequate outcome for you and your family?' (Huston, 2011). The response of CEOs indicates whether they recognize the need for an exit and their realism concerning the likely scale of the exit. A CEO who talks about wanting to 'pass the business on to his son' or indicates that this would be 'an inadequately lucrative exit' sends out clear warning signals to an exit-oriented angel investor.

At the due diligence stage the priority for an exit-oriented investor would be to identify any issues that would complicate an exit. For example, financial diligence would investigate the financial structure of the business, looking for such things as unusual kinds of paper being sold, complex shareholder structures, unacceptable legal structures, unrealistic valuations in the last financing round (making a future down round inevitable), bizarre valuation expectations, and an unwillingness to create a significant option pool to motivate current employees. Legal diligence would investigate intellectual property and its assignment. Investors would also investigate whether there were other factors that would complicate an exit. Examples include pre-existing agreements that could complicate an exit (for example, veto powers held by the founder, or a right of first refusal held by a strategic partner), too many family members on the payroll (which usually dampens the enthusiasm for a liquidity event because their jobs become vulnerable) and co-investors who are unlikely to be able to do more than one round.

An exit-oriented approach to investing would also give careful consideration to valuation. Of course, there is no recognized methodology for valuing early stage businesses because the value is in the future. Determining the value of an early stage investment is, therefore, highly subjective, with only rules-of-thumb available for guidance. However, it is critical that angels do not place too high a value on their investment. A business that is over-valued at the seed stage will not attract an investor at the next round. In fact, Shane (2009) suggests that successful angel investors tend to under-value as this increases their financial return. This is because the initial valuation has a curvilinear effect on the return on an investment, meaning that a 1 per cent decrease in the valuation of a company will increase the investor's return on investment by more than 1 per cent. Accordingly, exit-oriented angels do not settle on arbitrary valuations but base them on a thorough analysis of the company. Industry variations in valuation also need to be taken into account.

Exit considerations should also influence the initial term sheet. Achieving alignment between the entrepreneur and investor is critical. Both will, therefore, want to structure a deal that offers the most flexibility when it comes to an exit, whenever that will be. A key consideration here would be the class of share that angels accept. Preferred shares give investors more rights. Frequently, the stock clause specifies a convertible security, meaning that it can later be traded in or converted to another class of share. The strategy of seeking an early exit (see below) also encourages the use of convertible notes (a financial debt instrument that can be converted into another financial instrument, such as ordinary or preferred shares). These instruments have the advantage of avoiding negotiation on price with the entrepreneur, which limits option pricing issues for the company (because it does not change the price of ordinary shares) and secures a liquidation preference in the event the company does not grow (Amis and Stevenson, 2001). However, this may not be possible if the angel is investing under a particular government programme. For example, the UK's Enterprise Investment Scheme (EIS) requires investors to invest in ordinary shares. Other clauses in the term sheet also need to be considered because of their impact on an exit. These terms would include information rights, board rights, anti-dilution rights, pre-emptive rights and tag along rights, sale of shares to a third party, rights of first refusal if an owner decided to leave the company and any covenants on a company's finances or operations (May and Simmons, 2001). An angel is storing up potential difficulties at an exit if these provisions are not spelled out in advance. Bringing in a lawyer who is familiar with company and investment law to advise on the term sheet is, therefore, a sensible strategy. Similarly, the investor should ensure that the business meets standardized financial controls and accounting systems and that the tax position is optimum. Here again, involving an accountant is sensible (May and Simmons, 2001).

An exit-oriented investor would continue to have regular discussions on exit strategy after the investment is made. For example, the exit should be integral to the discussions at every board meeting. Hence every discussion topic and decision made would be influenced by its implications for an exit. If the angel is on the board, then he or she needs continually to ask exit-oriented questions. Keeping all parties aligned with the agreed exit strategy is also essential. It is also important that all the necessary documentation that a potential buyer would want to see in their due diligence, such as financial statements and tax returns, material contracts (such as insurance), trademarks, copyrights and any patent-related documents, sales funnel, product warranties and support obligations, leases, guarantees and banking agreements, are accessible and in good shape. When an exit is being actively sought, the angel should ensure that the CEO is not involved directly in the process, at least until the final stages, but should concentrate on keeping the business going. An 'exit coach' should be appointed to assist the CEO and Board in developing or aligning around an exit strategy, develop a budget and timeline to complete the exit, identify what specific action is necessary to complete the sale, and select mergers and acquisitions (M&A) advisers.

Exit Options

There are two critical exit-related choices facing angel investors: how to exit from their investment and when. In terms of the method of exit, the expectation among some investors and entrepreneurs is that the exit will occur through an IPO. The reality is very different. Johnson and Sohl (2012) examine 636 IPOs in the USA which occurred between 2001 and 2007: 268 of these firms had been venture capital backed whereas just 37 had been backed by angels, with a further 52 backed by both angels and venture capital funds. To put this into context US angels made investments in 55,000 businesses in 2009 alone (Sohl, 2012). Hence, as May and Simmons (2001, p. 177) comment, 'an IPO is to an exit strategy what a royal flush is to a poker hand. It's a rare event'. Moreover, the number of IPOs has been in decline in the US since the mid-1990s, averaging a little over 100 per annum since 2001 (Weild and Kim, 2010). Across all of the European exchanges since 2008, there have been fewer than 400 IPOs per annum (Mason, 2011). The most likely exit route for an angel investment is the acquisition of the business by a larger company. Companies that have been most active in making acquisitions in recent years include Apple, Cisco, Dell, EMC, Google, HP, IBM, Intel, Microsoft, Oracle and Qualcomm. Moreover, the acquisition rate has been increasing during the 2000s. Driving this trend for large companies to buy young entrepreneurial companies is their recognition that M&A is the best way for them to grow and is more effective than doing their own research and development (R&D). The trend is enabled by the large cash piles that these companies have accumulated and are under pressure from shareholders to spend.

What is also not well known is that most trade sales are relatively small, typically less than $30m valuation (Peters, 2009, 2012). All of the Ohio Tech Angels group exits have been in the $30m–$50m range (Huston, 2011). Gray (2011) cites data presented by Ascendant Corporate Finance that in the five years to 2010 over 50 per cent of the exits of UK and Irish technology companies have been at valuations of less than $25m. One of Google's senior M&A professionals is quoted as follows: '90 per cent of our transactions are small transactions. So that would be less than 20 people, less than $20 million and that is truly our sweet spot'. He goes on to say that 'we do prefer companies that are pre-revenue'. This is because what they are actually looking to buy are technical and engineering staff and strong engineering teams and it is 'important for us to use acquisitions in that manner' for the future success of Google (cited in Peters, 2010a). Google is by no means the only company taking this approach. The implication for exit-oriented angel investors is that their emphasis needs to be on getting their portfolio companies to breakeven as soon as possible where they can become an attractive acquisition target, rather than patiently seeking to build high growth companies. Although there is the possibility of hitting a 'home run' with the latter strategy, it also increases the risks of no return. The implication for exit oriented investors is that they should focus their investments on companies that need relatively little capital to reach their target exit valuation.

A further implication is that timing matters. There are two dimensions to this. First, value is not created linearly. Significant valuation increases usually occur in discrete steps rather than through smooth linear growth. These stepped increases in value occur when individual strategies – such as establishing strategic partnerships, developing new locations and introducing new products or services – are successfully implemented (Peters, 2010b). Investors, therefore, need to identify defined goals or objectives in conjunction with management. These create decision points for the investor either to retain their investment, make a follow-on investment or seek an exit. Second, investors need to be aware of industry cycles. Peters (2012) argues that the optimum exit time is three years after the investment. As it takes six to eighteen months to sell a company, it follows that the exit process needs to be started 18 months after the investment. Delaying the exit significantly beyond this point is likely to generate a much lower return and it may even not be possible to exit. He suggests two reasons for this. First, sectors which become 'hot' will attract venture capital firms – in true myopia style (Sahlman and Stevenson, 1985) – which will invest aggressively, with the consequence that the early innovators get driven out of business. Second, sectors get caught up in a consolidation wave driven by large companies seeking M&A opportunities which, in turn, flushes out companies that are willing to be acquired, resulting in a flurry of acquisitions in the sector. However, there will be a point at which buyer interest ceases. For companies that did not get acquired during the wave it will be virtually impossible to do so subsequently. Moreover, the competitive position of these companies deteriorates because their competitors are no longer underfunded small independently owned companies but are now subsidiaries of large companies that have access to huge amounts of capital, strong brands and other resources. The future of these companies that missed the opportunity to exit is, therefore, likely to be bleak, with profits under pressure and no opportunity to raise capital because investors recognize that the wave has ceased (Peters, 2012).

Financial versus Strategic Exits

The new thinking on exit-oriented angel investing also recommends that angels should invest in companies that will provide strategic rather than financial exits (McKaskill, 2009; 2010). Financial exits assign value to the future profit generating power of the entity being sold. Consequently, they need to be high growth companies that have increasing revenue and profits and thus involve high risk. However, from an investor perspective, investing in such companies will absorb significant capital to build sales, marketing, distribution and support channels and production capacity. As this is likely to require additional rounds of investment from other investors, such as venture capital funds, it will be dilutive for the angel. It also takes time to grow companies to the point where they are an attractive financial acquisition target. Moreover, such companies are likely to need to bring in new skills, notably management, which carries the risk that they may turn out to be ineffective, and to change their focus from product development to sales orientation.

On the other hand, a strategic buyer – typically an industry player – will assign value to the business not on the basis of the cash flow or profits it can generate but on the basis of what future profit could be generated by exploiting the underlying assets or capabilities of the business being acquired. One example of strategic value would be where the acquired firm has a product or service that has the potential to be scaled up and sold to the acquiring company's existing customers through its international distribution channels. By simply having the access to global customers, this might allow the acquirer to scale the revenue by 50 or 100 times. Another example is where a large company might like to develop a similar product or service but will instead make an acquisition to reduce the time to market and offset the risk that their own innovation may be unsuccessful. In short, businesses which appeal to strategic buyers will have developed some underlying assets or capabilities which a large company can exploit though its own organization. The key skills required are, first, to find a large corporation that can exploit this strategic value and, second, to communicate to this company the strategic value that can be accrued from acquisition.

Seeking a strategic exit has implications for the strategy of the angel's investee company. As discussed above, a strategic exit assigns value to the business not on the basis of what profits it can generate but what future profit could be generated by the acquiring company as a result of buying its non-physical assets. So from a valuation point of view, revenue, customers and profits are largely irrelevant to potential acquirers. The driver is the revenue opportunity for the buyer. Paradoxically, a business with too many sales might reduce its strategic value. The acquiring company will not be able to claim that the product is new to market, there may be duplication in sales operations (offices, warehouses), employees will require their contracts to be altered, and distribution methods may have to be changed. What an acquiring company wants to do is to build the market using their own branding and existing sales force. This has two implications for exit-oriented angel investors. First, their investments must create value for the company at the exit and should, therefore, be focused on enhancing the value proposition rather than simply growing revenue. Second, it again emphasizes the crucial significance of the timing of the exit.

This, in turn, has implications for valuation. Financial exits will be valued on a multiple of turnover or profits. Financial buyers will, therefore, carefully examine the books and analyse the financials, comparing them with others in the same industry. This is likely to discriminate against young companies which are typically loss-making as they build sales. In the case of strategic exits, the buyer needs to understand what its potential acquisition target company has to offer to the marketplace and how it adds extra value to its own business. The buyer is usually willing to pay more to secure this new leverage. However, the company that is being sold needs to work at effectively communicating the full strategic value to the buyer so that they are willing to pay the asking price. The strategic value to be derived from any particular acquisition will vary between different companies. It therefore follows that companies that are for sale need to attract multiple bidders if they are to maximize value from the sale. Peters (2012) argues that the number of companies looking to make small acquisitions, which are not confined to the global technology companies listed earlier, and the cash that large firms have available, means that the current M&A environment is a seller's market.

Fast Fail

An exit oriented approach to investing also has implications for portfolio management. It is inevitable that angels will have within their portfolios companies that are likely to fail, companies that will continue to trade but will not generate a profitable exit (the living dead) as well as those that offer good prospects of achieving a successful exit. There is an emerging realization that successful angel investing is about minimizing the losses as much as maximizing the gains. Two particular strategies are critical. The first is to have 'good' failures, by which it is meant that angels must adopt tactics that minimize the losses when an investee company is closed down. Huston's (2011) definition of a 'perfect loss' (sometimes termed 'falling upwards') is that the angel merely loses 100 per cent of their investment. The angel can take the tax deduction, suffers no ongoing litigation, no wind-down expenses, no media coverage, no reputational damage and no damage to relationships with co-investors.

The second strategy is to 'fail fast'. A big dilemma for angels concerns those companies in their portfolio that are underperforming but not failing – the so-called 'living dead' where the entrepreneurs do not want to give up because of what they have invested financially and emotionally. One of the most striking differences in Mason and Harrison's (2002) comparison of the returns profile of business angels and that of an early stage venture capital fund is that the venture capital fund had a much higher proportion of failed investments and a lower proportion that generated moderate returns, while both had similar proportions of high return investments. Venture capital funds would therefore appear to be more ruthless in dealing with these types of investments, preferring to close them down than letting them absorb further time and money. This is consistent with Gifford's (1997) view that venture capitalists, more so than business angels, consider the opportunity costs of giving attention (time) to their portfolio companies. In addition, it can be speculated that business angels have a greater emotional commitment to their investments.

The appropriate actions for business angels to take in such circumstances are threefold. First, they need to mentally write-off and emotionally detach from such investments. Second, they need to discontinue any more investment of time. Third, and hardest of all, they need to find ways in which to release the capital trapped in such companies, perhaps by selling their shares to a third party or to management. Alternatively, they might be able to create some kind of revenue sharing scheme in order to redeploy their capital. However, writing off their investment may actually be the most efficient strategy. A key requirement is, therefore, for angels to be able to recognize the symptoms of living dead investments at an early stage and take appropriate action (May and Simmons, 2001). Managing 'living dead' investments has attracted surprisingly little attention in the venture capital literature (Ruhnka and Feldman, 1992) and none in the business angel literature.

The Early Exits Strategy

A number of these themes are reflected in the early exits investment strategy developed by Peters (2009). His thesis is that the 'swing for the fences' approach to investing favoured by venture capital funds is no longer appropriate in the present economic conditions. This approach has been driven by the increasing size of the funds being managed. With all of the returns typically coming from 20 per cent of the investments, these investments have to generate a minimum of 10x to 30x to yield a respectable return for the fund as a whole. However, it takes longer to achieve such returns and the risks increase. Moreover, in an effort to achieve such returns, a venture capital fund is likely to block exits that would have been lucrative for the entrepreneurs and angel investors. Peters (2009), therefore, advocates that angel investors should focus their investments on early stage businesses with limited capital requirements that have the prospects of being sold in an M&A deal for less than $30m in three or four years. Although the returns will be smaller, there is less risk hence the overall returns will be greater.

Factors that favour this approach include the increasing difficulty of taking companies to IPO and the newly active market for small M&As by large cash-rich companies following a 'buy rather than build' high-growth strategy. Moreover, the much lower costs to start a business now compared with ten years ago combined with lean start-up techniques to provide capital efficiency (Ries, 2011), means that companies can now be launched for $500,000 or less and can sustain a low burn rate. This means that many new businesses need relatively little capital to develop a product or service and bring it to market, although significant capital is still needed to scale-up the business.

However, there are some important caveats to this discussion. First, Peters' experience comes from being a fund manager – albeit of an angel fund. Nevertheless, fund management has a different dynamic to the deal-by-deal approach that characterizes the vast majority of business angel investments because its objective is to maximize returns to the fund. Second, the types of exits being discussed here are likely to be sector specific, primarily in software, digital, Internet and social media. Third, most of the companies that these large technology companies are acquiring – around 80 per cent – are US based. Gray (2011) cites data from Ascendant Corporate Finance that only 9 of the 276 acquisitions made by major tech companies were of UK and Irish tech companies. Thus, there may be fewer potential acquirers for companies in the UK, Europe and other parts of the world and, as a result, selling prices might also be expected to be lower. Hence, the nature of the exit opportunities that angels encounter will vary depending on their location and the types of businesses that they have invested in. Whether the 'early exits' investment strategy can be applied in non-technology sectors, therefore, remains unclear.

Empirical Evidence

There is a paucity of empirical studies which have examined the process by which investors exit from their investee companies. Our own research – a small scale study based on ten cases of business angel-backed businesses that were successfully sold in trade sales – therefore provides a unique insight into this process. The exits varied in terms of their returns, ranging from 1.2 to 28.5 times the original investment.

The evidence tends to support the arguments above for an exit-centric investment strategy. These angels were consistently thinking about the exit. As one angel group manager noted, 'I think it's true to say it's always on our mind that there will be an exit'. Some went further, commenting that they thought about the exit before investing. 'You can't invest in something before you've thought about how you're going to get out'. Another noted that 'you always think about the exit. You may not call it that but you are always designing businesses to be attractive to buyers'. In all cases, there was an alignment between the investor and the entrepreneur: the entrepreneur also wanted to sell. Their motives were varied – to start another venture, to take the financial returns, because they could not scale the business, or because it was the only solution to a key challenge affecting the business. Six of the ten exits could be attributed to pro-active strategies. In the other cases, the exit was opportunistic, with a buyer approaching the business. This strategy was based on making the firm as appealing as possible to potential buyers but then waiting for an approach from a buyer instead of actively looking for an exit. In some cases, the exit was reluctant with the key drivers being investment fatigue and the inability to raise more capital.

CONCLUSION AND POLICY IMPLICATIONS

The exit stage in the entrepreneurial process has been largely ignored by researchers. In recent years calls have been made for scholars to devote more attention to the exit, and research agendas have been proposed (DeTienne, 2010; DeTienne and Cardon, 2012; Wennberg et al., 2010; Wennberg and DeTienne, 2014). However, this discussion has taken an entrepreneur-centric view which ignores investor-backed businesses that have raised finance from business angels, venture capital funds and increasingly through crowdfunding (Harrison, 2015). These investors require – and expect – an exit event to realize a financial return on what is otherwise an illiquid investment. This process has also been largely ignored in the entrepreneurial finance literature.

This chapter has focused on business angels who are the key source of risk capital for new and early stage businesses. The literature is quite limited. Whether business angel investing is 'worth it' for the majority of investors remains an open question. And who makes money from angel investing also needs further research. Vo's (2013) intriguing work on geographical variations in returns also warrants further investigation. The main focus of the chapter was on the challenges that angels have in achieving exits at the present time. Our discussion suggested that the lack of an exit-centric approach to investing by angels is a key factor. However, cyclical and structural factors are also likely to be relevant and need further investigation. Some empirical evidence on the exit process was presented which tended to support the argument for an exit-centric approach to investing. However, the tenets of this literature need empirical testing. Specifically, applicability of the early exits thesis of Peters (2009) in this context of fewer exits needs to be explored.

Fewer exits has implications for portfolio management, and specifically for how angels deal with their 'living dead' investments. Indeed, a paucity of exits – if it becomes a persistent feature of the market – has implications for the future of angel investing and how the market is organized and structured. Angel groups emerged because solo angels could not meet the demand for multiple funding rounds that resulted from the reduction in venture capital investment. This market development also prompted governments to introduce angel co-investment funds to help angel groups make larger funding rounds. It is possible that this challenging exits environment may prompt the emergence of a secondary market for angel investments to address many of the problems arising from the lack of exits. However, it is unclear whether this can emerge in the absence of government intervention (for example, allowing the transfer of tax incentives to secondary purchasers).

In summary, the exits dimension of angel investing is a critical part of the investment process with implications for the overall health of the angel market. It, therefore, needs to become a priority for researchers. It also requires attention from government: simply focusing on initiatives to stimulate more investment activity is not sufficient for a dynamic entrepreneurial economy; the exit dimension must also be considered.

NOTES

1. In conversation with the authors.
2. An exit-centric investor was defined as one who made 10 per cent or more of their comments about the exit.
3. See Note 2.

REFERENCES

Amis, D. and Stevenson, H. (2001), *Winning Angels: The 7 fundamentals of early stage investing*, London: Prentice Hall.

Brav, A and Gompers, P.A. (1997), 'Myth or reality? The long-run underperformance of initial public offerings: evidence from venture and non-venture capital backed companies', *Journal of Finance*, **52** (5): 1791–1821.

Brush, C., Edelman, L.F. and Manolova, T.S. (2012), 'Ready for funding? Entrepreneurial ventures and the pursuit of angel financing', *Venture Capital: An International Journal of Entrepreneurial Finance*, **14** (2–3): 111–129.

Clark, C. (2008), 'The impact of entrepreneurs' oral "pitch" presentation skills on business angels' initial screening investment decisions', *Venture Capital: An International Journal of Entrepreneurial Finance*, **10** (3): 257–279.

Covey, S.R. (1989), *The 7 Habits Of Highly Effective People*, New York: Simon & Schuster.

DeTienne, D.R. (2010), 'Entrepreneurship exit as a critical component of the entrepreneurial process: theoretical development', *Journal of Business Venturing*, **25** (2): 203–215.

DeTienne, D.R. and Cardon, M.S. (2012), 'Impact of founder experience on exit intentions', *Small Business Economics*, **38** (4): 351–374.

Feeney, L., Haines, G.H. and Riding A.L. (1999), 'Private investors' investment criteria: insights from qualitative data', *Venture Capital: An International Journal of Entrepreneurial Finance*, **1** (2): 121–145.

Freear, J. and Wetzel, W.E. (1990), 'Who bankrolls high-tech entrepreneurs?', *Journal of Business Venturing*, **5** (2): 77–89.

Gaston, R.J. (1989), *Finding Venture Capital for Your Firm: a Complete Guide*, New York: John Wiley & Sons.

Gifford, S. (1997), 'Limited attention and the role of the venture capitalist', *Journal of Business Venturing*, **16** (6): 459–482.

Gompers, P.A. (1996), 'Grandstanding in the venture capital industry', *Journal of Financial Economics*, **42** (1): 133–156.

Gray, N. (2011), *Present Business Angel Thinking on Exits*, Unpublished report for LINC Scotland.

Gregson, G., Mann, S. and Harrison, R. (2013), 'Business angel syndicisation and the evolution of risk capital in a small market economy: evidence from Scotland', *Management and Decision Economics*, **34** (2): 95–107.

Harrison, R.T. (ed.) (2015), *Crowdfunding and Entrepreneurial Finance*, London: Routledge.

Harrison, R.T. and Mason, C.M. (1992), 'International perspectives on the supply of informal venture capital', *Journal of Business Venturing*, **7** (6): 459–475.

Harrison, R.T., Mason, C.M. and Robson, P. (2010), 'Determinants of long-distance investing by business angels in the UK', *Entrepreneurship and Regional Development*, **22** (2): 113–137.

Huston, J. (2011), 'An American angel's view of producing economic value', presentation to the Young Company Finance Annual Conference, Stirling, Scotland.

Ibrahim, D M. (2008), 'The (not so) puzzling behavior of angel investors', *Vanderbilt Law Review*, **61** (5): 1405–1452.

Johnson, L. (2012), Q&A following presentation at UK Business Angels Association summer conference, July, London.

Johnson, W.C. and Sohl, J E. (2012), 'Angels and venture capitalists in the initial public offering market', *Venture Capital: An International Journal of Entrepreneurial Finance*, **14** (1): 27–42.

Kelly, P. and Hay, M. (2003), 'Business angel contracts: the influence of context', *Venture Capital: An International Journal of Entrepreneurial Finance*, **5** (4): 287–312.

Landström, H. (1993), 'Informal risk capital in Sweden and some international comparisons', *Journal of Business Venturing*, **8** (6): 525–540.

Lumme, A., Mason, C. and Suomi, M. (1998), *Informal Venture Capital: Investors, Investments and Policy Issues in Finland*, Dortrecht, NL: Kluwer.

Lynn, J. (2010), 'Want more angel investing in the UK? Then let's talk about returns', *Tech Cruch*, 5 August, http://techcrunch.com/2010/08/05/want-more-angel-investing-in-the-uk-then-lets-talk-about-returns/ (accessed 29 July 2015).

McKaskill, T. (2009), *Invest to Exit*, Ossining, NY: Breakthrough Publications.

McKaskill, T. (2010), *Ultimate Exits*, Ossining, NY: Breakthrough Publications.

Madill, J.J., Haines, G.H. Jr and Riding, A.L. (2005), 'The role of angels in technology SMEs: a link to venture capital', *Venture Capital: An International Journal of Entrepreneurial Finance*, **7** (2): 107–129.

Mason, C.M. (2006), 'Informal sources of venture finance', in S.C. Parker (ed.), *The Life Cycle of Entrepreneurial Ventures*, New York: Springer, pp. 259–299.

Mason, C.M. (2009), 'Public policy support for the informal venture capital market in Europe: a critical review', *International Small Business Journal*, **27** (5): 536–556.

Mason, C. (2011), 'Trends in IPO listings by SMEs in the EU', Discussion Paper, City of London, 25pp.

Mason, C. and Botelho, T. (2016), 'The role of the exit in the initial screening of investment opportunities: the case of business angel syndicate gatekeepers', *International Small Business Journal*, in press.

Mason, C.M. and Harrison, R.T. (1994), 'The informal venture capital market in the UK', in A. Hughes and D.J. Storey (eds), *Financing Small Firms*, London: Routledge, pp. 64–111.

Mason, C.M. and Harrison, R. (1996), 'Why business angels say no: a case study of opportunities rejected by an informal investor syndicate', *International Small Business Journal*, **14** (2): 35–51.

Mason, C.M. and Harrison, R.T. (2002), 'Is it worth it? The rates of return from informal venture capital investments', *Journal of Business Venturing*, **17** (3): 211–236.

Mason, C.M. and Harrison, R.T. (2004), 'Improving access to early stage venture capital in regional economies: a new approach to investment readiness', *Local Economy*, **19** (2): 159–173.

Mason, C.M. and Harrison, R.T. (2006), 'After the exit: acquisitions, entrepreneurial recycling and regional economic development', *Regional Studies*, **40** (1): 55–73.

Mason, C.M. and Harrison, R.T. (2010), *Annual Report on the Business Angel Market in the United Kingdom: 2008/09*, Department for Business, Innovation and Skills, 88pp.

Mason, C.M. and Harrison, R T. (2011), *Annual Report on the Business Angel Market in the United Kingdom: 2009/10*, London: Department for Business, Innovation and Skills.

Mason, C. and Rogers, A. (1997), 'The business angel's investment decision: an exploratory analysis', in D. Deakins, P. Jennings and C. Mason (eds), *Entrepreneurship in the 1990s*, London: Paul Chapman Publishing, pp. 29–46.

Mason, C. and Stark, M. (2004), 'What do investors look for in a business plan? A comparison of the investment criteria of bankers, venture capitalists and venture capitalists', *International Small Business Journal*, **22** (3): 227–248.

Mason, C., Botelho, T. and Harrison, R. (2013), 'The transformation of the business angel market: evidence from Scotland', Working Paper, Glasgow: Adam Smith Business School, University of Glasgow.

Maxwell, A., Jeffrey, S.A., and Lévesque, M. (2011), 'Business angel early stage decision making', *Journal of Business Venturing*, **26** (2): 212–225.

May, J. and Simmons, C. (2001), *Every Business Needs An Angel: Getting the Money You Need to Make Your Business Grow*, New York: Crown Business.

Megginson, W.L. and Weiss, K.A. (1991), 'Venture capitalist certification in Initial Public Offerings', *Journal of Finance*, **46** (3): 879–903.

NACO (2014), 2013 *Report on Angel Investing Activity in Canada: Accelerating the Asset Class*, Toronto: National Angel Capital Association.

OECD (2011), *Financing High Growth Firms: The Role of Angel Investors*, Paris: OECD Publishing, http://dx.doi.org/10.1797/9789264118782-en (accessed 4 August 2015). Also available as a hard copy, ISBN 978-92-64-11877-5 (print); or 978-92-11978-2 (PDF).

Ohio TechAngels (2009), '10 Exits', see www.ohiotechangels.com.

Ohio TechAngels (2012), Due Diligence 'Showstoppers', see www.ohiotechangels.com.

Paul, S., Whittam, G. and Johnston, J. (2003), 'The operation of the informal venture capital market in Scotland', *Venture Capital: An International Journal of Entrepreneurial Finance*, **5** (4): 313–335.

Peters, B. (2009), *Early Exits: Exit Strategies for Entrepreneurs and Angel Investors (but maybe not venture capitalists)*, Vancouver: Meteor Bytes.

Peters, B. (2010a), 'Google wants even earlier exits than in "Early Exits"', www.exits.com/blog/google-wants-even-earlier-exits-than-in-early exits/ (accessed 3 July 2012).

Peters, B. (2010b), 'Selling a business can increase the value 50% plus', www.exits.com/blog/selling-a-business-can-increase-the-final-value-by-50-or-more/ (accessed 29 July 2015).

Peters, B. (2012), 'How exits have changed in 2012', Presentation to the Angel Capital Association Annual Summit, Austin, TX, 5 March.

Politis, D. (2008), 'Business angels and value added: what do we know and where do we go?', *Venture Capital: An International Journal of Entrepreneurial Finance*, **10** (2): 127–147.

Riding, A.L., Dal Cin, P., Duxbury, L., Haines, G. and Safrata, R. (1993), *Informal Investors in Canada: The Identification of Salient Characteristics*, Ottowa: Carleton University.

Ries, E. (2011), *The Lean Start-Up*, London: Penguin.

Roach, G. (2010), 'Is angel investing worth the effort? A study of Keirtsu Forum', *Venture Capital: An International Journal of Entrepreneurial Finance*, **12** (2): 153–166.

Ruhnka, J.C. and Feldman, H.D. (1992), 'The living dead in phenomenon in venture capital investments', *Journal of Business Venturing*, **7** (2): 137–155.

Sahlman, W.A. and Stevenson, H.H. (1985), 'Capital market myopia', *Journal of Business Venturing*, **1** (1): 7–30.

Shane, S.A. (2009), *Fools Gold? The Truth Behind Angel Investing in America*, New York: Oxford University Press.

Smith, G. (2005), 'The exit structure of venture capital', *UCLA Law Review*, **53** (2): 315–356.

Sohl, J. (2007), 'The organization of the informal venture capital market', in H. Landström (ed.), *Handbook of Research on Venture Capital*, Cheltenham, UK and Northampton, MA, USA: Edward Elgar Publishing, pp. 347–368.

Sohl, J. (2012), 'The changing nature of the angel market', in H. Landström and C. Mason (eds), *The Handbook of Research on Venture Capital: Volume II*, Cheltenham, UK and Northampton, MA, USA: Edward Elgar Publishing, pp. 17–41.

Van Osnabrugge, M. and Robinson, R.J. (2002), *Angel Investing: Matching Startup Funds with Startup Companies – The Guide for Entrepreneurs and Individual Investors*, San Francisco CA: Jossey-Bass.

Vo, D. (2013), *The Geography of Angel Investment*, PhD Thesis, Victoria, Canada: University of Victoria.

Waddell, J. (2013), Evidence, *Official Report of the Scottish Parliament Economy, Energy and Tourism Committee*, 35th meeting, session 4, column 3697.

Weild, D. and Kim, E. (2010), *Market Structure is Causing the IPO Crisis and More*, Grant Thornton Capital Market Series.

Wennberg, K. and DeTienne, D.R. (2014), 'What do we really mean when we talk about 'exit'? A critical review of research on entrepreneurial exit', *International Small Business Journal*, **32** (1): 4–16.

Wennberg, K., Wiklund, J., DeTienne, D.R. and Cardon, M.S. (2010), 'Reconceptualising entrepreneurial exit: divergent exit routes and their drivers', *Journal of Business Venturing*, **25** (4): 361–375.

Wetzel, W.E. (1981), 'Informal risk capital In New England', in K.H. Vesper (ed.), *Frontiers of Entrepreneurship Research*, Wellesley, MA: Babson College, pp. 217–245.

Wiltbank, R.E. (2009), *Siding With the Angels. Business Angel Investing – Promising Outcomes and Effective Strategies*, London: NESTA.

Wiltbank, R.E. and Boeker, W. (2007), *Returns To Angel Investors in Groups*, Kansas City: Kauffman Foundation.

8. The role of UK government hybrid venture capital funds in addressing the finance gap facing innovative SMEs in the post-2007 financial crisis era
Robert Baldock and David North

INTRODUCTION

It is notable that virtually all of the flourishing venture capital markets globally have been stimulated by government support (Lerner et al., 2005; Lerner, 2009, 2010), with an increasing role for government hybrid venture capital fund (HVCF) programmes since the start of the millennium (Murray, 2007). Here, we apply Lerner's (2010) 'guide posts' for government VC interventions to the experience of three recent UK programmes providing equity finance to small and medium-sized enterprises (SMEs) in the aftermath of the 2007 global financial crisis (GFC).

Lerner (2010) highlights some successful government interventions in addressing equity gaps facing innovative small businesses, notably the United States (US) Small Business Investment Company (SBIC) and Israeli Yozma funds. These demonstrate that HVCFs can establish a community of knowledgeable early stage investors, business support services, entrepreneurs and R&D activity, which in turn build up a momentum of growth and development. It is crucial to provide the right catalyst of government support over time to generate sufficient critical mass of expertise before undertaking strategic withdrawal of government intervention. We explore five of Lerner's guiding principles in assessing recent UK HVCFs:

1. Let the market provide direction.
2. Resist the temptation to over-engineer.
3. Recognize the long lead times associated with public venture initiatives.
4. Avoid initiatives that are too large or too small.
5. Understand the importance of global interconnections.

After briefly describing the three HVCF programmes of interest and outlining the research methodology, we apply Lerner's guiding principles to them, drawing upon demand and supply side research evidence (North et al.,

2010; CEEDR, 2012). The conclusion summarizes the dilemmas facing HVCFs and considers their implications for future policy development.

THE EVOLUTION OF UK HVCF PROGRAMMES

The UK government HVCF programme expenditure has increased considerably in recent years, rising from £140.9m between 2000 and 2006 to £750m between 2006 and 2012 (CfEL, 2012). Programmes have evolved, with a greater focus on larger scale, specialist funds with expert private sector led fund management and co-investment, notably in the wake of the National Audit Office (NAO) review recommendations (NAO, 2009). The three HVCF programmes that we focus on here represent £602.5m of government expenditure since 2006 and address different market imperfections in terms of the nature of the finance gap and the kinds of businesses being targeted.

Enterprise Capital Funds

Enterprise Capital Funds (ECFs) are a rolling £440m programme of 16 funds,[1] established since 2006–2007, with a planned 10–12 year individual fund life cycle, addressing the equity gap facing high growth potential SMEs. Government funding is used alongside private sector funds to invest directly into businesses, targeting investments of up to £2m with potential to provide a good commercial return. Here we focus on the first tranche of eight ECFs operating under private sector VC fund management, with funds ranging from £10m to £30m. These ECFs focused on different stages of business development, including seed, early stage and expansion. Some were generalist, covering a broad range of sectors (for example, Seraphim Capital Fund), while others specialized for example in new media (Dawn Capital Fund) and medical and healthcare investments (Oxford Technology Management Fund), reflecting the areas of fund management expertise.

The Aspire Fund

The Aspire Fund, established in 2008, aimed to increase the number of successful women-led UK businesses, assisting those with high growth potential. It operates on a co-investment model[2] with £12.5m UK government funding matched by private sector funding from a lead investor. Investments have ranged between £200,000 and £2m, including the matched private investment.

The UK Innovation Investment Fund

The UK Innovation Investment Fund (UKIIF), established in 2010, aimed to stimulate private VC investment into intensive R&D sectors. The £150m of UK government funding was matched by a further £180m of public and private funding from two 'fund of funds' managed by the Hermes Environmental Innovation Fund and the European Investment Fund's UK Technologies Fund. UKIIF operates *pari passu* at arms' length under the scrutiny of the British Business Bank.[3] As it is private sector led and can invest in innovative businesses globally, there are no European Union (EU) state aid restrictions on the size of initial or follow on investments. The fund focuses on life sciences, cleantech, digital technology and advanced manufacturing sectors and must invest at least £150m into UK based businesses during its expected 12–15 year life cycle.

METHODOLOGY

Demand side evidence comes from 32 surveyed business recipients of the three HVCF programmes. Supply side evidence comes from interviews with 16 fund managers who dealt with applications for the government funds and 22 finance industry experts.

Business Manager Interviews

The owner-managers of 32 successful business applicants to the three HVCF programmes were interviewed face-to-face or by telephone, with purposive selection to provide sector and UK-wide coverage. These represented one-third of the programmes' funded businesses (32/94) at the time of the survey, with initial ECF and Aspire interviews undertaken in February 2010 and UKIIF interviews undertaken in February 2012 (Table 8.1). Survey questions included business characteristics, external financing requirements and knowledge, degree of success in obtaining external finance, terms and conditions, and the impact and additionality experienced and forecast from the funding received. Further follow up telephone interviews took place with 24 of the recipient businesses in May 2013 to assess development since the initial funding.

The surveyed businesses fitted each programme's target profile, being typically young, early stage businesses established since 2000. Over two-thirds of recipients were pre-trading at the time of interview, undertaking R&D and developing prototypes or in the initial stages of launching products and services. Most, including all 16 UKIIF businesses, were undertaking

Table 8.1   Business interviews by venture capital fund

Programme	Successful recipients	% of business investments*
ECF	12	21%
Aspire	4	100%
UKIIF	16	41%
Total	32	32%

Note: *At the time of survey.

market leading activities, developing leading edge software and medical technologies, and demonstrating global market leading export aspirations. Equity finance was perceived as the only viable option for raising finance due to a lack of financial assets, insufficient trading record, and owners' unwillingness to secure/guarantee debt finance against private property. The amount of equity sought by the 12 interviewed ECF recipients ranged from £300,000 to £3m (median £750,000), the four Aspire recipients sought between £500,000 and £2m, while the 16 UKIIF recipients sought between £75,000 and £10.4m (median £2.4m), demonstrating demand for early stage R&D equity finance at beyond the EU state aid cap of £2m.[4]

The majority of businesses were small when funded. ECF and Aspire recipients had a mean of 10 employees (median 5.5). UKIIF recipients had a mean size of 35 employees (median 8) and included three established medium-sized businesses undertaking new innovative product development cycles, including a recycling company diversifying into bio fuel production and a lightweight plastics manufacturer, both with over 150 employees.

Fund Provider Interviews

Face-to-face interviews were undertaken with eight UKIIF[5] and eight ECF fund managers, providing insights into their structure and operation, the type and range of applications, decision-making criteria, the effectiveness of their investments and assessment of whether funds were addressing an equity gap. These represented all of the programmes' operational funds at the time of survey (Table 8.2).

To enrich our understanding of the new and early stage VC market, interviews were also conducted with 22 expert informants. These comprised the British Venture Capital Association (BVCA), European Venture Capital Association (EVCA), three private VCs, two other public sector VCs, three mezzanine fund managers, six business angels, three bankers,

Table 8.2   Breakdown of fund manager interviews

Fund	Location
Enterprise Capital Funds (ECFs):	
The Catapult Growth Fund (ECF)	Leicester
IQ Capital Fund	Cambridge
Oxford Technology	Oxford
Seraphim Capital Fund	London
Sustainable Technology Partnership	London
Amadeus and Angels Seed Fund	Cambridge
Dawn	London
MMC	London
UK Innovation Investment Fund (UKIIF):	
Hermes GPE Environmental Innovation Fund	Fund of funds manager, London
European Investment Fund UK Future Technologies Funds	Fund of funds manager, Luxembourg
Underlying funds:	
Zouk Cleantech II	Hermes fund, London
Scottish Equity Partners Environmental Energies	Hermes fund, Glasgow and London
WHEB Ventures	Hermes fund, London
DFJ Esprit	EIF UKFTF fund, London and Cambridge
Advent Life Sciences	EIF UKFTF fund, London
Gilde Healthcare III	EIF UKFTF fund, Utrecht and Cambridge USA

one grant fund and two specialist support providers for technology based small firms (TBSFs).

We now consider the rationale for the UK HVCF programmes, before discussing our research evidence against five of Lerner's guiding principles.

ARE HVCF PROGRAMME INTERVENTIONS JUSTIFIED IN THE UK?

Supply Side Market Failure

Although less than 2 per cent of UK SMEs seek equity finance,[6] it is vital for many innovative and growth orientated enterprises who play a key role in developing new industries, thereby generating economic growth and jobs (Bank of England 1996, 2001; Siegel et al., 2003). These businesses exhibit higher levels of risk due to a lack of physical assets to provide collateral for debt finance and may also lack revenue streams needed to service loan repayments (Reynolds et al., 2000; Mason and Harrison, 2003). Recent evidence (Fraser, 2009; Cowling et al., 2012; North et al., 2013) also suggests that SME demand for equity finance has increased as bank credit rationing and moral hazard aversion have accentuated in the aftermath of the GFC.

The equity gap in the UK has long been recognized (Macmillan, 1931; HM Treasury, 2003), particularly for seed and early stage VC, with this market failure constraining innovation. The boundaries of the equity gap have increased over time; estimated at up to £0.5m in 1999, it is now on some estimates put at upwards of £5m, particularly for the longer investment horizon R&D intensive sectors (SQW Consulting, 2009; Rowlands, 2009). This is due mainly to information asymmetries between investors and young SMEs (Hughes, 2009) where information is not transparent and assets are knowledge based (Hsu, 2004). These businesses present high risk techno-logical, market and managerial uncertainties and in seed and early stage investment invariably require intensive managerial and consulting VC input to generate returns (MacMillan et al., 1989; Murray, 1999). The history of small specialist early stage European VC funds is characterized by low returns, failed funds (Murray, 2007) and established VCs retreating to safer later stage investments (Pierrakis and Mason, 2008; Harrison et al., 2010).

Lerner (2010) recognizes the importance of VC exit markets in attract-ing private investment. The UK has experienced a breakdown in the risk funding escalator (Mason et al., 2010, North et al., 2013) enabling innova-tive firms to reach a sufficient stage of market traction for a trade sale or initial public offering (IPO). The retreat of private VCs has increased pres-sure on business angel syndicates and HVCFs to follow-on fund, lengthen-ing timescales to exit to around seven years (Pierrakis, 2010; CfEL, 2013) and creating a funding gap for early stage businesses. Consequently, the equity gap now exists for projects that are too large for business angel syndicates to fund but below the level for most private VC investors, esti-mated at between £0.5m and £5m (Mason and Baldock, 2014).

Against this context there has been a growth in UK HVCFs, with public backed funds increasing from 20 per cent of early stage funding in 2000 to 68 per cent by 2008 (Pierrakis, 2010). Proportionally, government HVCF funding is even greater in real terms, as BVCA (2013; Figure 8.1) evidence demonstrates that apart from the twin peaks of the dotcom bubble (2000) and pre GFC (2006) boom, UK annual VC investment for 2010–2012 was similar at £340m to 1999. This suggests a growing need for UK HVCFs, without which the early stage VC market would be in a perilous state.

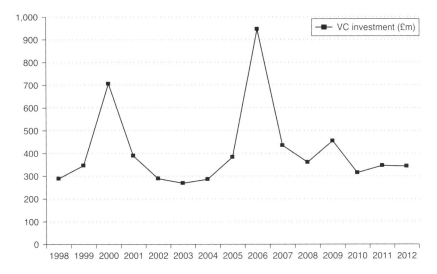

Source: BVCA (2013).

Figure 8.1   Value of UK VC (£m) funded per year by BVCA members

Demand-side Deficiencies

Oakey (2007) highlights the importance of being 'investor ready', with Mason and Kwok (2010) citing the key role of entrepreneurial support schemes offering training and experience in assessing and accessing external finance, particularly for equity finance. Few SME managers, except the small number of serial entrepreneurs, have the know-how to successfully apply for early stage VC (Gompers et al., 2010). The National Endowment for Science, Technology and the Arts (NESTA) (2009) found poor quality in much of the UK VC deal-flow, resulting in investors' difficulties in finding sufficient numbers of high growth potential firms. Mason and Harrison (2003) have, therefore, implied that the equity gap may be as much to do with demand-side deficiencies as supply side failures.

This view is supported by our exploration of the '*applications funnel*'. Interviewed fund managers typically received 500 annual applications per fund, with many rejected immediately for failing to meet basic criteria, only 10 per cent receiving interviews, and less than 2 per cent receiving funding. Fund managers rejected many early in the process because the businesses were not investment ready, underestimated their financial needs, or had a poor understanding of the requirements of investors.

More recent UKIIF fund manager interviews indicated that, despite recent improvements in application quality, they remained variable and that demand for equity finance was increasing as bank finance had become more difficult and expensive to obtain. They also stressed the importance of knowing the entrepreneurs before committing funds, requiring intensive work in selecting and managing small portfolios of investee businesses. The overall view from the equity investment specialists was that investors have become more cautious and stringent in their due diligence and negotiations, with greater attention to overcoming information asymmetries during the pre-deal completion stage.

Having considered the rationale for government intervention to address gaps in equity finance, we now consider the recent evolution of UK HVCFs over the last decade against five of Lerner's (2010) guiding principles, starting with two that he particularly emphasizes.

'LET THE MARKET PROVIDE DIRECTION' AND 'RESIST THE TEMPTATION TO OVER-ENGINEER'

During the past decade UK programmes have evolved along the lines of Lerner's principles, letting the market lead and resisting the temptation to micro manage funds. UK public officials are now far less involved in the management of funds than they were with some of the original publicly funded venture capital funds (Murray, 2007), even to the extent with UKIIF of wanting entrepreneurs to perceive them as entirely private funds. Recent UK HVCF programmes enshrine co-investment and 'fund of funds' principles, requiring minimal programme direction and setting broad fund aims such as sector, location and private matching fund requirements. Private sector managers make the investment decisions and assist in the management of their portfolio companies. In the case of UKIIF, private sector fund managers also lead the umbrella fund of funds, inviting competition from private VCs to run the specialist underlying funds. The British Business Bank provides light touch government monitoring, including early, mid-term and end of programme reviews which could lead to strategic operational changes.

Have UK Funds become too Private Sector Led?

The private sector-led format of recent UK HVCFs, notably UKIIF, raises questions as to whether they have become too market-led, chasing high performance and returns at the expense of assisting more marginal, but fundable cases (Rigos, 2011). Lerner (2010) states that public supported funds should not compete with private funds, yet our evidence suggests that they do once they are perceived by entrepreneurs to be private funds competing on equal terms to other private funds. For Lerner (2010) and Clarysse et al. (2009), the imperative is that government funds stimulate private VC activity and establish VC markets and then withdraw, rather than continue to compete and crowd out.

ECF, Aspire and UKIIF aim to balance generating commercial returns for investors with achieving wider economic objectives. Since the funds aim to demonstrate to private investors that early stage growth potential businesses can yield attractive returns, commercial investment decisions are devolved to private VC fund managers to ensure that investment decisions utilize rigorous commercial criteria. At the same time, by providing equity funding to innovative, high growth potential businesses that are struggling to raise sufficient funds from other sources, HVCFs aim to contribute to the UK's economic growth and job creation. This assumes that the government's wider economic goals can be achieved by first achieving the private fund managers' commercial objectives (Murray and Lingelbach, 2009).

Lerner also argues that HVCFs should not finance 'substandard firms' that cannot raise private capital. Defining 'substandard' is challenging because of the diverse range of investment propositions that fund managers are confronted with and the often subtle distinctions between them. For example, Oakey's (2003) model of funding viability and declining risk identifies 'immediately fundable' projects (hypothetically 10–20 per cent), a critical area of 'probably fundable' (hypothetically 10 per cent), 'probably un-fundable' (30 per cent) and 'clearly un-fundable' (50 per cent). He argues that from an economic development perspective public supported funds should be focusing on the 'probably fundable' only marginally more risky firms and developing them to a point where they would attract private sector VC.

Rigos (2011) argues that HVCFs addressing early stage equity gaps are assisting more risky and marginal business propositions and, therefore, should be expected to perform less well than their private VC counterparts operating at later stages. However, our surveyed UKIIF private fund managers' view strongly favoured delivering for their investors. These managers reported that it had been tough fund raising, particularly in 2009–2010, and that while the government funds were helpful, their main aim was to maintain a 'strong brand' and deliver high performance for their investors of 'at least two times investment return within eight years', with one respondent highlighting that 'we will out-perform other VCs, operating in the top quartile'.

It would seem that recent HVCF evolution has shifted towards greater emphasis on the 'immediately', rather than 'probably fundable' applicants.

This suggests the existence of a potentially important proportion of early stage ventures which may struggle to get private funding but which could be successful with the right support. Arguably, these are what HVCFs should focus upon, rather than the best applications that are likely to obtain private funding anyway, in order to reduce the risk of crowding out private investors (Leleux and Surlemont, 2003).

Finance and Project Additionality

Our surveyed HVCF recipients exhibited only moderate levels of financial additionality. More than two-thirds (69 per cent) of ECF and Aspire recipients believed they could have raised the required finance from elsewhere, while two-thirds of UKIIF recipients believed that they definitely would have raised alternative finance. However, many thought that alternative funding would have been more difficult to arrange and involve ceding greater equity share, particularly if it involved a business angel syndicate. Notably, several ECF and most UKIIF recipients mentioned other VC funds taking an interest, although they doubted that the terms and VC fit with their business would be as good. UKIIF recipients presented particularly strong business plans and managerial expertise, with globally innovative concepts and being fully prepared to cede ownership share for the business growth rewards that equity finance can deliver. These findings, therefore, also suggest that these latest HVCF programmes are supporting Oakey's (2003) 'immediately fundable' rather than more marginal 'probably fundable' businesses, particularly with UKIIF's dominant private sector ethos investing in only the very best projects in commercial terms.

Higher levels of project additionality were recorded (Table 8.3). Over two-thirds (69 per cent) of ECF and Aspire recipients indicated that their project would have been adversely affected in the absence of government funding; 31 per cent being slowed or reduced in scale and 38 per cent claiming inability to proceed in any format. Despite 15 out of 16 UKIIF recipients potentially being able to proceed without the funding, three-quarters of projects were likely to have been scaled down or slowed down (Table 8.4). A crucial point was that UKIIF VC managers 'really understand the business and take a hands-on approach to driving the business forward'. While other funding might have been available, UKIFF VC managers were considered far less constraining on business development plans than business angels or corporate investors. Consequently, additionality arises mainly from the management of the HVCFs being better suited to the needs and investment timescales of recipient businesses.

Table 8.3   Ability of recipient businesses to raise finance from elsewhere without government VC funding

	ECF/ Aspire	UKIIF
Definitely would not have raised finance from other sources	2 (12%)	1 (6%)
Probably would not have raised finance from other sources	1 (6%)	0 (0%)
No strong opinion	2 (12%)	0 (0%)
Probably would have raised finance from other sources	6 (38%)	4 (25%)
Definitely would have raised finance from other sources	5 (31%)	11 (69%)
Total recipient businesses	16 (100%)	16 (100%)

Table 8.4   Extent to which recipient businesses would have gone ahead with business plans without government VC funding

	ECF/ Aspire	UKIIF
Would not have gone ahead at all, in any format	6 (38%)	1 (6%)
Would have gone ahead at the same time, but on a smaller scale	1 (6%)	5 (31%)
Would have taken longer to go ahead, but at the original planned scale	2 (12%)	3 (19%)
Would have taken longer to go ahead and on a smaller scale	2 (12%)	4 (24%)
Would have gone ahead at the same time and at the same scale	5 (31%)	3 (19%)
Total recipient businesses	16 (100%)	16 (100%)

'RECOGNIZE THE LONG LEAD TIMES ASSOCIATED WITH PUBLIC VENTURE INITIATIVES'

Lerner (2010) emphasizes addressing the long investment horizon requirements for some types of innovative SMEs and the need to play the long game, despite the pressure from politicians for quick results. There can be a mismatch between the time required to demonstrate investment performance, with failed investments more likely to be realized before investment successes, and the time given to HVCFs to provide evidence of success (Murray and Lingelbach, 2009).

Recent UK TBSF financing research found that while expected investment returns on IT and electronics R&D were typically within three years, bio/life sciences could take considerably longer (up to ten years in some cases) (North et al., 2013). A recent European VC study also found that the time taken for investments to mature via trade sale or IPO exits is typically taking longer than before the 2007 financial crisis (Axelson and Martinovic, 2012). In the UK this may be due to finance escalator failures to ensure a continuous flow of external finance during the R&D funding rounds (Mason et al., 2010; Gill, 2010). Not only is this problem compounded by the inability of some HVCFs to make follow-on investments (Rigos, 2011), but our research also found examples of delays due to the greater demands of later stage investors and technical hurdles to get trading approvals.

Our fund manager interviews found that lengthening investment horizons apply to the more recent HVCF programmes. Fund managers commented; 'investments are taking longer to mature as exits are taking place further up the development cycle', and that 'client business managers are almost always over optimistic in their expectations'. In practice it takes between 18 months and three years for the benefits of investment to start to become evident, but often five years or more before the firm reaches profitability. Fund managers emphasized the need to spread investments and had little expectation of significant returns within the first five to seven years of the fund, with pareto principles applying; 'the key to the level of returns is how well the top 20–30 per cent perform'.

Actual and Likely Impact on Business Performance

The surveyed 32 recipient businesses managers expected the return on investment to take several years, typically presenting more optimistic growth forecasts than their fund managers. Our first round interviews were conducted within 12 months of receiving HVCF funding, when two-thirds of recipients were still at the pre-trading stage. Funding was mainly used for R&D, IP, prototyping and patenting. For those already trading, improved sales and profitability were typically judged as at least 50 per cent attributable to the funding, but in one-fifth of cases growth had been slower than expected because of poorer market conditions than anticipated.

A follow-up survey in May 2013 sought clearer assessment of recipients' progress and funding impacts. This revealed three business closures, five trade sale exits and five still pre-trading. Although trade sales may include failing businesses strategically acquired at low valuations, particularly in recessionary times (Baldock et al., 2013), the indications were that these

Table 8.5   *Total employment and sales turnover, actual change and future forecast*

Total Employment	ECF/Aspire			UKIIF			Total		
	N=	median	mean	N=	median	mean	N=	median	mean
Time of funding	16	4	9.5	16	11	38	32	5	26
1 year after funding*	16	10	12.9	16	20	58.4	32	15	39.5
2 years after funding	–	–	–	14	35	69.1	–	–	–
3 years after funding**	–	–	–	14	60	84	–	–	–
4 years after funding	10	26	25.7	–	–	–	–	–	–
5 years after funding**	10	30	29.4	–	–	–	–	–	–
Annual Sales Turnover (£m)									
Time of funding	16	0	0.56	16	0	6.2	32	0	3.85
1 year after funding	16	0	0.7	16	1.3	10	32	0.9	6.2
2 years after funding	–	–	–	14	1.5	14.3	–	–	–
3 years after funding*	–	–	–	14	3.25	18.9	–	–	–
4 years after funding	10	0.38	1.62	–	–	–	–	–	–
5 years after funding*	10	1.2	2.17	–	–	–	–	–	–

Notes:
* ECF/Aspire surveyed February 2010, UKIIF surveyed February 2012.
**Year 3 is the next year forecast for UKIIF.
**Year 5 is the next year forecast for ECF and Aspire.

represented at least double the original investment. The follow-up survey in May 2013 demonstrated the beginnings of the expected growth trend from these potentially high growth businesses (Table 8.5). For 14 UKIIF businesses (excluding two trade sales), two years after their first round funding, annual median sales had reached £1.5m, with median employment increasing more than threefold to 35 employees. In the case of ten ECF/Aspire businesses (excluding three trade sales and three business failures) four years after initial funding, annual median sales had reached £380,000 with median employment increasing sixfold to 26 employees. The re-surveyed businesses also forecast further exponential growth over the next year, with median annual sales turnover for UKIIF businesses doubling and more than trebling for ECF/Aspire businesses.

However, aggregate growth performance shields a trend of underperformance which underscores the fund managers' concerns. Focusing on the 24 re-surveyed businesses, Table 8.6 exhibits a trend of worsening performance over time, with three-fifths of ECF/Aspire respondents indicating that they were behind schedule four years after initial funding and projecting a median time to exit of 6.5 years, 1.5 years beyond original

Table 8.6   Business performance, time and type of investment exit expected

Performance	Year 1 All* (Column %)	Year 2 UKIIF (Column %)	Year 4 ECF/Aspire (Column %)
Better	30%	29%	0%
Same	48%	43%	40%
Worse	22%	28%	60%
Time to Exit			
Median	5 yrs	5 yrs	6.5 yrs
Range	2–7yrs	2–7 yrs	4–10 yrs
Longer	n/a	29%	80%
Same	n/a	64%	20%
Shorter	n/a	7%	0%
Type of Exit			
Trade Sale	67%	72%	80%
IPO	25%	21%	10%
Other	8%	7%	10%
N=	24	14	10

Note: * ECF/Aspire surveyed February 2010, UKIIF surveyed February 2012.

forecasts. Contributory factors included delays in technical development, regulatory compliance, lack of customer acceptance, poorly performing markets and lack of follow-on finance.

This investment horizon elongation (Table 8.6) supports Lerner's view that HVCFs need to be flexible/adaptable to changing circumstances. Some re-surveyed business managers voiced concerns that the 10–12 year ECF life cycle might require an earlier exit than ideal, creating uncertainty and a sub-optimal value trade sale or IPO. Other evidence (Baldock et al., 2013) found that the IPO exit route had become more difficult since the onset of the GFC, adversely affecting the development momentum of some innovative SMEs. Trade sales were the preferred exit route for most surveyed businesses (Table 8.6).

'AVOID INITIATIVES THAT ARE TOO LARGE OR TOO SMALL'

Lerner (2010) contends that HVCFs require sufficient funding and scale for sustainability. Rigos (2011) recommends an ideal UK fund size of

£50m operating over a ten year life cycle with global funds (for example, UKIIF) requiring at least £150m. Similarly, the Technopolis (2011) review of funding models for stimulating innovative new companies in Europe recommends that HVCFs should be large (>€50m), never regionally focused (as this constrains deal flow and the benefits of specialization) and properly aligned to realistic commercial incentives. The UK government's shift from regional to national, and even to pan national HVCFs, illustrates this more recent focus on scale and size.

Lerner is also clear that programmes must not be too large, or extend beyond their required life range, having sufficient scale and size to establish a sustainable VC ecosystem, enabling future government withdrawal. He points to the success of Israel's Yozma funds in encouraging high levels of foreign co-investment and achieving fund cycle completion and privatization within ten years, suggesting that once the mechanisms are demonstrably in place government can withdraw (Clarysse et al., 2009). Essentially, balance in the scale and size of HVCFs is required. They must not be so large as to crowd out existing private VC activities nor outlast their period of usefulness.

Funding Leverage

Scaling up HVCFs requires leveraging of matching private sector investment, achieved either through partnership and co-investment funding, or within the underlying fund's finance raising activities. UKIIF demonstrates the fund of funds model's scaling up potential: over and above the umbrella fund's £150m government finance input (Table 8.2), an additional 20x[7] match funding was raised (for example, from institutions, banks, family offices) including foreign investment.

Partnership funding is also important to developing a successful VC market. ECF, Aspire and UKIIF each adopted different models for leveraging additional finance for company portfolio investments. However, whether partnership funding is a programme requirement or not, it is widely adopted in early stage VC funding, being largely supported by both public and private VCs. Potential benefits include risk sharing, gaining key VC sector skills, opening up new and international market opportunities and presenting more viable exit cases (Hopp, 2010).

Typically, Aspire and ECF recipients sought additional finance at the outset. For example, for seven of the 12 ECF cases other funding followed (or was conditional upon) the ECF funding, including cases where business angel and bank loan finance was unlocked on completion of the deal, with £4.7m of ECF funding raising £7.9m from other sources within one year of the initial funding. UKIIF has no fund leveraging requirements, but with over four-fifths of investments in early stage R&D projects, other investors were often encouraged to prevent over exposure, strengthen human capital (for example, by partnering VCs with particular market knowledge) and provide sufficient funds to develop the business. Several UKIIF lead investor funds recommended other private VCs as junior investors in the financing round, with these alliances contributing to a more robust business case for future investment rounds. At the time of the research UKIIF had invested almost £46m out of total project financing of £96m, with 55 per cent of additional finance (£25m) attributed as leveraged through UKIIF. Leveraged funds came from a variety of sources, including private VCs, business angels, banks and mezzanine funds.

Follow on Funding

The NAO report (2009) highlighted that HVCFs require sufficient size to provide suitable follow-on funding. Our follow-on survey revealed four businesses experiencing lack of HVCF further finance with an innovative energy business CEO commenting: 'It is very tough with VCs backing off to later stage financing. Our early stage VC will not take us any further and we cannot raise sufficient funds from our HNW contacts. In the absence of any suitable government funding we will be forced to slow down development further'.

The follow-on survey also found that two-fifths (9/24) required further funding within the next 18 months, ranging from £150,000 to £13.3m (median £3m), with the largest amounts required by life sciences and advanced manufacturing businesses. The suggestion was that the larger investments required for later stage global sales development would be sourced from private and institutional investors, but that failure to secure follow-on funds would result in premature trade sales and the potential loss of the business overseas.

Several business managers voiced concerns that their fund managers were operating purely from an investment return perspective: 'VCs are more interested in their fund performance than their portfolio companies, do not like diluting their share of equity with later stage private or institutional equity investment, and may force trade sales that the business does not really want'. This minority viewpoint raises serious questions about how public backed VCs should operate. Those UKIIF fund managers favouring early stage partnering with other private VCs to share risk were clear that they wanted lead investor status and to avoid interim funding round partnership dilution where possible until they were ready to exit.

'UNDERSTAND THE IMPORTANCE OF GLOBAL INTERCONNECTIONS'

Lerner (2010) advocates a global perspective in establishing HVCF programmes, attracting foreign investment and VC skills which can be transferred into improved local VC spin out activities over time, as well as encouraging portfolio businesses to establish a multinational presence. The key proviso is that investment into businesses seeks a realistic return within the country where the funds are being established, creating a viable VC market and developing businesses which drive forward the national economy. UKIIF, which invests mainly into UK businesses but includes European private VC funds and can invest globally, embodies this philosophy.

UKIIF provides a government backed pan European funded programme at a size (£330m) that is comparable with successful US VC funds with a global reach which can assist the growth of leading edge, innovative high tech companies. Interviews with UKIIF's continental European fund managers clearly demonstrated that the programme was 'providing more emphasis to fund UK based companies', leading to matched foreign funding investment and high level experienced overseas fund manager participation with UK businesses.[8]

Around four-fifths of surveyed ECF/Aspire (12/16) and UKIIF (14/16) recipients reported trading overseas or planning on exporting, a far higher proportion than typical UK SMEs.[9] VC fund managers were often essential to their development, taking non-executive director (NED) roles or appointing specialists onto the board for guidance (for example, in sales and marketing), providing considerable perceived added value to the performance of the business (Manigart and Wright, 2013; Clarysse et al., 2011). For the UKIIF recipients in particular, a crucial aspect was the VC's assistance in opening up overseas market opportunities (Lockett et al., 2008). In some cases, this was achieved with the fund managers providing guidance and expertise in finding prospective customers, undertaking international trade negotiations 'which could be complex and daunting in the case of prospective large overseas business customers' and in overcoming technical market barriers. For others HVCFs partnered with overseas private VCs specifically to help establish entry into overseas markets, notably in North American for several life science and digitech businesses.

Lerner's (2010) proposition that overseas companies be invested in and establish a presence within the host HVCF programme country is more contentious. ECF and Aspire were aimed specifically at UK owned and based businesses, the economic development argument being that these businesses will grow and generate long term jobs in the UK. A commonly highlighted problem (Rigos, 2011) is that many of the assisted businesses will eventually trade sale, most frequently being acquired by overseas companies with the resultant loss of jobs and IP to the UK. Lerner's counter argument, which is broadly supported by current UK government policy, suggests that it is better to host innovation and enjoy the benefits of trade sale wealth, reinvestments, continued activity of the associated successful UK-based serial entrepreneurs and other related spin-out activities, than to be too prescriptive on retaining a national presence for these businesses.[10]

Our follow-up survey indicates that the vast majority (four-fifths) of recipient businesses will seek trade sale exits which will most likely be to an overseas buyer. Five out of the 32 originally surveyed businesses have so far been acquired, all by overseas companies (4 US, 1 Israeli), but some have retained a UK R&D and sales office presence. There is also some evidence that the entrepreneurs that sold out, or failed, are remaining in the UK and establishing new businesses. It is also evident that some of UKIIF's overseas investments have UK links which have led to strategic growth acquisitions and investments being made into the UK, indirectly resulting in jobs growth and financial spillover impacts. In an increasingly global economy, Lerner's position, therefore, makes considerable sense, provided that the host country remains an attractive and competitive place to do business.

CONCLUSIONS

In conclusion, UK government intervention for early stage equity finance is justified in addressing the finance gaps ranging from seed funding where there is insufficient business angel and grant funding at below £0.25m up to and possibly exceeding £5m for intensive R&D sectors.

Lerner's (2010) aim for HVCFs to catalyse the development of a sustainable private VC ecosystem appears highly appropriate for the UK. The British Business Bank is developing a new post GFC funding escalator involving the three HVCF programmes considered here alongside the Angel Co-investment Fund (£200k to £2m investment range) and Business Growth Fund[11] (£2m–£10m), both introduced in 2011. This requires a holistic approach (Hughes, 2009) to operate cohesively in overcoming finance escalator breakages and maximizing the synergies of government finance and related support programmes.

While UK programmes have evolved along the lines of Lerner's (2010) principles by letting the market lead, a critical question is whether the market driven, commercial private sector ethos is in danger of eclipsing the wider economic development rationale for public interventions in this area. Our evidence suggests that HVCF programmes should avoid cherry picking the 'immediately fundable' business projects that private VC managers prioritize, by focusing more on the 'probably fundable' in order to maximize wider economic benefits and minimize displacement.

It is critical that HVCFs have the timescale to match the extending investment horizons of highly innovative intensive R&D sectors and the associated technical and regulatory delays that lengthen exit horizons. Evidence suggests these business sector investments may well stretch beyond the 10–12 year lifespan of HVCFs, indicating the need for extended programme management, or transition to rollover or follow-on funds, to achieve optimal outcomes for funds and their portfolio businesses. HVCFs must also have the size and scale to achieve Lerner's ultimate sustainable legacy objective from investment returns and ongoing future private sector VC fund development, enabling strategic government withdrawal.

Finally, recent UK experience through the UKIIF endorses Lerner's view that in an increasingly global economic environment it is vital to encourage inward investment, collaborating with and encouraging the best VC funds to invest in the UK. However, a crucial remaining question which certainly merits further research is whether successful portfolio businesses will create sustainable jobs, investment and wealth creation within the UK economy rather than there being a leakage of these longer-term benefits.

ACKNOWLEDGEMENTS

The authors acknowledge the contribution of Adrian Lewis, a venture capital consultant, who undertook fund manager interviews. They also thank Daniel Van der Schans at the UK Department for Business Innovation and Skills (BIS) and project steering group members for their guidance. The findings and interpretations are those of the authors.

NOTES

1. Includes the Catalyst Fund which tops up multiple private funds to enable fund raising closure.
2. This model relies on a lead private investor finding potential investee businesses which they present to the fund manager who then decides whether to use the BIS funds to invest alongside the private investor based on an assessment of the latter's investment track record and the strength of the due diligence work undertaken.

3. Prior to the British Business Bank being formed in 2014, Capital for Enterprise Ltd (CfEL) was the UK government's body overseeing its equity programmes.
4. The EU state aid limit for the UK was subsequently raised in January 2014 from £2m to £5m.
5. Included the two umbrella funds not directly investing in companies.
6. Small Business Survey 2012 (BIS, 2013); Centre for Business Research (CBR, 2008); BDRC (BDRC Continental, 2010) Mid-cap finance survey.
7. Includes umbrella and underlying funds for which it is not possible to calculate the proportion of leveraged funds that would already have been committed.
8. Gilde Healthcare III fund, investing in the UK as well as across Europe and in the US, is managed by one of Netherland's most experienced VCs, established 1982.
9. The UK Small Business Survey 2012 (BIS, 2013) found that 19 per cent of SME employer businesses currently export.
10. While these arguments do apply to the UK, they are particularly relevant in the case of small economies such as New Zealand where the limited size of the equity and VC market combined with the limited size of the technological community can lead to successful TBSFs having to relocate abroad to develop further (Deakins et al., 2015).
11. Qualifying businesses are required to have £5m annual sales turnover. This is a private fund, established through the UK Government's Business Finance Task Force, backed by five UK banks (Barclays, HSBC, Lloyds, Royal Bank of Scotland and Standard Chartered) to provide growth funding.

REFERENCES

Axelson, U. and Martinovic, M. (2012), *European Venture Capital: Myths and Facts*, Report to the British Venture Capital Association, London: British Venture Capital Association.

Baldock, R., North, D., Supri, S., Macaulay, P. and Rushton, C. (2013), *Investigation into the motivations behind the listing decisions of UK companies*, CEEDR Report for the Department for Business Innovation and Skills, March 2013, London: CEEDR.

Bank of England (1996), *The Financing of Technology-based Small Firms*, London: Domestic Finance Division, Bank of England.

Bank of England (2001), *The Financing of Technology-based Small Firms*, London: Domestic Finance Division, Bank of England.

BDRC Continental (2010), *Results from the 2010 Finance Survey of Mid-cap Businesses*, Report to the Department for Business Innovation and Skills, URN10/P108, London: Department for Business Innovation and Skills.

BIS (2013), *Small Business Survey 2012: SME Employers*, Report by BMG Research to the Department for Business Innovation and Skills, April 2013, London: Department for Business Innovation and Skills.

BVCA (2013), *BVCA Private Equity and Venture Capital Report on Investment Activity 2012*, Report by the British Venture Capital Association, London: British Venture Capital Association.

CBR (2008), *Financing UK Small and Medium sized Enterprises: the 2007 Survey*, Cambridge: Centre for Business Research, University of Cambridge.

CEEDR (2012), *Early Assessment of the UK Innovation Investment Fund*, Report for the Department for Business Innovation and Skills, May 2012, London: CEEDR.

CfEL (2012), *Overview of Publicly backed Venture Capital and Loan Funds in the UK*, Capital for Enterprise Ltd, January 2012, London: CfEL.

CfEL (2013), *Survey of Fund Managers, Capital for Enterprise Ltd: 2013*, London: CfEL.

Clarysse, B., Bruneel, J. and Wright, M. (2011), 'Explaining growth paths of young technology-based firms: structuring resource portfolios in different competitive environments', *Strategic Entrepreneurship Journal*, **5** (2): 137–157.

Clarysse, B., Knockaert, M. and Wright, M. (2009), *Benchmarking UK Venture Capital to the US and Israel: What Lessons can be Learned?*, British Venture Capital Association (online), May 2009.

Cowling, M., Liu, W. and Ledger, A. (2012), 'Small business financing in the UK before and during the current financial crisis', *International Small Business Journal*, **30** (7): 778–800.

Deakins, D., North, D., and Bensemann, J. (2015), 'Paradise lost? The case of technology-based small firms in New Zealand in the post-global financial crisis economic environment', *Venture Capital*, **17** (1–2): 129–150.

Fraser, S. (2009), *Small Firms in the Credit Crisis, Evidence from the UK Survey of SME Finances*, Coventry: Warwick Business School, University of Warwick.

Gill, D. (2010), 'Collapse of the Funding Escalator', presentation to the Institute for Manufacturing, St John's Innovation Centre, Cambridge, 24 June 2010.

Gompers, P., Kovner, A., Lerner, J. and Scharfstein, D. (2010), 'Performance persistence in entrepreneurship', *Journal of Financial Economics*, **96** (1): 18–34.

Harrison, R., Don, G., Johnston, G.K. and Greig, M. (2010), 'The early-stage risk capital market in Scotland since 2000: issues of scale, characteristics and market efficiency', *Venture Capital*, **12** (3): 211–239.

HM Treasury (2003), *Bridging the Finance Gap: Next Steps in Improving Access to Growth Capital for Small Businesses*, London: HMSO.

Hopp, C. (2010), 'When do venture capitalists collaborate? Evidence on the driving forces of venture capital syndication', *Journal of Small Business Economics*, **35** (4): 417–431.

Hsu, D. (2004), 'What do entrepreneurs pay for venture capital affiliation?', *The Journal of Finance*, **59** (4): 1805–1844.

Hughes, A. (2009), 'Hunting the Snark: some reflections on the UK support for the small business sector', *Innovation, Management, Policy and Practice*, **11** (1): 114–126.

Leleux, B. and Surlemont, B. (2003), 'Public versus private venture capital: seeding or crowding out? A pan-European analysis', *Journal of Business Venturing*, **18** (1): 81–104.

Lerner, J. (2009), *Boulevard of Broken Dreams: Why Public Efforts to Boost Entrepreneurship and Venture Capital have Failed – and what to do about it*, Princeton: Princeton University Press.

Lerner, J. (2010), 'The future of public efforts to boost entrepreneurship and venture capital', *Small Business Economics*, **35** (3): 255–264.

Lerner, J., Moore, D. and Shepherd, S. (2005), *A Study of New Zealand's Venture Capital Market and Implications for Public Policy*, Report to the Ministry of Research Science and Technology, Auckland: LECG.

Lockett, A., Wright, M., Burrows, A., Scholes, L. and Paton, D. (2008), 'The export intensity of venture capital backed companies', *Small Business Economics*, **31** (1): 39–58.

Macmillan, H.P. (1931), *Committee on Finance and Industry Report*, The Macmillan Report, July.

MacMillan, I.C., Kulow, D.M. and Khoylian, C. (1989), 'Venture capitalist's involvement in their investments: extent and performance', *Journal of Business Venturing*, **4** (1): 27–47.

Manigart, S. and Wright, M. (2013), 'Reassessing the relationships between private equity investors and their portfolio companies', *Small Business Economics*, **40** (3): 479–492.

Mason, C.M. and Baldock, R. (2014), 'Government intervention in the entrepreneurial finance market: the case of the UK's Angel Co-Fund', Paper presented at the Institute for Small Business and Entrepreneurship Conference, Manchester, 5–6 November.

Mason, C.M. and Harrison, R. (2003), 'Closing the regional equity gap? A critique of the Department of Trade and Industry's Regional Venture Capital Funds Initiative', *Regional Studies*, **37** (8): 855–868.

Mason, C.M. and Kwok, K. (2010), 'Investment readiness programmes and access to finance: a critical review of design issues', *Local Economy*, **25** (4): 269–292.

Mason, C.M., Jones, L. and Wells, S. (2010), *The City's Role in Providing for Public Equity Financing Needs of UK SMEs*, Report to the City of London.

Murray, G. (1999), 'Early-stage venture capital funds, scale economies and public support', *Venture Capital*, **4** (1): 351–384.

Murray, G. (2007), 'Venture capital and government policy', in H. Landstrom (ed.),

Handbook of Research on Venture Capital, Cheltenham, UK and Northampton, MA, USA: Edward Elgar Publishing, pp. 113–151.

Murray, G. and Lingelbach, D. (2009), *Twelve Meditations on Venture Capital*, University of Exeter Business School, Paper No. 09/06, September 2009.

NAO (2009), *Venture Capital Support to Small Businesses*, Report of the National Audit Office to the House of Commons, 23rd Session, 2009–2010, London: NAO.

NESTA (2009), *From Funding Gaps to Thin Markets: UK Government Support for Early-Stage Venture Capital*, Research Report with British Venture Capital Association (BVCA), September 2009, London: NESTA.

North, D., Baldock, R. and Ullah, F. (2013), 'Funding the growth of UK technology-based small firms since the financial crash: are there breakages in the finance escalator?', *Venture Capital*, **15** (3): 237–260.

North, D., Baldock, R., Ekanem, I. and Lewis, A. (2010), *Early Assessment of the Impact of BIS Equity Fund Initiatives*, CEEDR Report for the Department for Business Innovation and Skills, July 2010, London: CEEDR.

Oakey, R.P. (2003), 'Funding innovation and growth in UK new technology-based firms: some observations on contributions from the public and private sectors', *Venture Capital*, **5** (2): 161–180.

Oakey, R.P. (2007), 'A commentary on gaps in funding for moderate "non-stellar" growth small businesses in the United Kingdom', *Venture Capital*, **9** (3): 223–235.

Pierrakis, Y. (2010), *Venture Capital: Now and After the Dotcom Crash*, NESTA Research Report, July 2010, London: NESTA.

Pierrakis, Y. and Mason, C.M. (2008), *Shifting Sands: the Changing Nature of the Early Stage Venture Capital Market in the UK*, NESTA Research Report, September 2008, London: NESTA.

Reynolds, P.D, Hay, M., Bygrave, W.D., Camp, S.M. and Autio, E. (2000), *Global Entrepreneurship Monitor 2000 Executive Report*, Kauffman Centre for Entrepreneurial Leadership, Babson Park MA: Babson College.

Rigos, S. (2011), *The UK equity gap: Why is there no Facebook or Google in the UK?*, Policy Paper for the Greater London Authority (GLA), London: GLA.

Rowlands, C. (2009), *The Provision of Growth Capital to Small and Medium Sized Enterprises*, Report for the Department for Business, Innovation and Skills, London: BIS.

Siegel, D.S, Westhead, P. and Wright, M. (2003), 'Science parks and the performance of new technology-based firms: a review of recent UK evidence and an agenda for future research', *Small Business Economics*, **20** (2): 177–184.

SQW Consulting (2009), *The Supply of Equity Finance to SMEs: Revisiting the Equity Gap*, Report to the Department for Business Innovation and Skills, Cambridge: SQW Consulting.

Technopolis (2011), *The Role of Different Funding Models in Stimulating the Creation of Innovative New Companies: What is the most appropriate model for Europe?*, Final Report to the European Research Area Board, October 2011, Brussels / Brighton: Technopolis Group.

9. Readiness for funding: the influence of entrepreneurial team diversity
Candida G. Brush, Linda F. Edelman and Tatiana S. Manolova

INTRODUCTION

Angel financing is defined as '[i]nformal venture capital-equity investments and non-collateral forms of lending made by private individuals . . . using their own money, directly in unquoted companies in which they have no family connection' (Harrison and Mason, 1999, p. 95). It plays a crucial role in financing growth-oriented ventures by filling the gap between informal family and friends and more formal institutional (venture capital) investment (Harrison and Mason, 1999; Van Osnabrugge and Robinson, 2000). However, comparatively little is known about the angel market, due in large part to its invisible nature (Mason and Harrison, 2008).

Given the private nature of angel investment data, getting exact investment numbers is difficult. Recent research in the US estimates the amount of capital provided by angels is nearly equal to the money provided by venture capital firms (Sohl, 2005). Worldwide, researchers estimate that angel investors provide up to 11 times the amount of funding provided by venture capitalists (Reynolds et al., 2003). In 2013, business angels invested $24.8 billion in 70,730 entrepreneurial ventures in the US (http://wsbe.unh.edu/cvr), while venture capitalists invested $29.6 billion in 3,382 companies (http://www.nvca.org). Further, the National Venture Capital Association (NVCA) suggests that the impact of angel financing from groups and individuals overall is approximately $100 billion in the United States alone. Angels focus much of their investment in early stage ventures (Figure 9.1). Researchers estimate that 45 percent of the 2013 angel investments were in the seed and start-up stage, up from 35 percent in 2012 (http://wsbe.unh.edu/cvr).

In this chapter, we are interested in discovering if firms with diverse top management teams are more likely to obtain critical early stage angel funding. Statistics indicate that women receive a small proportion of the total angel capital awarded and women also participate in the angel investment market at much lower rates than men do (Sohl, 2015). When women do apply for funding, the yield rate, which is the ratio of the number of deals funded to the number of proposals submitted, is about the same for men and women-led ventures (13.33 percent for women as compared with 14.79 percent for men) (Becker-Blease and Sohl, 2007).

We use the concept of 'readiness for funding' to explore the level of readiness of diverse top management teams to obtain early stage investments. Readiness is defined as 'the venture's state of willingness or preparedness to take a new investor' (Mason and Harrison, 2003, p. 30), coupled with the investor's perception of management skills, business model, market, and growth perspectives (Mason and Harrison, 2004; Douglas and Shepherd, 2002). Previous research examined three aspects of readiness (Brush et al., 2012); organizational readiness, or the capability and experience of the management team (Van Osnabrugge and Robinson, 2000); strategic readiness, or the track record of having customers and/or a product in an advanced stage of development (Wong, 2002; Freear et al., 2002); and technological readiness, or protectable intellectual property (Harrison and Mason, 1999). In the angel-investing context, the perceptions of readiness for funding could be influenced by the diversity of the top-management team. More specifically, we expect that diverse top management teams will perform better towards the achievement of organizational goals (readiness for funding, in our case).

To gain a better understanding of the readiness phenomenon, we used a proprietary database of 668 firms that over a four-year period sought angel investment from the members of a prominent angel investment group located outside of Boston, MA. We then divided this population into two sets, one in which top management teams were comprised only of men, and the other one with at least one woman on the top management team. We compared these two groups on our readiness criteria, and then looked at the effect of readiness in general across the entire population.

Our chapter proceeds as follows. After a review of the theoretical perspectives that guide our study, we formulate and test a set of hypotheses on the readiness for funding of new ventures with diverse top management teams as compared with their male-only counterparts. We then discuss our findings and conclude by presenting future research suggestions and theoretical and practitioner implications.

THEORY AND HYPOTHESES

Readiness

Readiness is 'the state of being fully prepared for something' (Dictionary. com, 2014). It is the 'state of being prepared or available for service, action, or progress' (http://www.thefreedictionary.com/readiness, 2014). Readiness has been explored through different theoretical lenses, including organizational behavior, strategic management, and management of technology. In organizational behavior, readiness is typically understood as readiness for change. Readiness for change generally begins with an organization member's perception of the benefits of change, perception of the risks of failing to change and perceived external demands of the change on the organization (Armenakis et al., 1993; Prochaska et al., 1994). Self-efficacy and confidence in coping with change as well as job characteristics also influence an individual organization member's perceived readiness (Prochaska et al., 1997; Armenakis et al., 1993). In all, organizational readiness for change has to do with factors internal to the firm such as the extent to which organization members have the attitudes, experience, perceptions, and confidence to move forward with a change.

Strategic readiness assesses how well prepared a company's people, systems and organizational culture are to carry out its strategy. The intangible assets, or the human, information, and organizational capital of the firm, are the foundation for strategic change (Kaplan and Norton, 2004). These assets typically involve new markets, products, or corporate transformation. In sum, strategic readiness has to do with the firm's response to external, product/market considerations such as the extent to which the organization's structure and systems are ready for strategic change, growth, or movement into new product/market arenas.

Technology readiness is different from organizational and strategic readiness. It is a measurement system that allows for comparison of maturity between different types of technologies (Mankins, 1995), and gauges the readiness of a technology for commercialization (Heslop et al., 2001), or an individual's readiness to use new technology in general (Parasuraman, 2000). In sum, technology readiness has to do with the proof of concept and acceptance of the innovation by a particular group.

We believe that an investigation of the concept of readiness from the perspective of the diversity of the top management team can enhance our understanding of the process of obtaining angel financing. When entrepreneurs submit a proposal to an angel investment group, they have made a determination that the venture is fully prepared, or ready to grow. In terms of organizational readiness, this would mean that the new venture is ready for change; in that it is a legitimate enterprise with a capable team and that the key management roles are filled (Van Osnabrugge and Robinson, 2000; Wong, 2002). New businesses showing strategic readiness would already have an investment in the business and hence a stronger resource base (Freear et al., 2002). Technology readiness is characterized by those businesses that have intellectual property (IP) that is protectable in some way (Harrison and Mason, 1999).

Research about angel investor decision-making suggests that all three aspects of readiness are important to passing the screening stage (Sudek, 2006). Hall and Hofer (1993) showed that venture capitalists (VCs) put more weight on aspects of the opportunity during the screening stage, while Haar et al. (1988) found that angels were interested in management's ability and market potential. Mason and Harrison (1999) found that the most common reasons for deal rejection were the state of the entrepreneurial team, marketing, and finance, resulting in the new ventures not being 'investment ready' (Mason and Harrison, 2003). Having a management team or a revenue stream is an indication to potential investors that the new venture has completed the initial research and development phases (Wong, 2002).

Readiness and Diversity of the Top Management Team

A maxim in organizational research is that the top management team (TMT) drives strategic choice, and that differences in choices can be explained by top management team demographics (Hambrick and Mason, 1984). Research suggests that greater top management team diversity leads to effective organizational functioning, greater variance in ideas, and enhanced creativity and innovation (Jackson et al., 1995). Diverse top management teams have been argued to have a higher degree of shared strategic cognition (Amason, 1996; Ensley and Hmieleski, 2005) and a higher degree of collective efficacy towards goal achievement (Sosik and Jung, 2002; Ensley and Hmieleski, 2005). In addition, research on entrepreneurial top management team indicates that diversity can be advantageous in turbulent and unstable environments (Beckman and Burton, 2008). In such environments, heterogeneous teams are found to problem-solve better, as they rely on different cognitive frames (Wiersema and Bantel, 1992), and have access to a more varied pool of networks and resources (Walske and Zacharakis, 2009). In essence, because a diverse top management team helps to ensure that the firm has the full range of capabilities and perspectives needed to manage (for example, Keck 1997; Randel and Jaussi 2003), diversity leads to better firm performance.

However, top management team diversity has been found to have negative effects as well. Teams that are more diverse have issues around group cohesion (O'Reilly et al., 1989) and exhibit greater interpersonal conflict, which is likely to negatively affect the performance of the firm. Interpersonal conflict reduces strategic consensus, and provokes disagreements about the overall direction of the firm. It is also likely to result in different perceptions or interpretations about what the current firm strategy actually is (Knight et al., 1999). In sum, diversity in the top management team can lead to problems with the frequency and quality of communication, and increase overall conflict (Eisenhardt and Schoonhoven, 1990).

Despite the possible negative effects of top management team diversity, evidence suggests that in the context of new ventures, many of the problems around top management team diversity are less salient. This is due to the voluntary nature of top management team participation in early stage firms. Because new top management team members both choose to join and are chosen by their peer incumbents, the interpersonal chemistry among top management team members should be less problematic. This leaves top management teams in an entrepreneurial context free of many of the negatives associated with diversity (Beckman and Burton, 2008). Therefore, greater diversity in the new ventures' top management team should lead to the new venture's higher ability to adapt to change, better overall strategic decision-making, and greater access to a multiplicity of resources; all indicators that the firm is 'ready for investment'. Formally:

H1: Compared with new ventures with male-only top management teams:

H1a*: New ventures with diverse top management teams are likely to have a higher degree of organizational readiness for investment.*

H1b*: New ventures with diverse top management teams are likely to have a higher degree of strategic readiness for investment.*

H1c*: New ventures with diverse top management teams are likely to have a higher degree of technological readiness for investment.*

We further expect that the higher degree of readiness along the three dimensions (organizational, strategic, and technological) will increase the likelihood of successfully passing through the administrative review stage of the angel investment process. Formally:

H2*: New ventures with diverse top management teams are more likely to pass the administrative review phase (stage-one, desk reject) of the angel investment decision-making process.*

METHODOLOGY

The data for the study comes from a portion of the investment proposals (N = 668) submitted to a large angel financing group located in the

Northeast United States over a four-year period (2007–2010). These new and small ventures applying for angel funding were on average less than five years old (mean = 4.38 years) and had fewer than 10 employees (mean = 7.09). Almost three-quarters of them operated in either the technology (54.20 percent) or the medical sector (19.99 percent) and close to 60 percent came from New England. The ventures in this sample are generally representative of those funded by angel investors in that biotechnology, medical devices, and software were most popular for angel investment (http://www.angelcapitaleducation.org).

The angel group has a four-step decision process (see Appendix). The investment proposal was reviewed by an administrative committee which made a decision to 'desk reject' the proposal or to move it on to a screening committee presentation. Ventures successful in passing the screening presentation were invited to present to the larger group of investors. Those successful at the large group presentation were in turn able to enter the due diligence process. The investment proposals were between one and five pages in length and offered detailed information about the qualifications of the founding team, the nature of the business, the amount of capital sought, cash flow, and the intended use of the funds, as well as a variety of additional product, intellectual property, market, and financial projections. The angel investment group provided us with the pool of investment proposals and the outcomes for each proposal as it moved through the angel investment decision-making process. However, we chose to focus on the initial administrative review or stage-one, desk reject decisions. The administrative review or stage-one, desk reject, is the decision closest to the submission of the investment proposal and hence there is the least amount of intervening and uncontrollable variance between the investment proposal and the decision.

To generate the initial dataset, two trained research assistants independently coded the investment proposals, following a specific coding scheme developed by the principal investigators, which consisted of 64 categories. We then calculated inter-rater reliability, implementing the kappa procedure in STATA, and utilized the linear weighted Cohen's Kappa statistics for the ordinal categories. The percent agreement across the coding categories ranged between 75.91 percent and 98.51 percent, well above the recommended .70 threshold (Stemler, 2004). One of the study's coauthors resolved coding inconsistencies, which occurred infrequently. Table 9.1 reports the descriptive statistics for all variables entered in the subsequent statistical analysis.

The dependent variable for this study was a binary variable, which captured whether the angel group's decision was to 'desk reject' the proposal. More specifically, if the new venture was desk rejected, the outcome of the

Table 9.1 Descriptive statistics

Variable	Min	Max	Mean	SD	Frequencies*	
					Category	%
TMT Diversity	0.00	1.00	0.31	0.46	Diverse	31.5
Readiness						
Organizational						
Number of employees	0.00	400.00	7.09	20.70		
Size of TMT	1.00	5.00	3.06	1.23		
Industry experience (% Yes)	0.00	1.00	0.86	0.35	Yes	86.4
Strategic						
Current customers (% Yes)	0.00	1.00	0.47	0.49	Yes	46.7
Expected revenues (Year 3, $)	0.00	93,207,204.00	188,503.41	3,676,524.36		
Premoney valuation ($)	0.00	60,000,000.00	3,945,883.72	5,293,850.53		
Stage of product development (1–5 scale)	1.00	5.00	3.60	1.27		
Technological						
IP (% Yes)	0.00	1.00	0.45	0.49	Yes	44.9
Demographics					*Industrial sector:*	
Company age (years)	0.00	34.50	4.38	3.52	Consumer Goods	25.9
Amount of capital raised ($)	0.00	65,000,000.00	1,130,602.31	4,568,819.90	Medical	19.9
Amount of capital sought ($)	0.00	50,000,000.00	1,552,557.25	2,942,242.96	Technology	54.2

Note: * Categorical variables only.

153

angel investment process was coded as '0'; if the new venture passed the desk rejection stage, the outcome was coded as '1'.

Top management team diversity was captured by a binary variable that took the value of '0' if all TMT members were male, and '1' otherwise.[1] *Organizational readiness* was captured by three variables: the *number of employees* of the new venture (self-reported), the *number of people on the top management team* (calculated as the tally of managers listed in the proposal) and the top management team's *industry experience* (extracted from the 'Management' section of the proposal and coded as '1' if the team had industry experience and '0' otherwise). *Strategic readiness* was captured by four self-reported variables: a binary measure of whether or not the company had *current customers*, an ordinal measure of the level of *new product development* ('concept', coded as '1', 'prototype', coded as '2', 'product in development', coded as '3', 'product ready', coded as '4', and 'revenue generated from sale of product', coded as '5'), *expected revenues in third year following the proposal*, and the *new venture's pre-money valuation*. Finally, *technological readiness* was captured by a binary measure that reflected whether the new venture had *intellectual property* in the form of a patent or patent-pending technology, trademark, or proprietary technology. The variable was extracted from the 'Competitive Advantage' section of the investment proposal.

RESULTS

Statistical Test Results

To test for the effect of diversity of the top management team on the different dimensions of organizational, strategic, and technological readiness, we performed analysis of variance (independent samples t-tests or cross-tabulations). Results are reported in Table 9.2. New ventures with diverse top management teams had a significantly higher number of employees and significantly larger top management teams. There were no significant differences in the percentage of top management team members who had industry experience. Thus with significant differences in two of the three aspects of organizational readiness we tracked, H1a receives partial support. New ventures with diverse management teams were also more likely to have current customers, were further along the stages of the product development cycle, and had significantly higher pre-money valuations. There were no significant differences in the expected revenues three years out. Thus, with significant differences in three of the four aspects of strategic readiness we tracked, H1b also receives partial

Table 9.2 Analysis of variance (N = 668)

Variable	Mean (continuous variables) or Percentage (categorical variables)		t-test or chi-squared
	Men-Only top management team	Diverse top management team	
	(n = 467)	(n = 201)	
Readiness			
Organizational			
Number of employees	5.98	9.95	−1.755†
Size of top management team	2.90	3.55	−7.354***
Industry experience (% Yes)	86.22%	83.00%	0.899
Strategic			
Current customers (% Yes)	44.18%	52.08%	3.394†
Expected revenues (Year 3, $)	252,274	39,007	0.654
Pre-money valuation ($)	3,715,643	4,780,000	−1.628†
Stage of product development (1–5 scale)	3.52	3.76	−2.353*
Technological			
IP (% Yes)	45.92%	43.01%	0.463
Demographics			
Company age (years)	4.20	4.92	−2.379*
Industrial sector:			
Consumer goods (% Yes)	25.32%	26.50%	0.102
Technology (% Yes)	56.22%	50.50%	1.848
Medical (% Yes)	18.45%	23.00%	1.820
Amount of capital raised ($)	1,067,214	1,245,601	−0.463
Amount of capital sought ($)	1,654,956	6,184,758	−0.911

Note: † significant at p<0.1; * significant at p<0.05; ** significant at p<0.01; *** significant at p<0.001.

support. There were no significant differences in the proportion of new ventures with intellectual property between new ventures with men-only and diverse TMTs. Thus, H1c was not supported.

To test for the effect of factors that determine the progress of the new venture in the initial, desk reject stage of the angel investment decision-making process, we used the logistical regression procedure in SPSS. To remedy for potential over-dispersion, we log transformed the variables 'expected revenues', 'pre-money valuation', 'amount of capital raised', and 'amount of capital sought' prior to entering them in the regression function. The regression coefficients are exponentiated and reported as odds ratios. Thus, they can be directly interpreted as the increase/decrease in the odds of the event happening (in our case, passing the desk-reject stage of the angel investment process) compared either to the baseline category (in the case of binary variables) or with one unit increase in the independent variable (in the case of continuous variables). Results are presented in Table 9.3. After controlling for the degree of readiness and other industry and firm-level variables, top management team diversity had no significant marginal effect on the likelihood of the new venture to be rejected at the administrative review stage. Thus, H2 was not supported.

DISCUSSION

One of the most important events in the life of a new venture is presenting the firm for funding. A new venture is considered to be 'investible' if the investor perceives that it has factors such as the requisite management skills, business model, market, and growth perspectives (Mason and Harrison, 2004). Our research takes this concept of 'investible' one step further, arguing that in order for a new venture to be investible it must be 'ready' for investment, and that 'readiness' can be divided into three distinct categories; organizational readiness, strategic readiness and technological readiness. We then suggest that readiness differs based on the diversity of the top management team. Our findings indicate that initially, at the desk rejection stage of the angel investment decision-making process, new ventures with a diverse top management teams are more ready for investment than their all male top management team counterparts. This suggests that greater numbers of new ventures with diverse top management teams will move through the administrative review portion of the angel investment decision-making process because angel investors prefer firms that are more 'ready for investment'. Interestingly, our findings do not support this logic.

Table 9.3 Logit estimates (n = 477)

Variable	Pass Desk Rejection	
	Odds Ratio	S.E.
Top management team diversity	1.03	0.26
Readiness		
Organizational		
Number of employees	**0.96†**	0.02
Size of top management team	1.17	0.13
Industry experience (% Yes)	1.37	0.51
Strategic		
Current customers (% Yes)	**3.05*****	0.77
Expected revenues (Year 3, $)	0.99	0.51
Premoney valuation (ln$)	1.02	0.07
Stage of product development (1–5 scale)	1.01	0.09
Technological		
IP (% Yes)	**1.89****	0.45
Demographics		
Company age (years)	0.94	0.04
Industrial sector:		
Technology (% Yes)	1.56	0.46
Medical (% Yes)	**1.90†**	0.68
Amount of capital raised (ln$)	**1.19***	0.09
Amount of capital sought (ln$)	**0.74****	0.08
Regression Function		
Log likelihood = −245.011		
Likelihood Ratio chi²(df = 14) = 58.71***		

Note: †significant at p<0.1; * significant at p<0.05; ** significant at p<0.01; *** significant at p<0.001.

Instead, when we look at the results from the logistical regression test, we find no support for team diversity. In sum, according to our criteria, new ventures with diverse top management teams are more ready for investment, yet top management team diversity in and of itself does not lead to a greater likelihood that the new venture will pass through the administrative review stage of the angel investment selection process. While we do find a small number of readiness indicators to be significant, they are significant for the entire sample (men-only top management team and diverse top management team). We discuss these findings below.

Readiness in New Ventures with Diverse Top Management Teams

Not being 'investment ready' is one of the most common reasons for deal rejection (Mason and Harrison, 1999), leading us to expect that the greater the readiness of the new venture, the more likely it will be to move through the angel investment decision-making process. Our findings indicate that firms with more diverse top management teams have greater strategic readiness and organizational readiness. In terms of strategic readiness, our findings indicate that new ventures with diverse top management teams have higher pre-money valuations, have current customers, and are further along in their product development processes. With respect to organizational readiness, new ventures with diverse top management teams have larger top management teams and have more overall employees. In addition, new ventures with diverse top management teams are significantly older than new ventures with all-male top management teams. In sum, based on our criteria, new ventures with diverse top management teams are more 'ready' for investment.

Yet despite prior research which finds that diverse top management teams have greater variance in ideas, enhanced creativity and innovation, and are overall more effective (Jackson et al., 1995), our findings indicate that top management team diversity in and of itself does not lead to a higher likelihood of passing through the review stage of the angel investment process. Firms that have all male top management teams move through the angel investment decision-making process in statistically significant similar quantities as firms that have diverse top management teams. This suggests top management team diversity may have a more nuanced effect on the new venture's success in securing angel financing. As the results from our statistical tests indicate, two of the criteria that differentiate the new ventures that pass through the administrative review stage of the angel investment process from those that do not are the number of employees and having current customers. In both of these categories, there were significant differences between new ventures with male-only TMTs and new ventures with diverse TMTs. Thus, we surmise that top management team diversity may affect the outcome of the angel investment process indirectly, through the qualities of the new venture. Once these characteristics are controlled for, the marginal effect of top management team diversity becomes insignificant. A future study exploring potential mediated or moderated relationships between TMT diversity, new venture readiness, and new venture progress through the angel investment process will be a fruitful extension of our research.

Readiness in All New Ventures

As discussed above, when we look at our entire sample, we do find some significant 'readiness' criteria. Specifically, at stage one, desk rejection level, one of our measures of organizational readiness, number of employees, was significant as well as one of our measures of strategic readiness, current customers.

New ventures that have a larger number of employees were less likely to receive funding. This surprised us as we thought that a critical number of employees would suggest that the new venture is legitimate, and is not merely a manifestation of the intentions of the founder; and hence more ready for funding. Given the negative relationship, we reasoned that angel investors perceived these ventures as 'too large' and hence more suitable for later-stage venture capital funding.

We did find that new ventures that reported securing customers were more likely to make it through the administrative review phase of the angel investment decision-making process. Having customers indicates that the new venture is no longer in the start-up phase and that the new firm has the potential to grow and become sustainable (Reynolds and Miller, 1992). This is a form of legitimacy and so indicates the overall readiness of the new venture to move through the angel investment decision-making process. More specifically, new ventures with current customers had three times the odds of passing through the administrative review stage of the angel investment process compared to new ventures without customers.

Our measure of technological readiness, intellectual property, was also significant at the stage one, desk rejection level. New ventures reporting some form of protectable intellectual property had almost two times the odds of passing through the administrative review stage of the angel investment process compared with new ventures without intellectual property. Having intellectual property protection suggests that the new venture has developed its technology (Haeussler et al., 2009). Previous literature has discussed the importance of patents in particular for young firms attempting to gain early stage financing (Lemley, 2001; Ueda, 2004). In the venture capital literature, researchers have found that an important selection criterion is proprietary products or products that can be otherwise protected (Hambrick and Macmillan, 1985). Therefore, the existence of intellectual property protection provides early stage angel investors with the confidence that they are investing in something that is protectable, and so helps the new venture move through the angel investment decision-making process.

In addition to our readiness indicators, a number of our control variables were also significant. Specifically, the amount of capital sought from the angel investors, the capital raised prior to applying for angel funding, and the industry sector, were significant in initially determining whether new ventures would move through the angel investment decision-making process. The importance of prior investment in early stage firms is well documented in the entrepreneurship literature (Shane and Cable, 2002; Wong, 2002). Even with a reputable entrepreneur, the illiquid nature of early stage financing makes it inherently risky. Therefore, the significance of the amount of both the capital sought from the angel investors and the capital raised prior to applying for angel funding is not surprising in the angel investment decision-making process.

Our findings also indicate that industry sector, and specifically the medical sector, is significant. Research suggests that entire industries can have legitimacy and that this legitimacy is conferred upon the firms operating within them (Aldrich and Fiol, 1994; Suchman, 1995; Zucker, 1988; Zimmerman and Zeitz, 2002). New ventures can use the past actions of the industry members, in conjunction with the industry's norms and practices to acquire legitimacy (Aldrich and Fiol, 1994; Zimmerman and Zeitz, 2002). The new ventures in the medical sector are known for their long product lead times, which present investors with few returns in the short run in exchange for the promise of significant payoffs later on. Firms operating in this sector are more likely to pass through the initial stage of the angel investment decision-making process.

FUTURE RESEARCH AND CONCLUSIONS

The objective of this chapter was to examine the role top management team diversity plays in new ventures moving through the angel investment decision-making process. Drawing from literatures of organizational, strategic, and technological readiness, we studied the extent to which the readiness of the top management team changes based on the diversity of that team. We then looked at how the readiness in all the new ventures in our sample, regardless of their top management team composition, affects the new venture's ability to make it through the angel investment decision-making process. Specifically, organizational readiness examines the extent to which organization members have the attitudes, experience, perceptions, and confidence to move forward with a change. Strategic readiness explores the extent to which an organization's structure and systems are ready for growth or movement into new product/market arenas. Technology readiness has to do with the proof of concept and acceptance of the innovation by a particular group. These three dimensions make up overall 'readiness' and capture the three subcategories of management, market, and technology as noted by Douglas and Shepherd (2002).

Our findings indicate that there are a number of differences between men-only and diverse top management teams. These differences indicate that diverse top management teams are more 'ready' for investment. Statistically, they are older, larger, have more customers, are further along in their product development, and have a higher pre-money valuation. However, despite these differences, diversity in the top management team in and of itself was not a significant predictor of firms moving through the angel investment decision-making process. In sum, top management team diversity has a complex effect on the likelihood of securing early private investment.

When we looked at the entire sample, we did find that number of employees, current customers, intellectual property protection, and a number of control variables were significant predictors of all firms making it past the stage-one, desk rejection stage. However, given the nature of our data, we only analysed our data up to the point where the new venture passed or failed the administrative review, or stage one, desk reject. While we can postulate that other, softer factors, such as persuasiveness, and ability to speak, reason and answer questions in front of an audience may outweigh the measureable factors we examined when we examine later stages of the angel investment decision-making process, this line of inquiry remains an open question for future research.

Other limitations of our study include that our data are collected from one angel investment group located in the greater Boston, MA area. While we are confident that our findings are replicable to other groups located on the East Coast of the United States, research has indicated possible differences in investment patterns between angel groups based on their location. Most angel investors are cashed-out entrepreneurs and their investment patterns are thus to a large extent imprinted by prior entrepreneurial activity within the respective geographic region (Harrison et al., 2010).

Limitations notwithstanding, this chapter offers a glimpse at the factors necessary for new ventures to move through the angel investment decision-making process. In addition, we find that despite quite compelling differences between men-only and diverse top management teams, and strong indications that diverse teams are 'more ready for investment', top management team diversity in and of itself does not help new ventures move through the angel investment decision-making process. For practitioners, our results suggest that while top management team diversity is purported to be positive, in terms of passing the stage-one, desk reject phase of the angel investment decision-making process and thus increasing the likelihood of obtaining early stage equity investment, our findings do not indicate that top management team diversity matters. In terms of readiness in general however, there are a few things that new ventures can do to enhance their readiness for funding such as protecting their IP, and securing a customer prior to applying for angel financing. In sum, our inquiry adds to the burgeoning literature on angel investment in general and in particular to the smaller but growing literature on women's entrepreneurial finance.

NOTE

1. There were 11 teams comprised of women only in our sample. Because of the small number of women-only TMTs (an interesting finding in and of itself), we could not run a three-group comparison (in other words, men-only teams relative to diverse teams and to women-only teams). We, therefore, excluded the women-only teams from the analysis. As a robustness check, we re-ran our analysis after adding the women-only teams to the 'diverse' group, with substantively the same results (not reported here because of space constraints and available from the authors upon request).

REFERENCES

Aldrich, H.E. and Fiol, C.M. (1994), 'Fools rush in? The institutional context of industry creation', *Academy of Management Review*, **19** (4): 645–670.
Amason, A.C. (1996), 'Distinguishing the effects of functional and dysfunctional conflict on strategic decision making: resolving a paradox for top management teams', *Academy of Management Journal*, **39** (1): 123–148.
Armenakis, A.A., Harris, S.G., and Mossholder, K.W. (1993), 'Creating readiness for organizational change', *Human Relations*, **46** (6): 681–703.
Becker-Blease, J.R. and Sohl, J. (2007), 'Do women-owned businesses have equal access to angel capital?', *Journal of Business Venturing*, **22** (4): 503–521.
Beckman, C.M. and Burton, M.D. (2008), 'Founding the future: path dependence in the evolution of top management teams from founding to IPO', *Organization Science*, **19** (1): 3–24.
Brush, C.G., Edelman, L.F., and Manolova T.S. (2012), 'Ready for funding? Growth-oriented ventures and the pursuit of angel financing', *Venture Capital: An International Journal of Entrepreneurial Finance*, **14** (2–3): 111–129.
Brush, C.G., Carter, N.M., Gatewood, E.J., Greene, P.G., and Hart, M.M. (2004), 'Gatekeepers of venture growth: a Diana Project Report on the role and participation of women in the venture capital industry', retrieved from http://sites.kauffman.org/pdf/diana_2004.pdf (accessed April 2014).
Coleman, S. (2000), 'Access to capital and terms of credit: a comparison of men and women owned businesses', *Journal of Small Business Management*, **38** (3): 37–52.
Douglas, E. and Shepherd, D. (2002), 'Exploring investor readiness: assessments by entrepreneurs and investors in Australia', *Venture Capital: An International Journal of Entrepreneurial Finance*, **4** (3): 219–236.
Eisenhardt, K.M. and Schoonhoven, C.B. (1990), 'Organizational growth: linking founding team, strategy, environment, and growth among US semiconductor ventures, 1978–1988', *Administrative Science Quarterly*, **35** (3): 504–529.
Ensley, M.D. and Hmieleski, K.M. (2005), 'A comparative study of new venture top

management team composition, dynamics and performance between university-based and independent start-ups', *Research Policy*, **34** (7): 1091–1105.

Freear, J., Sohl, J.E., and Wetzel, W. (2002), 'Angels on angels: financing technology-based ventures: a historical perspective', *Venture Capital: An International Journal of Entrepreneurial Finance*, **4** (2): 275–287.

Haar, N.E., Starr, J., and MacMillan, I.C. (1988), 'Informal risk capital investors: investment patterns on the east coast of the USA', *Journal of Business Venturing*, **3** (1): 11–29.

Haeussler, C., Harhoff, D., and Müller, E. (2009), 'To be financed or not . . . . The role of patents for venture capital financing', Working Paper 2009-02, retrieved from http://epub.ub.uni-muenchen.de/ (accessed April 2014).

Hall, J. and Hofer, C.W. (1993), 'Venture capitalists' decision criteria in new venture evaluation', *Journal of Business Venturing*, **8** (1): 25–42.

Hambrick, D.C. and Macmillan, I.C. (1985), 'Efficiency of product R&D in business units: the role of strategic context', *Academy of Management Journal*, **28** (3): 527–547.

Hambrick, D.C. and Mason, P.A. (1984), 'Upper echelons: the organization as a reflection of its top managers', *Academy of Management Review*, **9** (2): 193–206.

Harrison, R.T. and Mason, C.M. (1999), 'Editorial: an overview of informal venture capital research', *Venture Capital Journal: An International Journal of Entrepreneurial Finance*, **1** (2): 95–100.

Harrison, R.T., Mason, C.M., and Robson, P.J.A. (2010), 'Determinants of long-distance investing by business angels in the UK', *Entrepreneurship and Regional Development*, **22** (2): 113–137.

Heslop, L.A., McGregor, E., and Griffith, M. (2001), 'Development of a technology readiness assessment measure: the cloverleaf model of technology transfer', *Journal of Technology Transfer*, **26** (4): 369–384.

Jackson, S.E., May, K.E., and Whitney, K. (1995), 'Under the dynamics of diversity in decision-making teams', in R.A. Guzzo and E. Salas (eds), *Team Effectiveness and Decision Making in Organizations*, San Francisco, CA: Jossey-Bass, pp. 204–261.

Kaplan R.S. and Norton, D.P. (2004), 'Measuring the strategic readiness of intangible assets', *Harvard Business Review*, **82** (2): 52–63.

Keck, S.L. (1997), 'Top management team structure: differential effects by environmental context', *Organization Science*, **8** (2): 143–156.

Knight, D., Pearce, C.L., Smith, K.G., Olian, J.D., Sims, H.P., Smith, K.A., and Flood, P. (1999), 'Top management team diversity, group process, and strategic consensus', *Strategic Management Journal*, **20** (5): 445–465.

Lemley, M.A. (2001), 'Rational ignorance at the patent office', *Northwestern University Law Review*, **95** (4): 1497–1532.

Mankins, J.C. (1995), *Technology Readiness Levels*, White Paper prepared for the Advanced Concepts Office, Office of Space Access and Technology, NASA, retrieved from http://orion.asu.edu/Additional%20Reading/Mankins_trl.pdf (accessed April 2014).

Mason, C.M. and Harrison, R.T. (2003), 'Auditioning for money: what do technology investors look for at the initial screening stage?', *Journal of Private Equity*, **6** (2): 29–42.

Mason, C.M. and Harrison, R.T. (2004), 'Improving access to early stage venture capital in regional economies: a new approach to investment readiness', *Local Economy*, **19** (2): 159–173.

Mason, C.M. and Harrison, R.T. (2008), 'Measuring business angel investment activity in the United Kingdom: a review of potential data sources', *Venture Capital: An International Journal of Entrepreneurial Finance*, **10** (4): 309–330.

O'Reilly III, C.A., Caldwell, D.F., and Barnett, W.P. (1989), 'Work group demography, social integration, and turnover', *Administrative Science Quarterly*, **34** (1): 21–37.

Parasuraman, A. (2000), 'Technology Readiness Index (Tri)', *Journal of Service Research*, **2** (4): 307–320.

Prochaska J.O., Redding C.A., and Evers, K.E. (1997), 'The transtheoretical model and stages of change', in K. Glanz, F.M. Lewis and B.K. Rimer (eds), *Health Behavior and*

Health Education: Theory, Research and Practice (2nd edition), San Francisco, CA: Jossey-Bass, pp. 60–84.

Prochaska, J.O., Velicer, W.F., Rossi, J.S., Goldstein, M.G., Marcus, B.H., Rakowski, W., Fiore, C., Harlow, L.L., Redding, C.A., Rosenbloom, D., and Rossi, S.R. (1994), 'Stages of change and decisional balance for 12 problem behaviors', *Health Psychology*, **13** (1): 39–46.

Randel, A.E. and Jaussi, K.S. (2003), 'Functional background identity, diversity, and individual performance in cross-functional teams', *Academy of Management Journal*, **46** (6): 763–774.

Reynolds, P. and Miller, B. (1992), 'New firm gestation: conception, birth, and implications for research', *Journal of Business Venturing*, **7** (5): 405–417.

Reynolds, P., Bygrave, W., and Autio, E. (2003), *Global Entrepreneurship Monitor: Executive Report*, retrieved from http://www.gemconsortium.org/download/1311280723111/Replace mentFINAL ExecutiveReport.pdf (accessed April 2014).

Shane, S. and Cable, D. (2002), 'Network ties, reputation, and the financing of new ventures', *Management Science*, **48** (3): 364–381.

Sohl, J. (2005), *The Angel Investor Market in 2004*, University of New Hampshire, Centre for Venture Research, retrieved from www.unh.edu/news/docs/cvr2004.pdf (accessed April 2014).

Sohl, J. (2015), *The Angel Investor Market in 2014: A Market Correction in Deal Size*, Durham NH: Center for Venture Research, May 14, 2015.

Sosik, J.J. and Jung, D.I. (2002), 'Work-group characteristics and performance in collectivistic and individualistic cultures', *Journal of Social Psychology*, **142** (1): 5–23.

Stemler, S.E. (2004), 'A comparison of consensus, consistency, and measurement approaches to estimating interrater reliability', *Practical Assessment, Research & Evaluation*, **9** (4), retrieved from http://PAREonline.net/getvn.asp?v=9&n=4 (accessed August 2015).

Suchman, M.C. (1995), 'Managing legitimacy: strategic and institutional approaches', *Academy of Management Review*, **20** (3): 571–610.

Sudek, R. (2006), 'Angel investment criteria', *Journal of Small Business Strategy*, **17** (2): 89–103.

Ueda, M. (2004), 'Banks versus venture capital: project evaluation, screening, and expropriation', *The Journal of Finance*, **59** (2): 601–621.

Van Osnabrugge, M. and Robinson, R.J. (2000), *Angel Investing*, San Francisco, CA: Jossey-Bass.

Walske, J.M. and Zacharakis, A. (2009), 'Genetically engineered: why some venture capital firms are more successful than others', *Entrepreneurship Theory and Practice*, **33** (1): 297–318.

Weiler, S. and Bernasek, A. (2001), 'Dodging the glass ceiling? Networks and the new wave of women entrepreneurs', *Social Science Journal*, **38** (1): 85–110.

Wiersema, M.F. and Bantel, K.A. (1992), 'Top management team demography and corporate strategic change', *Academy of Management Journal*, **35** (1): 91–121.

Wiklund, J. and Shepherd, D. (2003), 'Knowledge-based resources, entrepreneurial orientation, and the performance of small and medium-sized businesses', *Strategic Management Journal*, **24** (13): 1307–1314.

Wiltbank, R. (2005), 'Investment practices and outcomes of informal venture investors', *Venture Capital: International Journal of Entrepreneurial Finance*, **7** (4): 343–357.

Wong, A. (2002), *Angel Finance: The Other Venture Capital*, unpublished PhD dissertation, University of Chicago, retrieved from http://papers.ssrn.com/sol3/papers.cfm?abstract_id=941228 (accessed April 2014).

Zimmerman, M.A. and Zeitz, G.J. (2002), 'Beyond survival: achieving new venture growth by building legitimacy', *Academy of Management Review*, **27** (3): 414–431.

Zucker, L.G. (1988), *Institutional Patterns and Organizations: Culture and Environment*, Pensacola FL: Ballinger Publishing.

APPENDIX

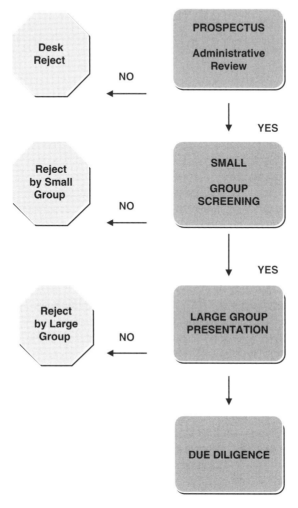

Figure 9A.1   Early stage angel investment decision-making process

10. Entrepreneurial finance of minority and migrant groups in Israel
Sibylle Heilbrunn and Nonna Kushnirovich

INTRODUCTION

Entrepreneurship among migrant and minority groups has growing significance for national and local economic and social development, since these populations are often disadvantaged in the labor market. Entrepreneurship and self-employment are, therefore, a bypass option for economic advancement and mobility for migrants and minorities. Entrepreneurship development is the cornerstone of successful economic development in general. Israel is characterized by its many cultures and ethnic and national groups (Heilbrunn et al., 2014b). Since immigration to Israel is ethnic, only Jews or members of their families can emigrate to Israel and obtain Israeli citizenship upon arrival. Therefore, in terms of ethnicity, immigrants to Israel are similar to the native majority, but are still different due to the culture of their country of origin. Israel perceives itself also as a democratic state, often described in terms of ethnocratic multiculturalism (Al-Haj, 2004) or as an ethno-nationalist country since, following the Law of Return, Jews entering the country have extensive rights and receive social acceptance (Bartram, 2011). Jewishness is the main sociopolitical indicator dividing Arabs and Jews; whereas pheno-typical and ethnic indicators are meaningful within the Jewish segment of society (Mizrachi and Herzog, 2012, p.419). Although there is a reality of multiplicity of cultures, subcultures and sectors, Israel is not a multi-cultural democracy in the classical sense (Kimmerling, 1998). As Smooha (2004) explains, normatively Zionism is not concerned with multicultural-ism. He maintains that when culture overlaps with class, cultural diversity inevitably turns into cultural hierarchy. Therefore, separate cultures such as the Ethiopian (even though Jewish) or the Arab Muslim culture might be a hindrance to social mobility.

Thus, the Israeli population is deeply divided along national, ethnic, and religious sectors (Al-Haj, 2004), with foreign-born persons (immi-grants) comprising about 21 percent of the total Israeli population, and Arab citizens, a national and ethnic minority, comprising about the same percentage (20.5 percent). Immigrants from the Former Soviet Union

(FSU) are the largest group that came within the last wave of immigration which began in 1989; they comprise about 80 percent of all immigrants who came to Israel in this period. FSU immigrants connect predominantly with co-ethnic individuals of the same origin (Kushnirovich, 2010; Litwin and Leshem, 2008; Remennick, 2004). As all Jewish immigrants to Israel, once they arrive in Israel, FSU immigrants are included in the social welfare system and mainstream societal context, and they have integrated well over the years in terms of education, labor market participation and political involvement (Semyonov et al., 2010). Over 69 percent of all FSU immigrants have at least some college education, whereas the percentage of college-educated among natives is only about 35 percent (HaCohen, 2002; Remennick, 2004). Thus, FSU immigrants who came to Israel in the 1990s constitute a highly skilled group with rich human assets as a major feature (HaCohen, 2002; Remennick, 2004).

The Ethiopian immigrants arrived in three waves: the first wave arrived in the mid-1980s, the second wave at the beginning of the 1990s, and the third wave is still ongoing. Since 1980, about 100,000 Ethiopian immigrants have arrived in Israel. The Ethiopian community is one of the poorest and most segregated communities in Israel, with extremely high levels of non-participation in the labor force, living in poverty and depending on welfare as their main source of livelihood. They also live primarily in disadvantaged neighborhoods (Offer, 2007; Dagan-Buzaglo, 2008). In addition, the blackness of Ethiopian immigrants positions them as the most visible minority among the Jewish Israeli population, thereby provoking for the first time a debate regarding race and Jewishness in Israel (Offer, 2007; Elias and Kemp,, 2010). Mizrachi and Herzog (2012) state that, although belonging as Jews to the dominant majority in Israel, their phenotype (being Black Jews) stigmatizes them and serves as the basis for discrimination.

Palestinian Arab citizens of Israel – named either Israeli Palestinians or Israeli Arabs – consist of approximately 20 percent of Israel's entire population. They constitute a distinct minority separated from the Jewish majority by national identity, religion, language, and culture (Heilbrunn et al., 2014b). The vast majority of the Israeli Arab population is Muslim with a minority of Christians and Druze (Ghanem, 2001; Mizrachi and Herzog, 2012). Formally included as citizens, as non-Jews, Israeli Arabs are socially excluded in terms of residence, land ownership, labor market participation, housing and political representation. Schnell and Sofer (2002) overview the literature on Jewish-Arab relations in Israel, and state that marginalization of the Arab population can be categorized into four main aspects: discriminatory state policies, a class structure that differentiates among ethnic groups, cultural and social-structural gaps, and socio-spatial segregation in the national and geographic periphery. In addition, in areas such as socio-economic status and education gaps continue to exist and the structural position of Arab citizens in Israeli Society limits their scope of participation to instrumental relations (Mizrachi and Herzog, 2012).

In this chapter we regard immigrant entrepreneurs as an immigrant business minority (as, for example, immigrants from the Former Soviet Union or from Ethiopia) and Israeli Arab entrepreneurs as an ethnic minority and investigate patterns of finance of these groups in comparison with the majority group. The chapter is constructed as follows. The next section provides the theoretical framework, and data collection and the methodology are then presented. Findings are presented, followed by conclusions and discussion in the last section.

THEORETICAL FRAMEWORK

In the academic literature, migrant and minority entrepreneurship have often been discussed in terms of structural push factors and cultural pull factors (Dana and Morris, 2007). This dichotomist approach is challenged by Kloosterman and Rath (2003) who maintain that when ethnic resources are mobilized in the presence of external constraints, a mixed embeddedness of structural constraints and cultural aspects evolves. Studies focusing on the impacts of gender, ethnicity and class on the entrepreneurial process (Brettell, 2007; Robinson et al., 2007; Heilbrunn et al., 2014a, 2014b) rely on the sociological notion of stratification in society (Weber, 1920/1978; Giddens, 2006; Marger, 2010) proposing that social stratification is the outcome of institutional processes that divide societies into advantaged and disadvantaged socially constructed groups (Robinson et al., 2007). The basis for social stratification includes groupings by gender, race, ethnicity, religion, nationality, wealth and class and emerging advantages and/or disadvantages of groups are often reinforced by the accumulation of power and resources by the advantaged group over time (Heilbrunn et al., 2014a). Robinson et al. (2007) maintain that stratification encounters entrepreneurship (at different intersections) where the latter is perceived as a means of social mobility, and where programs and/or support systems exist that aim at improving the situation of particular groups, often as an alternative to labor market entrance. Furthermore, the authors stress the fact that social stratification influences the entire entrepreneurial process, particularly for low-status groups. Assuming that social stratification based on race, ethnicity, gender or other characteristics influences the entrepreneurial process in general, and financing patterns in particular, we investigated the financing patterns of four groups of entrepreneurs in Israel. Furthermore, as a theoretical framework for investigating financing patterns of immigrants and minorities we use the literature on disadvantage. Individuals and groups that are disadvantaged and victims of discrimination often face resource and labor market constraints (Light and Rosenstein, 1995). Labor market constraints result from racial, gender, or ethnic discrimination, which is not necessarily related to the productivity of the group and resource disadvantage, occurs when a group struggling to enter the labor market has fewer adequate resources such as human capital, networks, and self-confidence (Light and Rosenstein, 1995). Labor market disadvantage stems from un- or under-employment, illegal status, lack of language proficiency, low educational qualifications (Valenzuela, 2001), and racism and discrimination (Lazaridis and Koumandraki, 2003). While restricted opportunity structures in the labor market often push people into self-employment, the same restrictions also constitute constraints when setting up a business (Jamali, 2009; Volery, 2007). Thus the disadvantage theory can explain the fact that in many societies, minorities and migrants have high rates of business ownership (Horton and De Jong, 1991; Smith-Hunter and Boyd, 2004), due to segregated labor markets that exclude minorities.

Immigrant and minority entrepreneurs encounter more barriers throughout the entrepreneurial process than do native-born entrepreneurs and have particular difficulties in obtaining initial capital (Constant, 2004; Pearce, 2005). Many studies provide evidence that they are discriminated in the small business credit market (Blanchflower et al., 2003; Cavalluzzo et al., 2002; Cavalluzzo and Wolken, 2005). Black entrepreneurs in the US were twice as likely to be denied credit in comparison to white entrepreneurs, after controlling for creditworthiness and additional factors (Blanchflower et al., 2003; Bruder et al., 2011). Studies conducted in the UK are less definite as to the disadvantage of ethnic entrepreneurs. Smallbone et al. (2003) found differences between non-ethnic and ethnic minority businesses' access to finance and business support but even more differences between ethnic minority groups. Their study revealed that African-Caribbean owned businesses were the most disadvantaged. Ram et al. (2003) concluded that access to bank credit continues to be problematic for ethnic minority businesses and also report on perceived discrimination based on racism. Fraser (2007) found that ethnic factors did not explain financial rejection but his results indicate discouragement among ethnic businesses. Hussain and Matlay (2007) reported that family and close associate networks were evaluated as very important for the support of ethnic minority owner-managers but the authors found the same results for non-ethnic owner-managers. The results of their qualitative study revealed that ethnic minority entrepreneurs reported less need for borrowing from bank institutions over the years and that they preferred more 'user friendly' financing options (ibid). In a study conducted in Germany, Lehnert (2002) revealed that immigrants perceived obtaining loans as a major obstacle twice as much as natives and that a higher percentage of immigrant businesses (22 percent versus 14 percent for natives) were financially restricted. In Germany about 80 percent of ethnic entrepreneurs finance their businesses with loans from friends and families or with personal savings (Bruder et al., 2011).

Leaning on the theoretical concept of resource disadvantage, based on the empirical findings and taking into account the Israeli context, we assume that migrant and minority entrepreneurs will have more difficulties acquiring financial resources for setting up their businesses than native born persons belonging to the majority. In order to investigate this assumption, we lean upon a classification of funding sources developed by Kushnirovich and Heilbrunn (2008) for immigrants' business (Table 10.1). This classification is relevant also for ethnic minorities since it relates to the ethnic character of the sources. According to this classification, all financial sources can be divided along the lines of formality and informality, and along ethnic and non-ethnic lines. Because of the capital constraints that are typical for business minorities and due to the fact that their social ties are often co-ethnic, minority entrepreneurs are more

Table 10.1   Funding sources for immigrant (and ethnic) businesses

	Personal savings:		
Equity	– money brought from the home country	Informal	Ethnic
	– money saved in the host country		Non-ethnic
Debt	Family		Ethnic
	Friends		Ethnic
	Rotating credit associations		Ethnic
	Government financial support	Formal	Non-ethnic
	Bank loans:		
	– non-ethnic commercial banking		Non-ethnic
	– ethnic banking		Ethnic
	Credit company		Non-ethnic
	Trade credit (business associates):		
	– from ethnic suppliers		Ethnic
	– from non-ethnic suppliers		Non-ethnic
	Miscellaneous sources		Non-ethnic

Source: Kushnirovich and Heilbrunn (2008).

likely to mobilize ethnic sources in order to finance their businesses. They also have access to specific formal sources intended for ethnic minorities' financial support from state schemes/donors on favourable terms. Thus, ethnic minorities should utilize informal ethnic sources and formal state schemes more than ethnic majorities.

DATA COLLECTION

The research population consisted of four groups of entrepreneurs: three groups of ethnic minority entrepreneurs and a reference group of Israeli-born entrepreneurs who represented the ethnic majority:

1. Israeli-born Jewish entrepreneurs who were regarded as the ethnic majority.
2. FSU immigrants who were regarded as an immigrant minority.
3. Immigrants from Ethiopia who were regarded as an immigrant minority.
4. Israeli Arabs who were regarded as an ethnic minority.

All respondents owned operating businesses at the time they responded to our questionnaire. The questionnaire was submitted in geographic locations all over the country.

Data collection was based on a combination of convenience and snow-ball sampling. The questionnaire included closed and open questions and was presented to the respondents in their native language. In order to control for misunderstandings and inconsistencies due to the translation process, we used the method of back-translation (Del Greco et al., 1987; Baker, 2011). We asked translators of the three groups (FSU, Ethiopian and Arab Israeli) who were not aware of the original questionnaire to translate the questions back into the original language (Hebrew). We then compared the back-translation with the original questionnaire, and examined discrepancies. A couple of questions were redrafted as a result of this process. Finally, research assistants belonging to the respective group (FSU, Ethiopian and Arab Israeli) submitted the questionnaires in person to the respondents, so that they were able to ask questions during the process. It took the respondents an average of 30 minutes to answer the questions.

We collected the data in three steps. In 2006 we surveyed 281 Israeli-born Jewish entrepreneurs and 218 FSU immigrant entrepreneurs. During 2010 we surveyed 350 Israeli-born Arab entrepreneurs, and in 2012 we surveyed 99 immigrants from Ethiopia. In total, our sample included 948 entrepreneurs. Although there is a six year gap between some interviews, these years were very similar with regard to the macroeconomic and business situation.[1] Since the Israeli labor force in this period was nearly 2.5 million persons, at the time of examination the minority groups (FSU and Ethiopian immigrants and Israeli Arabs) comprised about 40 percent of the labor force. At the same time the rates of entrepreneurship were about 12 percent among native-born Jews and about 5 percent among immigrants. Minority entrepreneurs in our sample represent nearly 1.4 percent of all minority entrepreneurs in Israel.

FINDINGS

Characteristics of Minority Businesses and their Owners

The groups of entrepreneurs differ in terms of human capital. FSU immigrant entrepreneurs are more educated than their counterparts; 56.3 percent of them have at least undergraduate academic education, while only 14.1 percent of the immigrants from Ethiopia and 16.6 percent of Israeli Arab entrepreneurs have academic degrees. Among Israeli-born Jewish entrepreneurs, 45.5 percent of entrepreneurs have academic education. Thus, immigrants from the FSU can be regarded as a high-skilled ethnic minority entrepreneurs, and immigrants from the Ethiopia and Israeli Arabs as low-skilled ethnic minority entrepreneurs.

The characteristics of businesses owned by minority entrepreneurs also differ significantly from those owned by non-minority entrepreneurs (Table 10.2).

Immigrant entrepreneurs, both from the FSU and from Ethiopia, are less likely to be engaged in production than the other two groups of entrepreneurs. Ethnic minority entrepreneurs (Israeli Arabs) are overrepresented in commerce and underrepresented in providing personal services. Low-skilled groups (both immigrants from Ethiopia and Israeli Arabs) are not engaged in financial and professional services.

Minority-owned businesses are smaller in terms of employees than those of non-minority ones, with ranges from 0.6 to 2.7 employees within different groups of ethnic minorities versus 5.6 employees for businesses owned by Israeli-born entrepreneurs. Minority-owned businesses are co-ethnic oriented in terms of their clients, workers, suppliers and partners. More than a half of their clients and suppliers, and almost all workers and partners, are from the same immigrant or ethnic community.

Table 10.2 Characteristics of businesses

Business characteristics	Groups of entrepreneurs				Test
	Israeli-born Jewish entrepreneurs	FSU immigrants	Immigrants from Ethiopia	Israeli Arabs	
Type of business:	100%	100%	100%	100%	χ^2 = 205.664***
commerce	30.9	41.0	41.4	65.2	
production	10.2	2.3	0.0	8.8	
personal services	35.3	39.2	43.4	26.0	
financial services	3.6	3.2	0.0	0.0	
professional services	14.9	12.9	0.0	0.0	
other	5.1	1.4	15.2	0.0	
Size of business in terms of employees	5.6	2.7	1.2	0.6	F = 43.084***
Mean duration of business activity, years	5.7	5.6	4.6	10.3	F = 56.411***
Businesses located at home	34.1	22.3	42.3	32.4	χ^2 = 23.462**
Education of business owner:	100%	100%	100%	100%	χ^2 = 278.079***
up to 12 years of schooling	2.5	0.5	21.2	7.7	
12 years schooling	28.0	9.3	34.3	16.3	
vocational studies	24.0	34.0	30.3	59.4	
undergraduate degree	31.3	25.1	13.1	13.4	
graduate degree	12.7	29.3	1.0	1.4	
doctoral degree	1.5	1.9	0.0	1.7	
Share of co-ethnic clients, %	–	72.2	97.0	59.0	F = 60.964***
Share of co-ethnic workers, %	–	95.1	100.0	99.7	F = 330.758****
Share of co-ethnic suppliers, %	–	53.0	78.0	67.2	F = 14.409****
Share of co-ethnic partners, %	–	81.4	100.0	100.0	F = 40.583***

Access of Entrepreneurs to Funds

As most scholars stress, the main peculiarity of minority entrepreneurship is capital constraints. Minority entrepreneurs encounter many barriers when mobilizing capital for setting up a business, because their income and savings that could be used as loan collaterals are often lower than those of the local majority population. Taking into account socioeconomic circumstances, they might not even have a personal banking track record. Thus, minority entrepreneurs are disadvantaged when trying to receive bank loans. Therefore, we examined whether minority entrepreneurs encounter more problems than non-minority ones when trying to obtain funds for setting up their businesses (Table 10.3).

The study revealed that minority entrepreneurs, both immigrant and ethnic, have more difficulties when accessing start-up capital. Immigrants from Ethiopia experienced the most overall problems (85.0 percent), followed by Israeli Arabs with 68.4 percent of entrepreneurs reporting on problems when seeking capital. Slightly more than half of the FSU immigrants (55.9 percent) had difficulties accessing capital and Israeli-born Jewish entrepreneurs reported the lowest rate (39.5 percent).

There is no significant difference among the groups in their application for bank loans, but there are substantial differences as to receiving a loan (Table 10.3). While almost all majority entrepreneurs received bank loans (95.5 percent), only about a half of minority entrepreneurs managed to obtain bank loans (49.3 percent of FSU immigrants, 40.5 percent of the immigrants from Ethiopia, and 49.7 percent of the Israeli Arabs). This is in spite of the fact that minority entrepreneurs asked for significantly lower sums. We conducted a post-hoc Scheffe test that indicated no differences in the requested sum of the loan between the groups of minority entrepreneurs. However, the test confirms a significant difference between native-born Jewish entrepreneurs and all groups of minority business owners.

The most frequently reported reason for refusal among FSU immigrants is a lack of collateral for receiving a bank loan. Immigrants from Ethiopia reported about two prominent reasons for not receiving the loan: (1) problems related to a bank account (overdraft, large credit commitments etc.); and (2) prejudice. For Israeli Arabs, there is no one outstanding reason; their answers are distributed almost evenly. Since the study is based on self-reported survey responses from entrepreneurs, we cannot know the real reasons for refusals by banks such as the bank's assessment of the viability of businesses and the risk of the non-repayment of loans. But the previous studies found that visible minorities in Israel believed that they were being discriminated against and that prejudice and discrimination

Table 10.3   Problems when recruiting funds

	Groups of entrepreneurs				Test
	Israeli-born Jewish entrepreneurs	FSU immigrants	Immigrants from Ethiopia	Israeli Arabs	
% encountered problems when recruiting start-up funds	39.5	55.9	85.0	68.4	χ^2 = 64.178***
% applied for a bank loan	55.8	49.3	40.5	49.7	NS
% received the loan (from those who applied)	95.5	73.0	45.2	26.1	χ^2 = 108.651***
Mean sum of the loan asked, NIS	104,667	44,302	19,484	25,977	F = 29.485***
Grounds for refusal (if refused):	100%	100%	100%	100%	χ^2 = 17.965**
– lack of collaterals[1]	n.a.	42.9	0.0	25.0	
– bank account related reasons (overdraft, large credit commitments etc.)	n.a.	14.3	52.9	28.1	
– prejudice	n.a.	21.4	47.1	22.9	
– other	n.a.	21.4	0.0	24.0	
Reasons for not seeking bank loan:	100%	100%	100%	100%	χ^2 = 134.060***
– no need	82.4	75.7	34.0	15.3	
– did not dare to ask	3.9	13.5	25.5	32.6	
– did not know how to ask	5.9	1.4	40.4	25.7	
– other	7.8	9.5	0.0	26.4	

Note: 1. Asset or property that borrower pledges when getting a loan. If borrower doesn't repay the loan, the lender is entitled to take collateral and sell it to regain the debt.

175

constrain them in the labor market and in business (Heilbrunn et al., 2010; Lipshits-Braziler and Tatar, 2012).

We also found differences in the reasons for not asking for a bank loan. The native-born and FSU immigrant entrepreneurs did not apply for a bank loan because they did not need it. Low-skilled minority entrepreneurs on the other hand needed a loan, but reported on lacking of information or did not dare to ask for it. About 40 percent of immigrants from Ethiopia did not know how to ask, and nearly a third of Israeli Arab entrepreneurs did not dare to ask. In terms of Han et al. (2009), these groups might be 'discouraged borrowers' who do not apply for loans because they feel that they will be rejected.

Sources of Financing and Scope of Capital of Business at Start-up

Minority entrepreneurs differ from the ethnic majority by the scope and sources of capital for setting up their businesses (Kushnirovich and Heilbunn, 2008). Table 10.4 shows the scope of initial investments of the different groups. Minority entrepreneurs invested less in their businesses than non-minority entrepreneurs did. Nearly half of Israeli-born entrepreneurs (47 percent) invested more than 50,000 Israeli New Shekel (NIS)

Table 10.4   Scope of investment of minority and non-minority entrepreneurs[1]

Scope of investment (in NIS[2])	Groups of entrepreneurs			
	Israeli-born Jewish entrepreneurs	FSU immigrants	Immigrants from Ethiopia	Israeli Arabs
No investment was made	3.7	6.0	24.5	13.6
up to 5,000	9.5	12.1	0.0	23.1
5,001–10,000	12.1	14.9	67.3	33.2
10,001–25,000	11.4	18.1	2.0	1.0
25,001–50,000	16.5	25.6	4.1	26.6
50,001–100,000	17.6	16.3	2.0	2.5
100,001–250,000	17.2	5.6	0.0	0.0
250,001–500,000	7.0	0.9	0.0	0.0
501,000–1,000,000	2.6	0.0	0.0	0.0
more than 1,000,000	2.6	0.5	0.0	0.0
Total	100%	100%	100%	100%

Notes:
1. 1 $ USA = 3.5 NIS.
2. $\chi2$ = 302.262, Sig. = 0.000.

in their businesses, while only a quarter (23.3 percent) of FSU immigrant entrepreneurs, and about 2 percent of Ethiopian immigrants and Israeli Arabs invested a similar amount. Immigrants from Ethiopia and Israeli Arabs were more likely to make no financial investment in their businesses at all (13.6 percent of immigrants from Ethiopia and 13.6 percent of Israeli Arabs versus 3.7 percent of Israeli-born entrepreneurs and 6.0 percent of FSU immigrants). Thus, capital constraints and problems when mobilizing start-up capital lead to the lower levels of initial investments in businesses owned by both ethnic and immigrant minorities.

When controlling for the type of business,[2] the ANOVA model revealed significant differences between types in terms of scope of investment (F = 5.942; sig. = .001). Owners of businesses providing personal services invested significantly less than all other business owners. Financial and professional services, which rated highest for the entire sample in terms of the scope of investment, are absent among Ethiopian and Arab Israeli entrepreneurs (see Table 10.2). Thus, when investigating the scope of investment along types of businesses and group, we can conclude that the impact of group affiliation is stronger than the impact of the type of business.

Relevant financial sources for Israeli entrepreneurs are personal savings, family, friends, bank loans and government financial support (see Table 10.2). Table 10.5 shows the sources of start-up capital for the businesses in our sample. The complementary value of each cell constitutes the share of entrepreneurs who reported obtaining capital from the specific source. Therefore, the total percentage can be over 100 because respondents may have more than one source.

Table 10.5   The sources of capital for setting up business

Financial sources	Groups of entrepreneurs				Test
	Israeli-born Jewish entrepreneurs	FSU immigrants	Immigrants from Ethiopia	Israeli Arabs	
Personal savings	88.5	78.6	59.2	57.3	$\chi^2 = 68.1***$
Family	20.2	22.6	71.8	89.4	$\chi^2 = 293.2***$
Friends	11.1	3.1	24.7	5.8	$\chi^2 = 32.4***$
Bank	29.3	31.7	17.3	12.8	$\chi^2 = 32.151***$
State schemes/ donors	12.3	2.5	21.3	9.6	$\chi^2 = 22.3***$

Note: *The values in the cells represent the percentage of respondents who reported use of specific source.

We found that the different groups of entrepreneurs finance their businesses from various sources. Moreover, the patterns of financing for setting up a business are different between the groups. Taking into account the data on education and type of businesses, it is not surprising that FSU immigrant entrepreneurs are more similar to the Israeli-born persons than Israeli-born Arabs or immigrants from Ethiopia. Immigrants from Ethiopia and Israeli Arabs more often receive finance from their families and are less likely to rely on their personal savings than FSU immigrants and Israeli-born entrepreneurs. However, as for other sources of start-up capital, there are differences between all groups. Immigrants from Ethiopia seek finance from their friends in order to mobilize capital more often than other groups of entrepreneurs, with about a quarter of them (24.7 percent) using this source.

Among the other groups, only a few received capital from friends (3.1 percent of FSU immigrants, 5.8 percent of Israeli Arabs and 11.1 percent of the Israeli-born Jewish entrepreneurs).

A bank loan is a popular source among all groups of entrepreneurs. Immigrants from Ethiopia and Israeli Arabs are less likely to use bank loans than other FSU and Israeli born entrepreneurs (12.8 percent and 17.3 percent respectively reported using this source). Nearly a third of Israeli-born entrepreneurs and FSU immigrants received bank loans when mobilizing start-up capital, whereas immigrants from Ethiopia (21.3 percent) are more likely to finance their businesses by receiving financial support from state schemes/donors. Financial support means designated loans on favorable terms that can be received from government agencies fostering entrepreneurship or from private funds that support specific groups of entrepreneurs (women, immigrants, people with disabilities etc.). Although Israeli-born entrepreneurs represent the ethnic majority, about 12.3 percent of them manage to receive financial support from state schemes/donors. This is more than FSU immigrants and Israeli Arabs who are the target groups of many of these schemes. One possible explanation for this could be familiarity with existing frameworks of support and higher ability to use it and achieve such support. FSU immigrants utilize this source to a very limited extent, which can be explained either through unfamiliarity with existing opportunities or a disinclination to apply to official institutions and funds that provide such assistance. Future research should attempt to clarify this issue.

According to the classification of funding sources of Kushnirovich and Heilbrunn (2008), family and friends are ethnic sources of finance, and public financial support encompasses a specific source for ethnic minorities that is designed to provide group-specific support. Our study revealed that immigrants from Ethiopia, who are the lowest-skilled and smallest group tend to invest less when setting-up a business and are more likely to mobilize start-up capital from both ethnic sources (family and friends) and specific sources (public schemes/donors) than the other groups of entrepreneurs. Also Israeli Arabs rely mostly on ethnic sources (family, but not friends). However, they use state schemes less than Ethiopians and the native ethnic majority. FSU immigrants used ethnic sources to a similar extent to majority entrepreneurs, and did not utilize target-specific support sources. This conclusion is consistent with our previous studies on the FSU immigrant entrepreneurs (Heilbrunn and Kushnirovich, 2007; Kushnirovich and Heilbrunn, 2008).

Financial Viability

The success of a business can be expressed in terms of business growth. If profit, number of clients and number of employees increased in the preceding years, business can be regarded as successful and viable finan-cially; decrease of the parameters can be a symptom of impending failure. Based on Lerner and Khavul (2003), we constructed an index of growth as described in Heilbrunn and Kushnirovich (2008). This index is calculated as a mean value of change that has occurred in profit, number of custom-ers and sales revenue during the year preceding the survey. The values of the index for different groups of entrepreneurs are as follows: 2.6 for Israeli-born Jewish entrepreneurs, 2.5 for FSU immigrants, 1.9 for immi-grants from Ethiopia and 2.0 for business owned by Israeli Arabs ($F = 4.756$, $p = 0.005$). Thus, the study revealed that the index of growth of minority entrepreneurs is lower than that of the native-born majority but varies within the groups.

CONCLUSIONS AND DISCUSSION

The overall patterns of financing businesses owned by minorities differ from those of ethnic majority entrepreneurs. These differences are expressed in access to start-up capital and financial constraints, sources of financial funds, scope of investments, and financial viability.

   In line with disadvantage theory, our study revealed that minority entre-preneurs encounter more problems than non-minority ones in obtaining funds for setting up their businesses. Although minority entrepreneurs asked for significantly less money than the business majority, their loan applications were less often approved than those of native-born entre-preneurs. This means that ethnic minorities need bank loans to the same extent as the ethnic majority but have difficulties in obtaining them.

Hence, our study revealed that problems accessing bank loans are affected by the affiliation of entrepreneurs to ethnic and immigrant groups, and minority entrepreneurs are disadvantaged when seeking bank loans. In the case of the Ethiopian and Israeli Arab entrepreneurs, the results of our study represents a classic case of resource disadvantage. Further investigation is needed concerning the group of FSU immigrants, who rate high on human capital, belong to the Jewish majority but nevertheless received significantly less bank loans than majority entrepreneurs.

The most frequently reported grounds for refusal are a lack of collateral and perceived prejudice. Especially for the Ethiopians, who constitute a visible minority with low human capital, perceived prejudice is the predominant reason for not receiving bank loans. Ethnic minority business owners, especially low-skilled, sometimes do not apply for a bank loan. The main reasons for this seems to be the fact that they do not know how to apply or do not dare to apply because they think that they would be refused. Thus, in line with Fraser (2007) we found that ethnic factors did not necessarily explain financial rejection but indicate discouragement among ethnic minority owned businesses. Future research should investigate these dynamics and attempt to determine whether non-application is demand failure in terms of poor application or is related to perception of discrimination of the business minorities.

Financial constraints and disadvantages when mobilizing capital result in the fact that minority entrepreneurs invest less in the start-up stage than the ethnic majority. We also found that various groups of entrepreneurs finance their business from different sources. Low-skilled ethnic minorities, namely immigrants from Ethiopia and Israeli Arabs, are more likely to use informal ethnic sources for mobilizing start-up capital, such as their families and friends, and are less likely to rely on their personal savings and bank loans than high-skilled FSU immigrants and native-born entrepreneurs. Designated loans on favorable terms are a specific source intended to be used by business minorities. Immigrants from Ethiopia managed to receive more financial support from state schemes/donors than all other groups of ethnic minorities. This can be explained by the dedicated work of public institutions providing support to this group of immigrants who are considered to belong to the Jewish majority of the country and are, therefore, subject to state-schemes aimed at improving their overall situation. Israeli-born entrepreneurs who form the ethnic majority, as well as Israeli Arabs, also managed to receive financial support from state schemes/donors. This might be due to their greater experience in Israel and hence familiarity with the existing framework of support and their high ability to deal within it. FSU immigrants are the only group that overall avoids this source of finance; future studies should investigate whether general aversion of state schemes, resulting from the FSU culture, simple unfamiliarity with these opportunities, or maybe both, are reasons for this aversion. Smaller start-up capital, unfamiliarity with existing opportunities in the local financial markets and co-ethnic orientation lead to lower financial viability of businesses owned by minority entrepreneurs than of those owned by majority entrepreneurs.

Concerning some characteristics of financing businesses, FSU immigrant entrepreneurs are more similar to the Israeli-born persons than Israeli-born Arabs or immigrants from Ethiopia. We found some similarities in success in receiving bank loans, reasons for not seeking a loan, sources of capital (using ethnic sources and bank loans), and even regarding the financial viability of businesses. The common characteristic of these two groups is their relatively higher level of education. In the case of FSU immigrants, it seems that education influences the finance of businesses sometimes in a stronger way than ethnic differences or being an immigrant. At the same time, as we explained in the introduction to this chapter, Jewishness is the main sociopolitical indicator dividing Arabs and Jews, whereas phenotypical and ethnic indicators are meaningful within the Jewish segment of society (Mizrachi and Herzog, 2012). Thus, the non-majority groups in our sample are heterogeneous offering a variety of findings, which is in line with other studies (Jones et al., 2014; Ram and Jones, 2008; Fairlie and Meyer, 2014; Smallbone et al., 2010).

Sociopolitical wise and along the lines of ethnic indicators, FSU immigrants belong to the Jewish dominant majority. Thus, they are not structurally disadvantaged. Nevertheless, it seems that education can smooth the gaps deriving from being from an ethnic minority. Future research on the two immigrant groups – FSU and Ethiopian immigrants to Israel – should, therefore, take into account acculturation of the first generations by their degree of education. Overall, our findings indicate that stratification encounters entrepreneurship also in financing patterns. Within the Israeli context, internal (education) and external (institutional) constraints lead to lower availability of financial resources, distributed and available along the lines of the social hierarchy of the groups under investigation.

NOTES

1. The net rates of new businesses (opened business minus closed business as a percentage of the total stock of businesses) were almost the same in these years: 2.2 percent in 2006, 2.6 percent in 2010 and 2.0 percent in 2012. These years were the years of very similar

economic growth rates (5.8 percent in 2006, 5.8 percent in 2010, and 3.0 percent in 2012) and rates of unemployment (8.4, 6.6. and 6.9 percent in 2006, 2010 and 2012 respectively). Thus, in spite of the time gap, the survey data in these years can be compared.
2.   We recoded the six types of businesses into four major types.

REFERENCES

Al-Haj, M. (2004), 'The political culture of the 1990's immigrants from the Former Soviet Union in Israel and their views towards the indigenous Arab Minority: a case of ethnocratic multiculturalism', *Journal of Ethnic and Migration Studies*, **30** (4): 682–696.
Baker, M. (2011), *In Other Words: A Course Book on Translation*, London: Routledge.
Bartram, D. (2011), 'Migration, ethno-nationalist destinations and social divisions: non-Jewish Immigrants in Israel', *Ethnopolitics*, **10** (2): 235–252.
Blanchflower, D.G., Levine, P.B., and Zimmerman, D.J. (2003), 'Discrimination in the small-business credit market', *Review of Economics and Statistics*, **85** (4): 930–943.
Brettell, C.B. (2007), 'Immigrant women in small business: biographies of becoming entrepreneurs', in L-P. Dana (ed.), *Handbook of Research on Ethnic Minority Entrepreneurship*, Cheltenham, UK and Northampton, MA, USA: Edward Elgar Publishing, pp. 83–98.
Bruder, J., Neuberger, D., and Räthke-Döppner, S. (2011), 'Financial constraints of ethnic entrepreneurship: evidence from Germany', *International Journal of Entrepreneurial Behavior and Research*, **17** (3): 296–313.
Cavalluzzo, K. and Wolken, J. (2005), 'Small business loan turndowns, personal wealth, and discrimination', *The Journal of Business*, **78** (6): 2153–2178.
Cavalluzzo, K., Cavalluzzo, L.C., and Wolken, J. D. (2002), 'Competition, small business financing, and discrimination: evidence from a new survey', *The Journal of Business*, **75** (4): 641–679.
Constant, A. (2004), 'Immigrant versus native businesswoman: proclivity and performance', Discussion Paper No. 1234, Bonn: Institute for the Study of Labor (IZA).
Dagan-Buzaglo, N. (2008), Non-discriminatory hiring practices in Israel towards Arab Citizens, Ethiopian Israelis and new immigrants form Bukhara and the Caucasus, Tel Aviv: ADVA Information on Equality and Social Justice in Israel.
Dana, L. and Morris, M. (2007), 'Towards a synthesis: a model of immigrant and ethnic entrepreneurship', in L-P. Dana (ed.), *Handbook of Research on Ethnic Minority Entrepreneurship*, Cheltenham, UK and Northampton, MA, USA: Edward Elgar Publishing, pp. 803–811.
Del Greco, L., Walop, W., and Eastridge, L. (1987), 'Questionnaire development: 3. Translation', *CMAJ: Canadian Medical Association Journal*, **136** (8): 817–818.
Elias, N. and Kemp, A. (2010), 'The new second generation: non-Jewish olim, black Jews and children of migrant workers in Israel', *Israeli Studies*, **15** (1): 73–94.
Fairlie, R. and Meyer, B.D. (2014), Ethnic and racial self-employment differences and possible explanations. UC Santa Cruz: Department of Economics, UCSC, retrieved from https://escholarship.org/uc/item/24p7v6gc (accessed April 29, 2015).
Fraser, S. (2007), Finance for small and medium size enterprises: comparison of ethnic minority and white owned businesses: a report on the 2005 UK survey of SME finances of ethnic minority, Booster Survey, Coventry: Center for Small and Medium-Sized Enterprises, University of Warwick.
Ghanem, A. (2001), *The Palestinian-Arab Minority in Israel, 1948–2000: A Political Study* New York NY: State University of New York Press.
Giddens, A. (2006), *Sociology* (5th edition), Cambridge: Polity Press.
Hacohen, D. (2002), 'Mass immigration and the demographic revolution in Israel', *Israel Affairs*, **8** (1–2): 177–190.
Han, L., Fraser, S., and Storey, D.J. (2009), 'Are good or bad borrowers discouraged from applying for loans? Evidence from US small business credit markets', *Journal of Banking and Finance*, **33** (2): 415–424.

Heilbrunn, S. and Kushnirovich, N. (2007), 'Immigrant and indigenous enterprises: similarities and differences', *International Journal of Business Performance Management*, **9** (3): 344–361.

Heilbrunn S. and Kushnirovich, N. (2008), 'Impact of ethnicity on financing of immigrant businesses', *International Journal of Business and Globalization*, **2** (2): 146–159.

Heilbrunn, S., Abu-Asbeh, K., and Abu, M. (2014a), 'Difficulties facing women entrepreneurs in Israel: a social stratification approach', *International Journal of Gender and Entrepreneurship*, **6** (2): 142–162.

Heilbrunn, S., Davidovitch, L., and Achdut, L. (2014b), 'Social cohesion in Israel: differences between migrants and minorities', in S. Boyd and M.A. Walker (eds), *Cultural Difference and Social Solidarity: Solidarities and Social Function*, Cambridge: Cambridge Scholars Publishing, pp. 98–111.

Heilbrunn, S., Kushnirovich, N., and Zeltzer-Zubida, A. (2010), 'Barriers to immigrants' integration into the labor market: modes and coping', *International Journal of Intercultural Relations*, **34** (3): 244–252.

Horton, H. and De Jong, G. (1991), 'Black entrepreneurs: a socio-demographic analysis', *Research in Race and Ethnic Relations*, **6** (fall): 105–120.

Hussain, J. and Matlay, H. (2007), 'Financing preferences of ethnic minority owner/manag ers in the UK', *Journal of Small Business and Enterprise Development*, **14** (3): 487–500.

Jamali, D. (2009), 'Constraints and opportunities facing women entrepreneurs in developing countries: a relational perspective', *Gender in Management: An International Journal*, **24** (4): 232–251.

Jones, T., Ram, M., Edwards, P., Kiselinchev, A., and Muchenje, L. (2014), 'Mixed embeddedness and new migrant enterprise in the UK', *Entrepreneurship and Regional Development*, **26** (5–6): 500–520.

Kimmerling, B. (1998), 'The new Israelis – multiplicity of cultures without multiculturalism', *Alpayim*, **16**: 264–308.

Kloosterman, R.C. and Rath, J.C. (eds) (2003), *Immigrant Entrepreneurs: Venturing Abroad in the in the Age of Globalization*, Oxford: Berg.

Kushnirovich, N. (2010), 'Ethnic niches and immigrants' integration', *International Journal of Sociology and Social Policy*, **30** (7/8): 412–426.

Kushnirovich, N. and Heilbrunn, S. (2008), 'Financial funding of immigrant business', *Journal of Developmental Entrepreneurship*, **13** (2): 167–184.

Lazaridis, G. and Koumandraki, M. (2003), 'Entrepreneurs in Greece: a mosaic of informal and formal business activities', *Sociological Research Online*, **8** (2), retrieved from http://www.socresonline.org.uk/8/2/lazaridis.html (accessed April 29, 2015).

Lehnert, N. (2002), 'Existenzgründungen durch Migranten in Deutschland. Ergebnisse des DtA-Gründungsmonitors 2002', *Wirtschaftsdynamik durch Existenzgründungen von Migranten*, Bonn: 35–54.

Lerner, M. and Khavul, S. (2003), 'Beating the odds in immigrant entrepreneurship: how does founder human capital compare to institutional capital in improving the survival of immigrant owned businesses?', Working Paper No. 4/2003, *Babson College*, Babson Park, MA.

Light, I.H. and Rosenstein, C. (1995), *Race, Ethnicity, and Entrepreneurship in Urban America*, New Brunswick, NJ: Transaction Publishers.

Lipshits-Braziler, Y. and Tatar, M. (2012), 'Perceived career barriers and coping among youth in Israel: ethnic and gender differences', *Journal of Vocational Behavior*, **80** (2): 545–554.

Litwin, H. and Leshem, E. (2008), 'Late-life migration, work status, and survival: the case of older immigrants from the Former Soviet Union in Israel', *International Migration Review*, **42** (4): 903–925.

Marger, M. (2010), *Social Inequality: Patterns and Processes*, Boston MA: McGraw-Hill.

Mizrachi, N. and Herzog, H. (2012), 'Participatory destigmatization strategies among Palestinian Citizens, Ethiopian Jews and Mizrachi Jews in Israel', *Ethnic and Racial Studies*, **35** (3): 418–435.

Offer, S. (2007), 'The Ethiopian community in Israel: segregation and the creation of a racial cleavage', *Ethnic and Racial Studies*, **30** (3): 461–480.

Pearce, S.C. (2005), 'Today's immigrant woman entrepreneur', *Immigration Policy in Focus*, **4** (1): 1–17.

Ram, M. and Jones, T. (2008), 'Ethnic minority business: review of research and policy', *Environment and Planning C – Government and Policy*, **26** (2): 352–374.

Ram, M., Smallbone, D., Deakins, D., and Jones, T. (2003), 'Banking on "break-out": finance and the development of ethnic minority businesses', *Journal of Ethnic and Migration Studies*, **29** (4): 663–681.

Remennick, L. (2004), 'Language acquisition, ethnicity and social integration among Former Soviet Immigrants of the 1990s in Israel', *Ethnic and Racial Studies*, **27** (3): 431–454.

Robinson, J., Blockson, L., and Robinson, S. (2007), 'Exploring stratification and entrepreneurship: African American women entrepreneurs redefine success in growth ventures', *The ANNALS of the American Academy of Political and Social Science*, **613** (1): 131–154.

Schnell, I. and Sofer, M. (2002), 'Unbalanced embeddedness of ethnic entrepreneurship: the Israeli Arab case', *International Journal of Entrepreneurial Behavior and Research*, **8** (1/2): 54–68.

Semyonov, M., Haberfeld, Y., Rebecca, R., Bar-El, R., Amit, K., Heilbrunn, S., and Chachashvili-Bolotin, S. (2010), *Ruppin Index of Immigrant Integration in Israel*. Emek Hefer, Israel: Institute for Immigration and Social Integration, Ruppin Academic Center.

Smallbone, D., Kitching, J., and Athayde, R. (2010), 'Ethnic diversity, entrepreneurship and competitiveness in a global city', *International Small Business Journal*, **28** (2): 174–190.

Smallbone, D., Ram, M., Deakins, D., and Baldock, R. (2003), 'Access to finance by ethnic minority businesses in the UK', *International Small Business Journal*, **21** (3): 291–314.

Smith-Hunter, A.E. and Boyd, R.L. (2004), 'Applying theories of entrepreneurship to a comparative analysis of white and minority women business owners', *Women in Management Review*, **19** (1): 18–28.

Smooha, S. (2004), 'Jewish ethnicity in Israel: Symbolic or real?' in U. Rebhuhn and C.I. Waxman (eds), *Jews in Israel: Contemporary Social and Cultural Patterns*, Hanover NH: Brandeis University Press, pp. 47–80.

Valenzuela Jr, A. (2001), 'Day laborers as entrepreneurs?', *Journal of Ethnic and Migration Studies*, **27** (2): 335–352.

Volery, T. (2007), 'Ethnic entrepreneurship: a theoretical framework', in L-P. Dana (ed.), *Handbook of Research on Ethnic Minority Entrepreneurship*, Cheltenham, UK and Northampton, MA, USA: Edward Elgar Publishing, pp. 30–41.

Weber, M. (1920/1978), *Economy and Society: An Outline of Interpretive Sociology*, Oakland CA: University of California Press.

11. Bridging the equity funding gap in technological entrepreneurship: the case of government-backed venture capital in China
Jun Li

INTRODUCTION

China's economic growth over the last three decades has been widely viewed as a 'miracle' (Li and Wang, 2014). While China's economic bandwagon continues rolling on, a sense has taken hold that growth will need to be driven primarily by entrepreneurship and innovation, simply because the long-standing low-tech manufacturing-based, export-oriented growth model is 'unstable, unbalanced, uncoordinated, and unsustainable development' as described by Wen Jiabao, the former Premier, in his speech at the 18th National Congress on 12 November 2012.[1] The year 2006 marks another milestone in Chinese economic development when the country proclaimed the building of an innovative economy as its new national strategy. At the core of this strategy is the endeavour to drive independent innovation. In the landmark document, the 'Outlines of Medium and Long-term National Plan for Science and Technology Development (2006–2020)' (MLNP), independent innovation is defined to include three types of innovation, namely original innovation, integrated innovation, and re-innovation based on assimilation and absorption of imported technologies.[2] With such inspirations came a series of policy initiatives aimed at boosting technological entrepreneurship and mitigating the funding gap facing entrepreneurial firms in the early stage of their venture development. A significant development, above all, was the launch of the public venture capital scheme, called venture capital guiding funds (VCGFs), in 2008. Like similar efforts elsewhere, underlying the venture capital guiding fund initiative in China were the viewpoints that there is a close relationship between venture capital and technological entrepreneurship and that China was under-provided in the supply of this type. Where the private sector was unable to provide sufficient capital to new firms, the government was of the view that it could use VCGFs as a lever to direct more risk capital into entrepreneurial firms that will ultimately yield high social returns.

Internationally, while these efforts have proliferated, evidence on whether such schemes have delivered as anticipated remains elusive (Rigby and Ramlogan, 2013). As Lerner (2009) states, the challenge results from little understanding as to how to structure such programmes to ensure their effectiveness and to avoid political distortions. This chapter uses China as a case study to examine how the country has used public-backed venture capital to bridge the funding gap in technological entrepreneurship. It addresses three questions: What are the background conditions that explain the need for public venture capital? What are the distinct features of programme design? What is the impact of government-backed venture capital? Reflecting the early state of the programme and a lack of empirical evidence, I relied on qualitative interviews, case studies of the programme, and the review of a large number of documents from official sources to research the topic.

The chapter is organized as follows. After the introduction, the literature review section reviews the empirical evidence on major public venture capital schemes in a number of countries and identifies the key factors influencing the performance of those schemes. This is followed by a section that profiles the developments of the public venture capital initiative in China. The fourth section looks in greater detail at the national level venture capital guiding fund in terms of its principles, funding models and governance. The fifth section provides a tentative assessment of the impact of the public venture capital funds in China.

LITERATURE REVIEW

The role of public venture capital falls into two broad and interconnected categories. At the macro level, public venture capital is used to stimulate the supply side of venture capital markets without any direct government involvement; at the micro level, governments take a hands-on role in directly implementing programmes to fill financing gaps of various kinds over the short or medium term (Hood, 2000). The rationale for public sector involvement in this area is founded on the deficiencies within the existing private sector provision. It is noted that many early stage investments require significant pre-project investigation and project preparation relative to the size, scale and likely rewards from the venture – hence a 'gap' not readily filled by the private sector (Commission of the European Communities, 2009).

Two policy objectives can be identified in a variety of public venture capital schemes. The first policy objective is to fill an equity gap in the provision of finance to growing or growth-potential smaller businesses

(Harrison and Mason, 2000). This arises from the recognition of the catalytic role venture capital plays in the entrepreneurial process and of 'market failure'. Availability of venture capital will allow companies to exploit significant growth opportunities which they will otherwise not do because they are unable to fund this growth from internally generated sources of finance and debt finance and are too small to access public equity markets (Harrison and Mason, 2000). The second policy objective is to redress spatial variations in venture capital investment activity that may lead to uneven spatial economic development within a country (Hood, 2000) resulting from a concern that there is an extreme geographical concentration of venture capital firms and their investments. The creation of public venture capital hence is aimed at stimulating and directing its supply capital to achieve equitable economic development goals.

So far, empirical evidence on the performance of public venture capital funds established in a number of countries has shown mixed results. There is evidence of positive outcomes in a few public venture capital schemes, for instance, the Small Business Investment Research programme (SBIR) in the US and the Yozma Venture Capital in Israel.

SBIR was created by the US federal government in 1982 and was the largest public venture programme in the United States (US). The programme aimed to drive demand for venture capital in the US. Lerner (1999) analysed the long-term impact of the program, by matching SBIR awardees to companies that did not receive SBIR financing. He found that, while the awardees and matching firms did not differ significantly in the likelihood of receiving VC in the years prior to the awards, in subsequent years the awardees were significantly more likely to receive such financing. Awardees also enjoyed substantially greater employment and sales growth. The study suggests that the SBIR programme played an important catalytic role in high-technology sectors, by both reducing some of the information gaps faced by investors and helping the certified firms to obtain venture funding. However, the research also finds that the superior performance was confined to awardees in areas that already had private venture activity, suggesting that the programme failed to redress the spatial unevenness in venture capital supply to achieve economic and development goals.

Yozma was set up by the Israeli government in 1992. It was widely viewed as a success, measured by the indicators of the high returns to funds that served as precursors to larger, follow-on funds, a good number of spin-offs of local Yozma funds partners, increased capitalization of the ten original Yozma groups, and a higher ratio of venture investment to GDP (Lerner, 2009; Senor and Singer, 2011).

Evidence of the performance of other schemes has been mixed, however.

The Small Business Investment Companies (SBICs) scheme is another US government-backed venture capital programme designed to address the supply side of venture financing. It was perceived as a success early on but a later review (SBA, 2004; cited in Clarysse et al., 2009) of fund performance over the years 1994–2000 finds that the composite IRRs were −12.3 per cent for the scheme as opposed to 20.4 per cent for the private investors and that the estimated total value to capital was 0.78, compared to 1.3 for the private partners, indicating underperformance of the scheme. Baygan (2003, cited in Clarysse et al., 2009) in his analysis of the same scheme found that SBIC investments were not addressing gaps in the private funding process, such as industrial segments or firms neglected by financiers and that it may be contributing to over-funding of particular sectors and crowding out purely private funds.

In the UK, NESTA's (2009) review of the impact of investment from six government-backed venture capital schemes on 782 funded firms over the period 1995–2008 finds that these schemes have had a positive, yet modest, impact on firm performance when compared with a matched control sample. More specifically, the review finds that while the schemes overall produce a positive effect on employment and are likely to produce positive high quality jobs, the size of the effect is relatively small. It also finds that there is a 'U-shaped' relationship in gross profit margins over time since investment, that is, funded firms' gross profit margins collapse substantially and immediately in the three years after receiving the initial investment, level out by the fourth year and increase dramatically by year six, and that funded firms do have higher than average labour productivity. While the review acknowledges that government funding does have a positive effect on intended firm behaviour in which firms make a trade-off between short-run growth and longer-run profit as they reconfigure and invest in new products, technologies and processes for future growth, and that these schemes do play a role in the allocation of financial and managerial resources to help grow firms that have an impact on productivity in the economy, it concludes that these schemes are a relatively expensive means of short-term job creation. In the examination of three public-backed venture capital funds, the National Audit Office (NAO) (2009) finds that 84 per cent of businesses surveyed reported that the initial funding had made it easier for them to obtain additional finance from other sources, that 32 per cent of businesses reported they would have been unable to obtain any finance without support from the funds, and that the financial performance of the funds is likely to be poor, although not untypical when compared to private venture capital returns over the same period. On the basis of the NAO's (2009) report, the House of Commons Public Accounts Committee (HCPAC) (2010) raises a number of concerns, that is, the disproportionate distribution of funding from national funds to London and the South East, the underperformance of the government-backed funds, and the substantial and high costs of managing the funds. They conclude that the funds were structured in a way that meant the taxpayer bore a disproportionate share of the risk and hence greater losses, and that there is a risk that the ongoing pattern of investment, concentrated in London and the South East, reinforces inequalities between regional economies.

Elsewhere, Cumming and MacIntosh (2006) analysed the labour fund initiative in Canada and found no evidence that the programme boosted the aggregate amount of venture spending in each province. Da Rin et al. (2006) examined the level of venture capital funding across 14 European countries over two decades and found that for every dollar being handed out by a government-sponsored programme or fund, private investors put a dollar less into the sector.

Harrison and Mason (2000) sum up the potential drawbacks of the public sector provision of venture capital. First, the effect of these programmes may simply be to replicate and reinforce existing spatial biases in the venture capital industry. Second, an increase in the supply of venture capital as a result of direct or indirect government programmes may create market distortions that over the longer term could drive out or displace private sector venture capital funds. Third, the supply of capital is not the only or the most important constraint on economic development, so simply making venture capital available will not automatically generate the conditions under which entrepreneurship can flourish. Fourth, in the case of direct public sector provision of venture capital funds, the long-term financial viability and sustainability of these funds are doubtful. Fifth, if there are geographical constraints on the investments of the fund (reflecting the territorial interests of the government department or agency involved) deal flow may be constrained, investments made in non-competitive businesses and lower fund portfolio returns generated, making more difficult the attraction of additional venture capital into the region from either public or private sources.

Lerner (2009) suggests that public venture capital initiatives could fail as a result of design imperfections and implementation failure. Design imperfections are manifested in two respects. First, such initiatives may ignore the realities of the entrepreneurial process: (a) the programme may have a short-term orientation, not understanding that initiatives take many years to bear fruits; (b) the programme may have requirements that run counter to the nature of the entrepreneurial process and the mission of the programme (for example, profitability or self-sufficiency); and (c) reasonable programmes may have been too tiny to have an impact, or so large that they swamp the already-existing funds. Second, such initiatives may ignore the market's dictates, namely pressure to 'spread the wealth'. Government officials usually encouraged funding in industries or geographic regions where private interest simply did not exist. Implementation failures manifest themselves in failure to build in incentives, failure to design appropriate evaluative mechanisms, and ignorance of the international nature of the entrepreneurial process.

Hood (2000) draws a few lessons from the Scottish experience. These include: (a) clear and consistent objectives of a public venture capital organization – a measure of accountability in respect of objectives and performance of public venture funds, (b) operating and taking a medium to long term view of outcomes, (c) necessity to attract, reward and hold together experienced and committed venture capital executives to manage public funds, and (d) interaction between public and private sector venture capitalists.

THE CHINESE PUBLIC VENTURE CAPITAL INITIATIVE

The concept of venture capital did not feature in any policy agenda in China until 1985 when its relevance to the Chinese economy was first deliberated in the major document of the ruling communist party – 'Decisions on Reforms of the Science and Technology (S&T) System'. It was proclaimed for the first time that venture capital funds can be set up to support high-tech development. In September 1985, the central government approved the establishment of the China New Technology Venture Capital Corporation (CNTVC), China's first home-grown VC firm. CNTVC was a US$10 million fund in which the State Science and Technology Commission and Ministry of Finance (MOF) had a 40 per cent and 23 per cent stake respectively. Its remit was to provide finance to support the country's 'Torch Programme', that is, the development of technology firms in high-tech development zones. In March 1991, the State Council granted permission to the national high-tech development zones for setting up VC funds and VC firms. Thereafter, there was a sudden spurt of activity at the local level.

In 1999 the establishment of the Innovation Fund for Small Technology-based Firms (InnoFund) represented the central government's new effort to address the funding gap confronted by high-tech SMEs. The InnoFund was designated to support technological innovations of small technology-based firms and to facilitate R&D commercialization. InnoFund differs from other nongovernmental fund or commercial venture capital in two respects. First, it is policy-oriented, intending to maximize the government's role in guiding the development of new and high-tech industries and innovation of technology-based SMEs. Secondly, it serves as a 'priming-pump', aiming to leverage more investment in technology-based SMEs by local governments, large firms and financial institutions. InnoFund offers finance in the forms of grants, loan interest subsidy, and equity investment.

The major push to address the finance gap came in July 2007 when MOF and the Ministry of Science and Technology (MOST) co-issued the Interim Regulation on the Management of Venture Capital Guiding Fund for High-tech SMEs (the Interim Regulation). It was intended to provide guidelines to local governments for the set-up of such schemes at the local level. Soon afterwards, MOF and MOST jointly launched the first ever national level VCGF. Building on what was perceived as a promising start, the Chinese government announced in January 2015 it would launch a RMB 4 billion ($6.5bn) VC fund to support start-ups in emerging industries.

In the meantime, the tax system has been streamlined to support public venture capital initiatives. For example, new tax policies were announced in 2007 as supporting measures to the implementation of the MLNP-related action plan. Also, second board markets were opened to offer additional exit routes for VC investments. Significantly, the Small and Medium Enterprise Board was launched in Shenzhen Stock Exchange (SSE) in May 2004, and it was followed by the opening of the Growth Enterprise Market (GEM) in SSE in 2009. Highlights of the evolution of the public venture scheme in China can be seen in Figure 11.1.

VCGFS: PRINCIPLES, FUNDING MODELS AND GOVERNANCE

The public venture capital scheme in China shows an apparent influence of the Israeli Yozma model. The preference was to take a relatively hands-off approach to managing the fund. In the 'Directives on Establishment and Management of VCGFs' jointly issued by the National Development and Reform Commission (NDRC), MOF and the Ministry of Commerce (MOC) in October 2008, two key principles were laid down for the establishment of VCGFs in accordance with this line of thinking:

1) *Government guidance.* Governments are not encouraged to assume the role of lead investors both in the VC fund and in venture investments, instead they are expected to use public finance to leverage and guide more private capital toward investment in the priority areas of

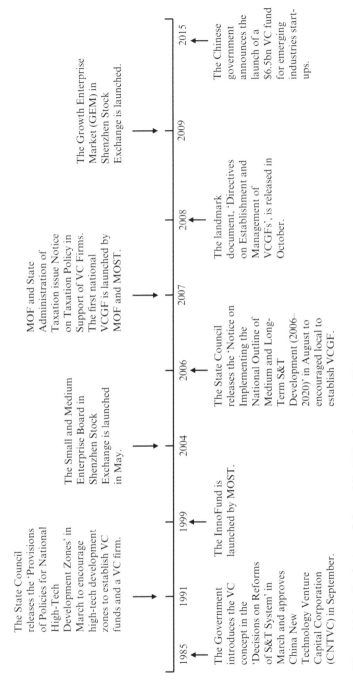

Figure 11.1   *Evolution of the public VC schemes in China*

national and regional strategic importance, thereby speeding up the industrialization of independent innovation and the development of emerging, strategic industries.

2) *Market-based management.* In VCGF invested VC funds, fund managers are given responsibility for managing funds and investments, and the VCGF participates in investor governance decisions on the same terms as private investors, with the same voting rights. By adopting market practice in investor governance arrangements, the VCGF relies on the well-tried and tested VC model world-wide to maximise impact. In other words, the VC fund will take full responsibility to identify good investment opportunities and make investment decisions on the basis of the due diligence process, market analyses, and fund management experiences, while the VCGF will use its capital contribution to gear private VC investment toward early stage companies to fulfil its own strategic goal.

The Funding Models

Five funding models in the VCGF scheme can be identified, with each model serving different purposes.

Fund-of-funds
In this model, the VCGF invests in private VC funds. Investments in the VC fund are structured as equity and can be bought out by investors. Government investments in the fund are on the same terms as those of private investors. This funding model can ensure that the government can distance itself from risk and liability for investments made. It also ensures the fund's independence in decisions about the appointment of VC fund managers and in individual investment decisions. This funding model has become popular for two reasons. First, by investing directly in many VC funds, the VCGF can achieve its policy objective by multiplying the amount of venture capital available for new, technology-based companies. Second, it offers the VCGF an opportunity to invest in a number of VC funds so as to diversify investments and minimise risks.

Co-investment
In this model, both the VCGF and the VC fund invest together in early stage SMEs. The main objective of this approach is to bring decent size private venture investment firms on board to invest in high-tech start-ups in the government's priority areas and to share investment risk with VC investors.

VC investment subsidy

This model is very similar to co-investment, except that the VCGF subsidises a VC fund's investment costs with a non-repayable grant without having any shareholding in the venture-backed company. As such, the VCGF can help the VC fund to withstand risks arising from its investments in early stage ventures. A subsidy is open to all VC funds who have invested in early stage firms – a grant worth up to 5 per cent of the VC fund's actual investment in one project or a maximum of RMB 5 million.

Investment guarantee

The main objective of this funding model is to encourage VC funds to nurture early stage high-tech firms with a follow-on investment commitment. To be eligible, the VC fund will first need to recruit a prospective early stage high-tech firm, dubbed 'firms under supervision', and then apply for a grant for the firm. If successful, the firm can use the grant worth up to RMB 1 million to subsidise its R&D expenses. As a binding condition, the VC fund should first provide free mentoring services to the candidate company for up to two years and invests in the company when the supervisory period ends. To go with the VC fund's investment, the VCGF shall offer to the venture-backed company a second grant of up to RMB 2 million to subsidise the costs of mass production of the new product.

Financing guarantee

This model aims to support VC funds to borrow money through debt financing. In this way, the VCGF helps reduce the creditor's risk and encourage small investors and banks to invest in high-growth ventures through the platform of VC funds. VC funds can also improve their financial performance as debt creditors will only receive relatively low fixed rate interest. Using information from credit rating agencies, the VCGF can provide financing guarantee to those VC funds with excellent credit record and supports them to use debt financing to consolidate their funding resources.

Governance of VCGFs   As an example, the MOF- and MOST-funded VCGF adopts a three-tier governance structure to ensure an orderly and risk-controllable operation.

On the top tier of governance are MOF and MOST who are responsible for setting rules of fund management, making decisions on directions of strategic investment, and determining capital allocation. On the second tier is the Expert Review Committee (ERC). Members of the ERC are appointed by MOF and MOST and are responsible for reviewing applications and short-listing projects for consideration by MOF and MOST. On the third tier is the Innovation Fund Management Centre (IFMC), which is the government agent charged with the following responsibilities: (1) managing funding applications, conducting initial screening, and recommending candidates to ERC; (2) managing VCGF's shares in all invested interests on behalf of MOF and MOST; and (3) monitoring the VCGF's investment projects and reporting periodically to MOF and MOST.

When using either fund-of-funds or co-investment, the VCGF would use a bundling strategy to package together investments from both the VCGF and the VC fund into one bundled solution. The strategy is such that the VCGF shall only use its equity capital investment to leverage more similar investment from other parties and that it shall not commit to an investment of more than 25 per cent of the total sum of subscribed funds. This is deliberate in order to achieve two objectives – sharing the VC fund's investment risk and reinforcing the fund's responsibility.

The development of VCGFs   According to the MOST survey in 2011, from 2006 to 2010, 55 VCGFs were established at all levels with a total committed fund of RMB 43 billion. On the top of all this, there were three super funds set up by the central government, that is, a RMB 1 billion VCGF for High-Tech SME set up jointly by MOST and MOF in 2007, a RMB 1 billion New Industry Venture Capital Programme (NIVCP) set up by NDRC and MOF in October 2009, and a RMB 5 billion China Development Finance (CDF) set up by China Development Bank (CDB) in conjunction with Suzhou Ventures Group (SVG) in December 2010. Of all VCGFs, 35 were established by governments at the city level and 20 at the provincial level (Table 11.1). In terms of fund size, city-level VCGFs overall were smaller with nearly half having a total capital of less than 500

Table 11.1   VCGFs at three administrative levels

		All	State level	Provincial level	City level
Number of VCGF		58	3	20	35
Promised capital, billion		45.21	7.16	15.47	22.58
Fund scale distribution, per cent	More than 1 billion	35	100	33	32
	500 million to 1 billion	22	0	29	20
	100–499 million	33	0	33	34
	Less than 100 million	10	0	5	14

Source: Ding and Li (2015).

Table 11.2   Source of capital in VCGFs

	VCGF		Capital	
	Number	per cent	Billion	per cent
Fiscal special fund	51	79.69	34.30	63.49
Listed/non-listed companies	6	9.38	0.33	0.60
Solely state-owned investment companies	2	3.13	5.9	10.92
Banks	4	6.25	8.5	15.73
Other	1	1.56	5	9.26

Source: Ding and Li (2015).

Table 11.3   Forms of financing by VCGFs

	Use of fund	per cent	Capital allocation, billion	per cent
Fund-of-funds	54	93	44.95	99
Co-investment	34	58.62	31.26	69
Financing guarantee	5	8.62	1.6	4
Investment subsidy	7	12.07	4.46	10

Source: Ding and Li (2015).

million. Province-level VCGFs were better resourced with near two-thirds owing capital of more than RMB 500 million.

A special fiscal fund from the government budget was the main source of capital in VCGFs. This is a fund from special accounts set up by MOF or departments of finance at the local level for earmarked, transitory activities. This source of funding was used in the establishment of 51 VCGFs and contributed almost two-thirds of capital in all VCGFs. As can be seen in Table 11.2, banks contributed another 15.73 per cent to VCGFs. These mainly refer to CDB's contribution to three VCGFs and Eximbank's contribution to the Chengdu VCGF.

The VCGF initiative in China started with a more conventional approach such as an investment subsidy but over time fund-of-funds have gradually become the main funding model (Table 11.3). As of 2010, 93 per cent of VCGFs had used this method to leverage private VC investments. Capital contribution-wide, this funding model even has a much higher percentage of VCGF involvement. Clearly, this is a very positive sign of development in the public-backed venture capital sector.

IMPACTS OF PUBLIC VENTURE CAPITAL SCHEMES

In 2008 the Chinese government set out two policy objectives in the 'Directives on Establishment and Management of VCGFs' for the public venture capital scheme: (a) to increase the supply of venture capital through the catalytic role of fiscal funds, and (b) to encourage venture capital to invest in seed or start-up businesses. Early evidence so far has seemed to suggest that VCGFs have done well in increasing the availability of venture capital. By the end of 2009, 14 out of 43 VC funds were selected by the MOF and MOST-backed VCGF to set up fund-of-funds and received VCGF funding worth RMB 309 million. These VC funds went on to raise an additional RMB 2.382 billion. As such, the VCGF maximised its investment impact by a factor of 7 (Ding and Li, 2015). For the VC sector as a whole, a sharp increase in the availability of VC after 2006 was evident as displayed in Figure 11.2. By 2012, VC under management had increased by five-fold to RMB 331.1 billion from RMB 66.4 billion in 2006.

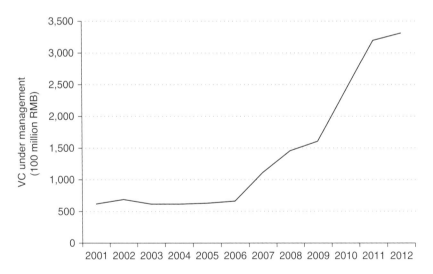

Source: MOST online database.

Figure 11.2 VC capital under management, 2001–2012

However, impact assessment based on overall increases in the availability of venture capital can be rather narrowly focused and sometimes misleading, as Harrison and Mason (2000) suggested. The increase in the volume of VC does not reveal the extent to which government funding does not crowd out other investment, the rate of return of funds and the cost of managing funds relative to the investment. As can be seen in Table 11.4, multiple aims can be identified in various VCGFs but these aims were not defined as clear, measurable objectives. In particular, none of the funds had laid out an explicit financial performance objective. Of course, this does not appear to be a unique problem to China's VCGF initiative. Similar concerns were raised about schemes of other countries (for example, NAO, 2009). In late 2008 MOST commenced an interim evaluation of the economic benefits of VCGFs but it is not clear how performance was measured against their objectives. None of the VCGFs have reached the end of their life and hence the matter of financial performance evaluation is yet to be on the top of those funds' agenda. It will be important, though, that robust evidence to measure the achievement of all of the stated objectives is produced by the time when funds come to the end of their life.

The second objective of China's public venture capital scheme is to leverage VC into new firms in the seed and start-up stages. Yet, evidence of focused targeting of the equity gap so far has been ambiguous. As can be seen in Figure 11.3, the percentage of VC investment in the seed and start-up stages since 2008 has not shown a significant increase for the VC sector as a whole. From 2003 to 2012, VC investment in the seed stage averaged 10.8 per cent but there were seven years in that period the share of seed stage investment was below the average level. This may suggest that the public venture capital scheme were not very effective in focused targeting of the equity gap as stated in the scheme. Alternatively, it may suggest that the public venture capital scheme might have crowded out private VC investments in seed and start-up ventures.

The performance of VCGFs can also be impacted upon by their design. Recent academic research identifies a number of factors which tend to improve the chances of a successful venture capital fund, including a flow of good quality deals; the timing of investments; broad geographic coverage; larger fund sizes; and the ability to make follow-on investments and to exit individual investments on a timely basis (Lerner, 2009). There is evidence that local government policymakers made decisions based on 'buzz'. Many local governments may have started their own VCGFs to promote high-tech industries, in the hope of creating a cluster of activity. Realistically, however, only a handful of these regions had the necessary scientific resources and infrastructure to support a successful cluster,

Table 11.4 Selected venture capital guiding funds by region

Region	Scheme objectives	Year of establishment	VCGF size	Source of capital	Target of leverage
Provincial and 1st tier municipality level					
Zhejiang	Industrial restructuring and upgrading	March 2009	500 million	n/a	Early stage high-tech SMEs; growth SMEs
Anhui	n/a	September 2009	Originally 500 million with a target of 1 billion	Budgetary revenue of 500 million RMB	50% of capital to set up fund-of-fund; 50% to support Hefei, Wuhu and Benbo in the establishment of municipality-level VCGFs
Shanxi	n/a	2008	200 million originally with a target of 1 billion	150 million from Department of Finance; 50 million from Development and Reform Commission	Early stage high-tech SMEs; SME M&A
Provincial capital city level					
Nanjing	The development of a VC market and an innovative city	December 2009	200 million	Special budgetary revenue; fund earnings; central and provincial VCGFs	Growth ventures
Hangzhou	The development of a VC market and an innovative city	April 2008	200 million	Budgetary revenue	Early stage ventures

199

Table 11.4 (continued)

Region	Scheme objectives	Year of establishment	VCGF size	Source of capital	Target of leverage
Provincial capital city level					
Shijiazhuang	The development of high-tech industries	September 2009	300 million	Equity capital of Shijiazhuang Development Investment Ltd; fund earnings, and others	Early stage high-tech SMEs; SME M&A
City level					
Haidian, Beijing	The development of VC firms and small and medium-sized innovative ventures	June 2007	70 million with a target of 500 million in five years	Special budgetary revenue; enterprise development grants from central and Beijing government; fund proceeds; donations	Early stage and growth stage enterprises
Minghang, Shanghai	Industrial upgrading	May 2010	100 million with a target of 500 million in five years	Budgetary revenue; operating public asset earnings; fund exit proceeds and earnings; donations	n/a
Binghai, Tianjin	The development of a national modern manufacturing and R&D commercialization base	March 2007	2 billion	1 billion from Binghai Management Commission; 1 billion from China Development Bank	Fast growth high-tech firms
Shaoxing, Zhejiang	Implementation of an entrepreneurship and innovation strategy	September 2008	200 million	Budgetary revenue; existing budgetary enterprise development funds, and others	Business ventures

Jiangde	n/a	September 2008	5 million	Budgetary revenue; existing budgetary enterprise development funds, and others	Early stage high-tech SMEs
Fuyang	The development of an innovative city	December 2008	20 million	Budgetary revenue; existing budgetary enterprise development funds	Early stage high-tech SMEs
County level					
Tonglu	n/a	August 2008	5 million	Budgetary revenue; existing budgetary enterprise development funds	Early stage SMEs
Anji	n/a	January 2009	30 million	Budgetary revenue; existing budgetary enterprise development funds; fund exit revenue and earnings	Seed stage and early stage SMEs
Nanhu, Jiaxin	Implementation of an entrepreneurship and innovation strategy	October 2009	15 million	Budgetary revenue; existing budgetary enterprise development funds; fund exit revenue and earnings	Business ventures

Sources: Complied from respective government documents.

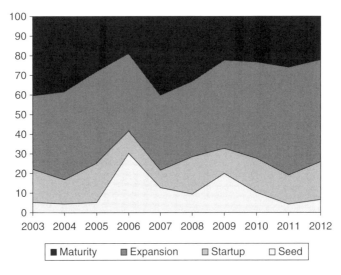

Source: MOST online database.

Figure 11.3   Percentage of VC investment by stage of venture development

so the bulk of these funds could be ineffective. Concerns were already expressed about whether it is desirable for a city at the county level to establish a VCGF.[3] Entrepreneurship is commonly drawn towards areas where entrepreneurial talent, locally embedded social capital and supporting infrastructure prevail: there are powerful forces that lead firms to cluster in particular places (Li and Geng, 2012). Thus, much of the impact can be diluted as funds that could be very helpful in a core area end up where they are not helpful.

Local governments' enthusiastic replication of the national model of VCGFs at the local levels came with caveats. In many local initiatives, VCGFs have been conditional on funds investing in specific regions, local registration and the threshold of registered capital for a new fund-of-fund. For example, the 2010 MOST survey found that 87 per cent of local VCGFs demanded their partner VC funds to invest a certain percentage of subscribed capital locally and that 68 per cent of VCGFs requested the new fund to be registered locally, and that 61 per cent set the minimum size of a new fund. The survey also found that 49 per cent of VCGFs had included all three restrictive clauses in their initiatives, that 25 per cent had included two restrictive clauses, that 24 per cent had one restrictive clause, and that only 3 per cent did not set any restriction. There was a tendency that the further down the local levels the more restrictions were placed on

VCGF's partners in obtaining local government's contribution. In a separate survey in 2011 conducted by Zero2IPO, it was found that a condition on a fund-of-fund to invest 60–70 per cent of its subscribed capital locally was a common practice.[4] This local protection tendency counters against one of the principles of VCGFs, namely, market-based operation. The extent to which a local VCGF can impact on the local economy should be considered from a demand-side perspective. It is reasonable to suggest that not every region has a large group of high potential firms that are capable of earning the exceptionally high returns sought after by venture capital investors. By placing restrictions on the VC fund in regions where a strong deal flow of attractive, high-potential firms is lacking, these VCGFs are in danger of creating a mismatch between demand and supply in a specific region and compromising fund performance.

Finally, it appears that the public venture capital scheme has not had an impact on reversing the uneven spatial concentration of venture capital investment activity, although this is not a stated objective of the scheme. Figure 11.4 shows that 54 per cent of VCGF-backed VC investments were concentrated in the Yangtze River Delta that made up of 34 per cent of the country's GDP. Comparatively, the less developed South-West region had only a 6.8 per cent share of all VCGF-backed VC investments against its 12.7 per cent share of the national GDP. Investments from the national level VCGFs also suggest a similar pattern. For example, in 2012, the national level VCGFs approved 299 investment projects, of which only

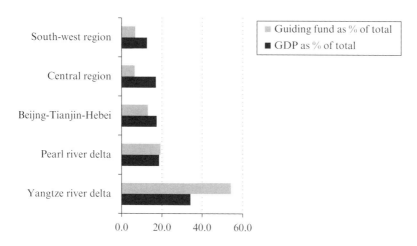

Source: MOST online database.

Figure 11.4 Spatial distribution of investments by VCGFs, 2012

nine projects were in the west region. All projects received funding worth RMB 530 million and only five million investments went to the west region.

CONCLUDING REMARKS

China has aspired to overhaul its growth model by vigorously promoting technological innovation and entrepreneurship. Like many other countries, there is a funding gap facing new and technology ventures in the early stage of venture development. To address this challenge, China has used government-backed venture capital to plug the gap. Four super-sized central government backed VCGFs have been set up and dozens of similar schemes are in operation at the local levels. Framed in the mould of the Yozma model, fund-of-funds and co-investment have been the dominant models to leverage private VC investments. In the two objectives the government has set out for the scheme, early evidence seems to suggest that such schemes have had a desirable catalytic effect. Nevertheless, the true impact is yet possible to assess until VCGF-backed funds complete their funding cycle and exit.

NOTES

1. See 'Wen pinpoints key tasks facing China in five years', retrieved from www.china.org.cn/china/18th_cpc_congress/2012-11/10/content_27067312.htm (accessed 15 December 2014).
2. See the document in the Chinese version at www.gov.cn/jrzg/2006-02/09/content_183787.htm (assessed 12 February 2014).
3. See a report on Caijing Net on 10 April 2009, 'Emerging concerns behind the fever of venture capital guiding funds', at www.caijing.com.cn/2009-04-10/110137001.html (accessed 15 December 2014).
4. See a report in China Jingji Daobao on 7 January 2012, 'the butterfly effect of government guiding funds to reshape the driver of regional development', at http://www.ceh.com.cn/ceh/cjxx/2012/1/7/97382.shtml (accessed 15 December 2014).

REFERENCES

Clarysse, B., Knocjaert, M. and Wright, M. (2009), *Benchmarking UK Venture Capital to the US and Israel: What Lessons Can Be Learned?*, London: BVCA.
Commission of the European Communities (2009), *Financing Innovation and SMEs*, Commission Staff Working Document, Brussels: European Commission.
Cumming, D. and MacIntosh, J. (2006), 'Crowding out private equity: Canadian evidence', *Journal of Business Venturing*, **21** (5): 569–609.
Da Rin, M., Nicodano, G. and Sembenelli, A. (2006), 'Public policy and creation of active venture capital markets', *Journal of Public Economics*, **90** (8–9): 1699–1723.

Ding, X.D. and Li, J. (2015), *Incentives for Innovation in China: Building an Innovative Economy*, London and New York: Routledge.

Harrison, R.T. and Mason, C.M. (2000), 'Editorial: the role of the public sector in the development of a regional venture capital industry', *Venture Capital*, **2** (4): 243–253.

Hood, N. (2000), 'Public venture capital and economic development: the Scottish experience', *Venture Capital*, **2** (4): 313–341.

House of Commons Public Accounts Committee (HCPAC) (2010), *Department for Business, Innovation and Skills: Venture Capital Support to Small Businesses*, Seventeenth Report of Session 2009–10, London: The Stationery Office.

Lerner, J. (1999), 'The government as venture capitalist: the long-run impact of the SBIR program', *Journal of Business*, **72** (3): 285–318.

Lerner, J. (2009), *Boulevard of Broken Dreams: Why Public Efforts to Boost Entrepreneurship and Venture Capital Have Failed and What to Do about It*, Princeton NJ: Princeton University Press.

Li, J. and Geng, S. (2012), 'Industrial clusters, shared resources, and firm performance', *Entrepreneurship and Regional Development*, **24** (5–6): 357–382.

Li, J. and Wang, L.M. (eds) (2014), *China's Economic Dynamics: A Beijing Consensus in the Making?*, London and New York: Routledge.

National Audit Office (NAO) (2009), *The Department for Business, Innovation and Skills: Venture Capital Support to Small Businesses*, London: NAO.

NESTA (2009), *From Funding Gaps to Thin Markets: UK Government Support for Early-Stage Venture Capital*, Research Report, September, London: NESTA.

Rigby, J. and Ramlogan, R. (2013), *Access to Finance: Impacts of Publicly Supported Venture Capital and Loan Guarantees*, NESTA Working Paper 13/02, London: NESTA.

Senor, D. and Singer, S. (2011), *Start-up Nation: The Story of Israel's Economic Miracle*, London: Random House LLC.

12. Informal lenders and small/marginal farmers in India: an unregulated sociological symbiotic relationship?

Navjot Sandhu, Javed G. Hussain and Harry Matlay

INTRODUCTION

In the context of lending in developing countries, formal and informal sectors co-exist, although there are major differences in the interest rates charged. This is compounded by the paradigm of imperfect information, legal monitoring and enforcement that explains the sectors' underperformance and strained co-existence (Hoff and Stiglitz, 1990; Conning, 1996; Bell et al., 1997; Madestam, 2014). Despite the tacit acknowledgement of the importance of formal and informal finance,[1] the plight of marginal farmers has not received much attention in empirical or theoretical underpinnings or within microfinance literature (Ghatak and Guinnane, 1999; Ghatak, 2000; Sandhu, 2007; Chaudhuri and Dwibedi, 2014). The economic and strategic significance of informal lending and borrowing for the farming sector in developing economies has been overlooked in the finance literature. This study attempts to overcome the gap within the extant literature and in particular investigates how informal providers make lending decisions for small/marginal farmers.

This chapter, therefore, examines the unique structural characteristics of informal lenders such as retail merchants (*arthiyas*), local private moneylenders (*sahukars*), wealthy entrepreneurs, wholesale sellers, friends and family in comparison with their formal counterparts. The survey and analytical results indicate that informal financing from moneylenders and family friends, at least in India, is significant. We find evidence of a small farm bias, for whom the majority of income comes from agriculture produce that is seasonal, hence dependents are more likely to use informal financing. The evidence shows that whether or not a farmer had at one point been denied a loan does not affect the choice of using informal sources, nor does the denial of a previous loan disqualify the farmers (borrowers) from obtaining a formal loan since no information histories are kept. Thus this study seeks to answer the following research questions – 'what makes informal lenders successful?' and 'why will informal lenders lend to farmers?' – by taking farmers' credit requirements as the dependent variable, and the linkage between the borrowers and lenders from different backgrounds as the unit of analysis. This chapter pursues these relationships and identifies the reasons why small/marginal farmers (SMFs) incline towards informal lenders, leading to the development of a conceptual model of informal financing activities, and highlighting distinctive characteristics of informal lenders which sets out to make informal lending more competitive. Finally, the chapter ends with a summary of the issues covered, as well as identifying the implications and limitations of the study.

THE PREVALENCE OF THE INFORMAL SECTOR IN INDIA IN THE PRE- AND POST-COLONIAL ERA

The survival of moneylenders since the colonial era, despite the existence of basic networks of credit cooperatives, has been well-documented (for example, Central Banking Enquiry Committee (CBEC) in 1929 and Madras Provincial Banking Enquiry Committee (MPBEC) in 1930 cited by Shah et al., 2007). The major findings from both reports suggested that the repayment of prior loans was the major factor that entrapped marginal farmers in the clutches of informal lenders who exploited them through charging high rates of interest and confiscating their land. The lending practices of informal lenders often lacked transparency and often adverse means were used to extract high charges and capital repayment. In 1935 a report on Agricultural Indebtedness provided instances where moneylenders kept accounts of balances but never revealed them to the debtors as no receipts or written documents were made available, hence exploitation of the poor and illiterate was excessive. The colonial administration was aware of this and made several meagre efforts to tackle this problem by passing Acts such as the Deccan Agricultural Debtor Relief Act (1879); the Land Improvement Act of 1883 for long-term loans; the Agriculturists Loan Act of 1884 for current needs; the Cooperative Credit Societies Act in 1904, followed by the more comprehensive Cooperative Societies Act of 1912. Moreover, in 1918 the Usurious Loans Act was passed to control debts (where the interest rate could never exceed the principal). The Debt Conciliation Acts in 1933 and 1936, the Punjab Regulation of Accounts Act (1930) and the Debtors Protection Acts of 1935 were introduced for compulsory licensing and registration of moneylenders and proper recording of transactions. Despite all the concerted efforts made by the central government, the debt mechanisms and their functioning remains a contentious issue in India (Naidu, 1946; Chandavarkar, 1983; Shah et al., 2007; Rajeev et al., 2012; Gill, 2014).

During the post-colonial period, the first All India Debt and Investment Survey in 1951 found that 93 per cent of rural households relied heavily on informal finance and similar findings are reported by Bouman et al. (1989). To counter the informal sector throughout the 1950s and 1960s, the government actively promoted the expansion of cooperatives to enhance the availability of credit and alleviate poverty (Reserve Bank of India, 1954). To enhance credit outreach, the Indian Rural financial system went through another expansionary stage with the establishment of Regional Rural Banks (RRBs) in the mid-1970s and also the nationalization of seven commercial banks in 1980 (Shah et al., 2007; Rajeev et al., 2012).

Reforms and the introduction of new institutions led to an increase in the distribution of institutional credit for agricultural purposes. However, Regional Rural Banks proved to be financially unsustainable and inefficient in loan delivery (Bhatt and Thorat, 2001). Over the last decade, the Indian agriculture sector has witnessed unprecedented changes in terms of the control of imports of many agricultural products and the gradual removal of restrictions to comply with the demands of the World Trade Organization (WTO) (Datta and Deodhar, 2001). These changes were taking place at the time when in India, however, RRBs proved to be financially unsustainable and inefficient in loan delivery; and the growth of agricultural credit was slowing down during the 1990s as compared with the 1980s (Chavan, 2001). Concurrently, there was a sharp decline in the prices of many agricultural commodities, depriving farmers of income that had financial consequences which led many farmers to commit suicide in many states, especially in the Punjab (Deshpande, 2002). As a result of these exceptional transformations, changes took place in the indebtedness profile of the farmers' households. Despite efforts made in the colonial and post-colonial era to bring transparency and to increase the supply of informal lending, the moneylenders still have a significant presence and market share. The National Situation Assessment Survey (NSSO) of farmers (2003) reported that 52 per cent of farmers are still heavily reliant upon informal lenders. It is well recognized in the literature that larger farmers have access to formal credit, while small farmers rely on informal sources due to a lack of collateral, moral hazards, high borrowing costs for being illiterate and urgency of having money to buy seeds for new crops and other commodities to survive (Sarap, 1991; Swaminathan, 1991; Sandhu, 2007). This status quo is supported by several studies which have focused on agricultural credit including indebtedness of rural households, including those of farmers in India (Shivamaggi, 1986; Bell, 1988;

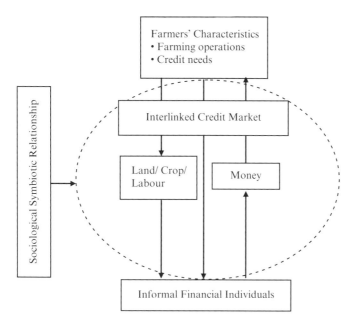

Figure 12.1   A conceptual model of informal lending for Punjabi farmers

Desai, 1988; Mujumdar, 1988, 1999; Swaminathan, 1991; Ramachandran and Swaminathan, 2001; Vani and Rajeev, 2011; Rajeev et al., 2012; Chaudhuri and Dwibedi, 2014). These studies and government legislation to address the gap show the importance of small/marginal farmers and the need to address their finance gap. This chapter attempts to study the different characteristics of informal lenders in the context of the Indian Punjab, why the gap still exists, and how the banks make lending decisions. In the following section, conceptual models are proposed (Figures 12.1 and 12.2) that outline the informal lending practices between farmers and various types of informal lenders and evaluate the motivations of small/marginal farmers to use informal moneylenders.

INFORMAL LENDING: UNREGULATED SOCIOLOGICAL SYMBIOTIC RELATIONSHIP?

Figure 12.1 outlines a conceptual model that highlights the process of borrowing money from informal sources. This tentative model illustrates that farmers have a choice of different arrangements which suit an individual borrower and hence there is no one structure to fit all.

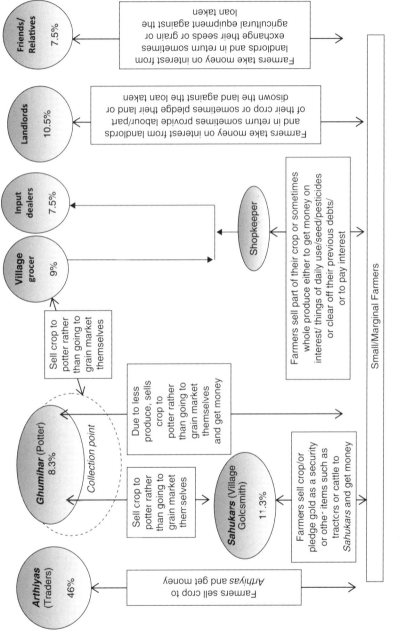

Figure 12.2   Typology of informal lenders and their characteristics

This relationship between moneylenders and farmers is similar to that of Bhaduri's (1981) framework where alternative relationships are depicted among the ruling classes. In the first case, farmers' borrowing and moneylenders' lending maintains a relationship of strict complementarities. In this case, private investment by the moneylenders or *arthiyas* (in the form of loans given to farmers) helps farmers to fulfil their needs to attain profit in production. These *arthiyas* or commission agents make arrangements to receive their return in the form of purchasing their crops at lower than market prices. Thus moneylenders play a dual role and transactions made by them are called Interlinked Credit Transactions (ICTs) (Gill, 2003, 2014). The ICTs are mapped out in Figures 12.1 and 12.2. Different types of credit-tying of labour services in some green revolution areas of India have been reported by Bhalla (1976) and Bell (1988). In this situation, both the moneylender and farmers obtain benefits from one another. In biological models of interdependence among species, such a situation of mutual benefit from expansion in production and in forced commerce could be seen to correspond to a symbiotic pattern characterized by mutualism[2] and could be called a sociological symbiotic relationship.[3]

The loan (consumption or business) taken by the farmers puts them into the clutches of unregulated lenders that unlock the possibility of abuse through high charges and at times physical punishment. However, this grip becomes weakened by income or employment opportunities offered by the moneylenders (who are at times landlords) throughout the year, which consequently enables the farmers to reduce their dependence on consumption loans.[4] Failure to repay a loan often leads the moneylenders to take over assets, land or other items until the loan is repaid by the farmer. This leads to entrapment that could adversely affect the borrower and his family for years. A loan taken to expand farming has unintended consequences, an effect similar to ecological models of antagonistic association among the species, describing an episitic competitive extinction[5] or struggle for survival. In these situations, the farmer and his family become slaves, sometimes called *badava* or belong to the informal moneylender/s until the debt is clear.

The situation becomes worse especially when the farmers fail to pay the interest in one season, with the result that the compound interest effect deepens, repayments become high (debt burden); this leads to land seizure by the moneylenders and this land is often sold at a higher price than the actual loan amount outstanding including interest money, a transaction often lacking transparency. Therefore, from this analysis it becomes clear that in the whole process of this nexus between farmers and moneylenders, the moneylenders, *arthiyas* or commission agents are in a win–win situation and grow like parasites attached to the poor farmers and eventually destroy them. The relationship or deal that offers flexibility to farmers and moneylenders which begins with mutualism leads to a disastrous end (Gill, 2003, 2014).

It is evident that extreme poverty propels farmers to enter into a financial deal that is heavily weighted in favour of moneylenders and has exploitative traits. The loan advanced to a farmer is often not monitorable and, consequently, an investment loan often becomes a consumption loan. Such a loan investment is unproductive, as it is not directed towards raising the output potential of the economy and burdens the individual. Indeed, within the framework of conventional national income accounting, the moneylenders' savings used for advancing consumption loans is matched by borrowers' dissaving and such fresh loan arrangements cannot even be counted as an investment because moneylenders are outside the national accounting system. Nevertheless, it remains an important channel for the deployment of private saving by the merchant and moneylending class in an agrarian economy (Sandhu, 2007). As a matter of fact, most of this exploitative network of forced commerce is sustained by the indebtedness of the poor farmers who are the direct beneficiaries of such forced relationships. Depending upon the nature of the agrarian class structure, such productive investment activities are predominantly carried out by the moneylenders/commission agents/*arthiyas* or by another distinct class of rich farmers and progressive landlords. In this context, it is important to distinguish between various types of informal lenders and their borrowers, although it is not clear whether finance or microfinance researchers or academics recognize this distinction or differentiate different categories of lenders. The next section outlines the specific methodological approaches used to explore the specific issues relating to informal financing.

RESEARCH METHODOLOGY AND SAMPLE

The majority of the research output in this field is based on interviews with borrowers (farmers) and not the banks or moneylenders (the supply side) mainly due to the unwillingness of moneylenders to participate in any academic work because of a lack of trust or to keep quiet or hide their informal lending business from their relatives, families or competitors, many of whom may be working illegally. Within this study, we explore farmers and informal lenders' perspectives. In our research, a qualitative approach is employed involving in-depth, face to face interviews based on a semi-structured questionnaire among 185 farmers (demand side), and 10 informal lenders (supply side) located in five districts (Gurdaspur, Amritsar, Jalandhar, Nawanshahr and Patiala) of the Punjab, India.

Hence the primary data for this study has been collected from the five districts, representing different agro-climatic zones of the Indian Punjab. The location was seen as particularly relevant because of the geographical location of its agriculture sector; in particular, this Indian State has been on and off the political agenda for the last 50 years. The questionnaires and semi-structured interviews were carried out face to face and in focus groups with respondents from both the supply and demand side.

Supply Side

In order to get an insight into the various issues related to informal lending, the detailed interviews focused on moneylenders. And, furthermore, to examine the market from the moneylender's point of view and to learn about their business practices, we interviewed 10 informal lenders. To access a range of informal lenders from different backgrounds, one of the authors made use of personal contacts and her familiarity with particular selected districts of the Indian Punjab. The researcher had relatives in each of these districts and through them she was able to access 10 interviews with moneylenders.

The aim was to interview around 20 moneylenders. Despite the personal relationships with the interviewees and going through very strong contacts, a few moneylenders (6) chose not to reveal very much about their business and four moneylenders refused to participate in the research. Given that we have a small sample of moneylenders, there are limitations in terms of the generalization of the research results. The difficulty in obtaining access to informal lenders is that they are not registered, nor do they have any office from where they operate. The cash they receive is not banked and hence they never fall into any formal establishment, nor do they wish to be recognized as such. They do not wish to operate openly for the fear of legalities or punishment (attracting a government agency's attention and risking fines) and/or closure of their business. Similarly, the details of these transactions are typically kept secret. Therefore, it was not surprising when some moneylenders were not comfortable with answering some questions. The assurances given by, and trust of, the introducer ensured a degree of co-operation and openness to provide some information, although the lead researcher did become aware after a certain point that they would not provide any information and, therefore, she did not insist on their answering every question. The interviews involved both specific and open-ended questions.

To ensure the reliability of data gathered and the process, several measures were taken. Firstly, the appropriateness of the questionnaire was verified by undertaking a pilot survey with 10 per cent of the sample that confirmed that the approach employed was suitable for proceeding with interviews. To overcome confidentiality issues, excerpts cited were anonymized and only relevant data for this study was used, not the whole set of conversations that took place during the interviewing process. Ten interviews with informal lenders, each lasting an hour, were undertaken to examine the interaction between borrowers and lenders. For this purpose, interviews were digitally recorded, transcribed verbatim by the researcher and analysed.

Demand Side

From the five districts, 350 farmers participated in this research via semi-structured interviews. The districts selected were chosen on the basis of the lead author's familiarity with them and the available social networks. This approach enabled her to use the government's records maintained by the each village's land revenue collector (*Patwari*) to identify small/marginal farmers. From the records, 500 farmers were selected using non-systematic sampling from the five districts. At the second stage, on the basis of classification, 70 farmers were selected for each category and when the contacts were made, only 200 farmers were willing to participate in the research. 15 respondents within this sample did not answer all the questions and they were excluded from the analysis. Fear of how the information may be used and repercussions may have ensured that farmers were reluctant to provide information freely. Therefore, it was only after reassurances and confidence-building measures that the participants felt at ease to respond to the questions.

The sample was stratified into five groups according to the size of the holding: marginal (less than 1 acre), small (1–2 acres), medium-sized (2–4 acres), large (4–10 acres) and very large (10 acres and above). The selected farmers were approached by the lead author directly to avoid any impression that there is pressure from the *Patwari* or a third party. Some farmers were very open and they shared almost all of the details (loan size, reasons for indebtedness, sources used, etc.) and concerns related to financing and farming practices, while some farmers, especially medium-sized and large farmers, were worried about their financial indebtedness becoming public which may have consequences for their reputation, and consequently they were reluctant to answer questions directly or openly. However, as the results below illustrate, once personal assurances were given and familiarity with the researcher was established, this reluctance and the related barriers were mitigated and there was a free flow of information from the respondents.

Table 12.1 Proportion of formal and informal borrowings

Size of landholdings	Households in the sample N=185	Farmers borrowing formal loan	Farmers borrowing informal loan	Borrowed from both sources
Less than one acre	30	Nil	30	Nil
1–2 acres	36	3	20	13
2–4 acres	32	4	13	15
4–10 acres	34	10	11	13
10 acres and above	53	16	6	21
Total	185	33	80	72

RESULTS AND DISCUSSION

Access or Distribution of Formal and Informal Credit

From the selected sample of 185 respondents, we were able to establish that they had some form of debt either from formal or informal sources and most of them could be apportioned under the two categories as listed in Table 12.1. From the sample of 185, a total of 33 farmers (17 per cent) had borrowed from formal credit institutions, 80 farmers (43 per cent) used only informal sources and 72 (40 per cent) used a combination of both. The findings suggested there was a positive correlation between the proportion of formal borrowings and the size of landholdings. It is quite evident from the findings in Table 12.1 that none of the marginal farmers had borrowed from the formal institutions due to lack of collateral. On further investigation, it was found that for SMFs, informal sources of finance such as *arthiyas* (retail merchants), *ghumihars* (potters), grocers, *sahukars* (village goldsmiths) and landlords (Table 12.2) are the main sources. Sixty-three SMFs among the sample of 66, as shown in Table 12.1, borrowed large amounts of money from informal sources for their families' subsistence because of low income due to lower landholdings. Small/marginal farmers are at a disadvantage as they do not have a choice; they cannot borrow from financial institutions because of their inability to provide the required collateral. Therefore, SMFs are reliant on loans from informal financial sources at a significantly high cost. Interest rates charged vary from region to region and according to the power of the lender.

The analysis suggests financial constraints are a major impediment to the adoption of technological innovations. Farmers' inability to use the most appropriate source of finance and size of credit impacts on the

Table 12.2   Proportion of borrowing from various informal lenders according to land size

Size of landholdings	Borrowed from both sources	Banks	Co-op societies/bank	Arthiyas	Ghumihar	Village grocer	Input dealer	Landlords	Sahukar	Friends/ family
Less than 1 acre	Nil	Nil	Nil	Nil	8	4	Nil	8	8	Nil
1–2 aces	13	Nil	3	11	3	4	Nil	4	6	4
2–4 acres	15	3	2	16	2	Nil	4	2	1	3
4–10 acres	13	2	3	14	Nil	Nil	5	Nil	Nil	3
10 acres and above	21	7	Nil	20	Nil	Nil	1	Nil	Nil	Nil
Total	72	12	8	61	13	8	10	14	15	10

efficiency of smaller farmers. Responses of farmers suggest the cost of seeds, pesticides, fertilizers and machinery are too much to bear for small/ marginal farmers, but to remain active they have to purchase these items without which they cannot survive. This vicious cycle means that they have to borrow from informal sources because of their exclusion by the formal financial institutions. Lack of access to finance is a hindrance for the survival of small/marginal farmers. Formal credit constraint threatens farmers' existence and limits their expansion. The analysis of responses suggests SMFs are solely dependent on informal lenders.

Reasons for Multiple Sources

As shown in Tables 12.1 and 12.2, the findings suggest that 83 per cent of farmers access finance from multiple lenders. The reasons for using multiple sources could be either to overcome the finance gap (a lower credit amount received from the bank) or to satisfy their specific needs from distinctive sources. The farmers, especially the new borrowers, do not get a sufficient amount of loan from one lender, hence they borrow from multiple lenders. Since there are no records shared between the lenders, the borrower's excessive borrowing leads them to financial distress and the associated problems of debt collection. Multiple borrowing from formal institutions is lower as they are more rigorous in ascertaining full information from the borrower. However, respondents often suggested that their reluctance to approach banks was due to excessive information sought by the banks and corruption in the form of bribes sought by bank officials, hence their preference to visit *arthiyas* for funds (see Table 12.3 and Figure 12.2).

Moreover, 70 per cent of the farmers mentioned that the cost of accessing and setting up informal finance is negligible, while the cost of accessing formal finance is significantly higher. However, the biggest driver of high informal lending is their easy accessibility. It has been observed during the interviews that the farmers have ties with different lenders to fulfil their distinctive needs. It has been found that if the farmer is an old client then the lender has more accurate information set and is willing to extend credit, sometimes possibly on lowering the cost of capital, and the credit facility remains open for many years. Informal lenders emphasized relational lending practices and lending decisions are made independently based on local and family knowledge; often they have in-depth knowledge of the household and at times credit may be extended to different family members without the knowledge of other family members.

The above analyses illustrated that there is an interesting range of reasons for choosing particular sources of funds (low cost, availability,

Table 12.3   Borrowing from various informal sources

Types of informal providers	Land/farm size (in acres)					
	>1	1–2	2–4	4–10	10 and above	Total N=133
Arthiyas	Nil	11	16	14	20	61
Landlords	8	4	2	Nil	Nil	14
Sahukars	8	6	1	Nil	Nil	15
Ghumihar	5	4	2	Nil	Nil	11
Village grocer	8	4	Nil	Nil	Nil	12
Input dealer	Nil	Nil	4	5	1	10
Friends/family	Nil	4	3	3	Nil	10

personal relationship, information asymmetry) or for having to rely on those sources that are eventually used. In terms of how these might differ from farmers who do or do not have access to finance, we cannot simply suggest that farmers who have chosen informal sources are more likely to be marginal farmers who, therefore, have no access to funds from formal institutions because of a lack of collateral. There is some evidence of outright rejection among most of the farmers (medium-sized and large farmers), leading to reliance on savings or family support and *arthiyas*, but not as much as might be expected from SMFs. However, 17 per cent of farmers borrowed only from formal financial institutions, 43 per cent from informal sources and 40 per cent from both formal and informal sources. Reasons for small/marginal farmers accessing informal finance included familiarity and an ability to obtain small amounts as and when required without having to follow complex procedures. The choice is based on economic rationality. As illustrated in Figure 2.2, lack of choice means that farmers are habitual borrowers and are reliant on *arthiyas*, as they purchase farmers' produce. Due to market imperfections, farmers at times do not have a readymade market for their produce and the government does not purchase crops directly from the farmers. Therefore, this is the basic reason or the starting point of the interaction between farmers and *arthiyas* that enables them to build a personal relationship on the basis of provider and recipient of finance. Hence if the government wants to keep farmers out of *arthiyas*' clutches, it needs to formulate an effective policy to develop a crop procurement system, to give basic training to farmers to understand borrowing and paying back, and to establish a framework to regulate this informal system.

Characteristics of Informal Lenders

As discussed above, informal lenders are a dedicated and bespoke source of finance for farmers, a well-established informal institution among farmers for generations and serve a large number of small and medium-sized farmers.

Tables 12.2 and 12.3 illustrate the position and activities of *arthiyas*; they are influential and familiar institutions, which operate from their homes and have no administration or other costs among the farming community. *Arthiyas* are easily accessible, well-established informal institutions, who live and operate among farmers for generations and serve a large population of farmers, and have built up their reputations and have acquired a high level of local knowledge and specialization. There is an informal accounting system showing how much money is borrowed from them, a book kept called *Khyta* to kept *Hisab* (account). A majority of the *arthiyas* in the sample were from the Jat caste (70 per cent), the Hindu religious community (25 per cent) and were *ghumihar*/potters only (5 per cent); all of them were male. *Arthiyas* provide collateralized loans and sometimes the pledged land can be at risk too. Despite *arthiyas* being the dominant party in the transaction, farmers still feel that *arthiyas* can better understand them than bank managers do, as they share a common background. Farmers do not need to explain their requirements to the *arthiyas* while the bank managers are more inquisitive, require more personal information and there were issues where the lending managers were from a different caste, hence were reluctant to provide full information. Moreover, lending managers are often from middle-class families and, although they are well educated, they are less aware of the problems faced by small/marginal farmers.

Figure 12.2 and Tables 12.2 and 12.3 show that farmers are heavily reliant (46 per cent) on customized sources of finance, varying according to the size of landholdings. Interest rates also vary from region to region, as also do the lending source and the final use of the credit itself (for instance, for consumption or investment in durable goods). In the sample, *arthiyas* declined to disclose the size of their business book and number of borrowers. Only one out of 10 disclosed informal accounts that he held, but such books of accounts are neither disclosed to tax authorities, nor does any audit trail exist. This importance and role of informal lenders appears to be critical for the farmers, without which the marginal farming community would have a major finance gap, especially for short-term finance. Agricultural business is often seasonal and the shortfall may only be for a few months. Formal institutions were reported to take a longer time to approve the loan and often took much longer to process the applications. Hence the loans provided by *arthiyas* are mainly seasonal short-term loans. There is evidence in the literature and in our findings that there is a social stigma attached to borrowing generally and especially from banks. Borrowers fear being exposed in society, as the farmers' community looks down upon indebted farmers; whereas *arthiyas*' loans are non-documented and confidential and the borrower is only exposed to his peer group. Therefore, farmers prefer to deal with *arthiyas* for money despite the high cost involved.

There was a commonly held view among the sample interviewed that banks are bureaucratic in that they strictly follow formalities and procedures; there are elements of patronage, arbitrariness and the corrupt practices pursued by the officials of formal institutions. These findings are corroborated (Bedbak, 1986; Sarap, 1991; Chaudhuri, 1993; Chaudhuri and Gupta, 1996, 1997; Sandhu, 2007; Sandhu et al., 2012a, 2012b). Twenty-seven per cent of the respondents reported that banks did not even bother to acknowledge the receipt of a loan application; 57 per cent of the surveyed farmers never approached the banks as they reported that there is a commonly held view that banks never lend unless you have someone who will be a guarantor. Banks, on the contrary, suggest farmers often rely on rumours due to their lack of education, awareness and reluctance to experience for themselves. Nonetheless, often they prefer an intermediary to deal with banks on their behalf rather than approaching the banks directly, and frequently they do not even have an account. One banker said, 'Farmers have a herd mentality and they react on the basis of a rumour rather than fact'. Such a view does not give confidence to small farmers when dealing with banks and 'bank approaching phobia' continues to prevail. With this background, *arthiyas* have a competitive advantage and continue to thrive on the basis of local knowledge of farmers' families and their financial credibility. The analysis suggests that the banking structure, management practices and lack of training for managers in dealing with farmers makes it difficult to compete with informal lenders.

Landlords are the rich and wealthy farmers who collect rent and also lend money as and when required. Figure 12.2 suggests that farmers take money on interest from landlords and in return sometimes provide labour or a part of their crop or sometimes pledge their land or disown the land against the loan taken. Such loans have severe implications for borrowers as there is no external monitoring; this point is dealt with in the section on 'Informal lending: unregulated sociological symbiotic relationship?' above.

Relatives/Friends: There is evidence of a pecking order when it comes to borrowing money for investment and consumption purposes. However, 80 per cent of respondents have borrowed money from their family and friends to fulfil their consumption needs. Interviews and discussions revealed that farmers repay their borrowing using agricultural commodities produced. Farmers normally borrow to either buy fertilizers or acquire seeds. Normally, farmers tended to store one-tenth of the harvested quantity as seeds but SMFs often fail to adopt this practice. Acquisition of good seeds is essential to improve the crops' yield. Landlords and wealthy farmers at times use this leverage over SMFs to extract labour or excessive returns. *Arthiyas* too supply loans for seed renewals but banks often are reported not to consider such applications for loans. This too explains banks' failure to understand farming needs and practices. Larger farmers which have finance can acquire technology and high-yielding seeds and adopt advanced practices but SMFs suffer from the finance gap. The findings suggest that there is an informal practice of seed exchange, hiring the equipment and providing labour among relatives and neighbours. The social structures and networks serve as a safety net and often farmers who may have a poor track record to either repay or return an equivalent amount of the produce are also provided seeds. However, this practice varies between locations and is strongly influenced by traditions and relationships.

Farming is a technology-intensive business that requires education to enable farmers to adapt emerging technologies and practices. However, this study suggests that there is a lack of education among the SMFs which has implications in terms of understanding the needs of formal banks to provide finance and in managing agriculture strategically. Lack of access to finance for acquisition of technology means SMFs continue to be labour intensive and rely on family labour, a practice evident in South Asian families in the West (Ram and Smallbone, 2001; Howorth, 2001; Atherton, 2006; Hussain and Scott, 2006; Mascarenhas-Keyes, 2007). The findings from this study are consistent with Howorth (2001) and Atherton (2006) in that SMFs tend to seek finance first from their own resources, friends and families, and then from other sources such as banks. The money from family and friends is used as leverage to unlock support from financial institutions. However, informal providers are in a better position to know the financial position of the family or borrower as they have networks to ascertain information, consequently information asymmetry is mitigated.

Sahukars (Village Goldsmith): One other group reported to play an important role is *sahukars* in the Indian Punjab. This group also acts as a safety net for women in case they need to raise funding for rainy days. Other moneylenders tend to have a concentration among one ethnic group. However, *sahukars* offer loans to multi-ethnic groups. Like *arthiyas*, they have been involved in moneylending for generations but their clientele base is restricted, and tends to serve borrowers from their own village, especially SMFs (as shown in Table 12.2). They tend to provide various types of loans (mainly consumption loans) and take gold or land or cattle as collateral. From the sample, seven farmers reported to have experienced some form of exploitation by *sahukars*, while others were reluctant to say anything due to the fear of loan denial in future.

Ghumihar (Potter): This group of lenders is less significant in terms of their market share but they too provide loans to local small/marginal farmers. Their modus operandi tends to be that, in return for the loan, they buy crops from the poor farmers at less than the market price. As illustrated in Figure 12.2, they act as a collection point, particularly in the villages situated in the remote areas. As these farmers' outputs are small and – due to transportation and communication problems – they sell locally, potters tend to exploit small farmers. However, they act as arbitrageurs, as they buy crops from marginal farmers, village grocers and *sahukars* at a lower price and sell them in the market at a higher price.

Sources of Financing of Informal Lenders

The study found that six out of ten informal lenders have accumulated money that they lend to others. The moneylenders often come from families which have been moneylending for many generations. However, a few new start-ups relied on family members who have acquired surplus money from family members working abroad. Four of the respondents mentioned that they are financing their lending business with a loan taken from the bank, they borrow at a lower interest rate and lend at a higher rate. The use of bank finance by moneylenders is consistent with the findings of Sinha and Martin (1998) and Borchgrevink et al. (2005). Management of the default rate is a key consideration, something that is managed by using information acquired through a network and, at times, respondents acknowledged, using coercion and bullying techniques. According to the surveyed moneylenders, they tend to remain small as they do not register their business transactions and prefer informality. Although a high default rate can have consequences, there is no data to assess their bad debt, nor were they willing to comment on this aspect of the business. The informal lenders acknowledged that internal constraints limit growth of even very successful moneylenders beyond a certain point as they tend to have no formal structures; but felt that improved flows of information and technological developments and the expansion of financial institutions will drive out their business and make access to finance more of an issue for SMFs.

Lending Criteria Adopted by Informal Lenders (Lending Decisions)

The moneylenders provided credit services involving innovative and novel credit contracts to cater for an individual's need: something banks can never do. All the lending decisions are made intuitively by the money-lender himself. The terms of the loan are informally determined by setting up an interest rate, time period and handling of any delinquent accounts. Within this context, relational lending practices are prominent among all the informal lenders. Moneylenders suggested that relying on relation-ships and recommendations of other clients served to minimize bad debts but limited their business growth, risk diversification and the ability to exploit economies of scale. Seven out of 10 informal lenders stated that they are very selective about their client: 'only lend to those people we know or to those referred by the guarantor, to whom the informal lender knows'. The informal lenders especially emphasized that the collateral of gold and land is very important rather than solely relying on social networks. Interestingly, almost all the lenders reported that they avoid lending to relatives as they cannot be objective in assessing risks and it can cause conflicts if money is not returned. Consequently, it also has a nega-tive impact upon the families. For instance, married women are put under pressure by their husbands to ask for money from their rich relatives, etc.

The legal structures and systems are not effective to enforce an agreed contract. Therefore, moneylenders rely on screening borrowers to ensure repayment of loans. Eight moneylenders reported that approximately 35–40 per cent of the defaulters are SMFs who borrowed for investment in farming. Interestingly, in the case of landlords, they reported low default rates. This may be explained by their political, strong social influence and their potential use of force to demand repayment of loans. As suggested in the literature and reported in Figure 12.1, informal lenders, especially landlords, rely on interlinked loans. These results corroborate earlier research findings (Sarap, 1991; Basu, 1997).

The results suggest that informal lenders tend to offer loans of differ-ent amounts with various maturity dates to suit individual clients' needs. Therefore, interest rates charged tend to vary according to the loan type and also the previous background of the farmers and their personal rela-tionship with the informal lenders. Often the interest rates charged are not disclosed in writing and only sums in excess of the amount lent is disclosed. It was not uncommon for landlords to charge a rate in excess of 20 per cent per month. Lenders did use the track records of borrowers to lend for a second time; 60 per cent of the moneylenders reported that a successful repayment of a small loan meant a larger amount was lent the next time. The average number of loans per borrower over time varied across various types of informal lenders. Two informal lenders reported that each borrower has taken 15–20 loans over a decade but this practice was not reported by the other eight moneylenders, but often the loan was renewed just before the harvest was ready.

CONCLUSIONS

This chapter makes an important contribution to the literature on informal lending to small/marginal farmers by providing an empirical examination of the financial lending and borrowing structures which exist in the Indian State of Punjab. The chapter sought to explore lending practices to SMFs among moneylenders in India and made a number of novel contributions. First, the study is the first of its kind that specifically examines the experiences of SMFs when dealing with informal lenders in the state of Punjab, India. This chapter has investigated why the informal lenders are the dominant players for small/marginal farmers and the consequences of such structures. Second, the chapter provides an analysis of bank failure in supporting SMFs. The study examined the causes and consequences of the finance gap for SMFs from both the demand and supply side to determine policies and measures to overcome these emergent issues. The findings from this chapter suggest that there exists an unregulated, complex, sociological symbiotic relationship between our units of analysis: farmers and informal lenders. It became apparent that, despite the usurious nature of loans, forced commerce and other illegal traits adopted by informal lenders, they are popular among the farmers due to their relational lending techniques and interlinked commerce (Figure 12.2). Informal transactions are preferred as formal institutions are constrained by the bureaucratic practices. Furthermore, there is a social stigma attached to borrowing and often banks failed to maintain the confidentiality of their borrowers. The results of interviews, therefore, show that informal lending was attractive to borrowers due to factors such as confidentiality, flexible terms of loan and time periods. On the other hand, lenders preferred unrecorded non-taxable income and repayments in the form of hard cash or produce from the farms. The qualitative findings suggested that informal lenders exploited social structures, ties and peer pressure to minimize bad debts. Borrowers often feared humiliation if the lender disclosed their borrowing: consequently this reduced the default risk.

Thus the literature review and empirical analysis provides evidence that informal lenders, especially *arthiyas*, are a significant part of the farming community and, in fact, dominate the borrowing activity in the Indian Punjab. A majority of the sample are farmers (78) and, of those,

30 per cent are SMFs. However, with increased fragmentation as families expand, the numbers are increasing (Singh and Joshi, 2008; Sangra, 2010). Such a large group's reliance on informal lenders is an issue for policymakers within India and there are lessons to be learned by other agriculturally dominated economies too. There is a need to regulate this informal lending sector, set some parameters for their operations and to deal with the malpractices adopted by the informal lenders. Notwithstanding empirical support for informal lenders to SMFs, it is important to emphasize that SMF financing cannot be merely provided by informal lenders, and policymakers and financial institutions need to develop strategies to cater for this unmet niche. How best the banks and government may provide appropriate finance for SMFs is an issue to be addressed in future studies.

NOTES

1. Informal finance is defined as contracts or agreements conducted without reference or recourse to the legal system to exchange cash in the present for promises of cash in the future (Schreiner, 2000). Formal finance is borrowing from financial institutions such as banks and credit unions, and other non-financial institutions subject to state supervision and regulation.
2. In biology, symbiosis is a broad term representing a variety of patterns between associating organisms. Mutualism is a narrower concept of reciprocal or mutual benefit from associating organisms (Whitefield, 1979).
3. Mutualism between two strictly separate classes may require such cheap labour obtained by merchants and moneylenders to be offered to the rich farmers at lower than the market wage rate in exchange for other assured benefits, because the merchant moneylending class has no direct use for much of the labour service they obtain. In effect, they then operate as convenient labour contractors for the rich farmer class. Mutualism becomes a distinct sociological possibility when the two classes are economically separate, but are interlinked through a caste or kinship network.
4. Consumption loans are those which are given by the banks to a customer in order to meet consumption needs which may range from medical emergencies, marriage purposes, educational purposes and so on.
5. Episitic dependence in biology entails when one species kills another for food (Lotka, 1956).

REFERENCES

Atherton, A. (2006), 'Pecking order theorisations of finance re-visited: prior experiences and founder heuristics as a determinant of start-up finance acquisition', Paper presented at Annual Conference of the British Academy of Management, 12–14 September.
Basu, S. (1997), 'Why intuitional credit agencies are reluctant to lend to the rural poor: a theoretical analysis of the Indian rural credit market', *World Development*, **25** (2): 267–280.
Bedbak, H. (1986), 'Institutional financing for priority sector: an assessment of delay and analysis of attitudes of agencies towards loanees', *Indian Cooperative Review*, **24** (2): 65–76.
Bell, C. (1988), 'Credit market and interlinked transactions', cited in H. Chenery and

T. Srinivasan (eds), *Handbook of Development Economics*. Vol. I. Holland: Elseneia Science Publishers, pp. 763–830.

Bell, C. Srinivasan, T. and Udry, C. (1997), 'Rationing, spillover, and interlinking in credit markets: the case of rural Punjab', *Oxford Economics Papers*, **49** (4): 557–558.

Bhaduri, A. (1981), 'Class relations and the pattern of accumulation in an agrarian economy', *Cambridge Journal of Economics*, **5** (1): 34–46.

Bhalla, S. (1976), 'New relations of production in Haryana agriculture', *Economic and Political Weekly*, **XI** (3): A23–A30.

Bhatt, N. and Thorat, Y. (2001), 'India's regional rural banks: the institutional dimensions of reforms', *Journal of Microfinance*, **3** (1): 65–94.

Borchgrevink, A. Woldehanna, T., Gebrehiwot, A. and Teshome, W. (2005), 'Marginalized groups, credit and empowerment: a study of the dedebit credit and savings institution of Tigray, Ethiopia', a Report Commissioned by Norwegian People's Aid and the Association of Ethiopian Mircofinance Institutions. Vol. 1, Ethiopia: Association of Ethiopian Microfinance Institutions.

Bouman, F. Bastiaansen, R. Boggard, V. Gerner, H. Hospes, O. and Kormelink, J. (1989), *Small, Short, and Unsecured: Informal Rural Finance in India*, New York NY: Oxford University Press.

Chandavarkar, A. (1983), 'Money and credit, 1858–1947' in D. Kumar and M. Desai (eds), *The Cambridge Economic History of India*, Vol. 2: c.1757–c. 1970, Cambridge: Cambridge University Press, pp. 300–387.

Chaudhuri, S. (1993), *Problems of Institutional Credit and Small Farmers: A Study of two Selected Villages of West Bengal*, Unpublished PhD Thesis, Princeton, NJ: Princeton University.

Chaudhuri, S. and Dwibedi, J. (2014), 'Horizontal and vertical linkages between formal and informal credit markets in backward agriculture: a theoretical analysis', retrieved from http://mpra.ub.uni-muenchen.de/55666/1/MPRA_paper_55666.pdf (accessed 10 September 2014).

Chaudhuri, S. and Gupta, M. (1996), 'Delayed formal credit, bribing and the informal credit markets in backward agriculture: a theoretical analysis', *Journal of Development Economics*, **51** (1): 433–449.

Chaudhuri, S. and Gupta, M. (1997), 'Formal credit, corruption and the informal credit market in agriculture: a theoretical analysis', *Economica*, **64** (1): 331–343.

Chavan, P. (2001), *Some Features of Rural Credit in India with Special Reference to Tamil Nadu: A Study of the Period after Nationalisation*, Unpublished MPhil dissertation, Mumbai: Indira Gandhi Institute of Development Research.

Conning, J. (1996), *Mixing and Matching Loans: Complementarity and Competition Amongst Lenders in a Rural Market in Chile*, Transcript, Yale: Yale University.

Datta, S. and Deodar, S. (eds) (2001), *Implications of WTO Agreements for Indian Agriculture*, CMA Monograph No. 91, Ahmedabad: Indian Institute of Management.

Desai, B. (1987), 'Credit: summaries of group discussion', *Indian Journal of Agricultural Economics*, **42** (3): 326–355.

Desai, D. (1988), 'Institutional credit requirements for agricultural production – 2000 A.D', *Indian Journal of Agricultural Economics*, **41** (3): 326–355.

Deshpande, R. (2002), 'Suicide by farmers in Karnataka: agrarian distress and possible alleviatory steps', *Economics and Political Weekly*, **37** (26): 2601–2610.

Ghatak, M. (2000), 'Screening by the company you keep: joint liability lending and the peer selection effect', *Economic Journal*, **110** (465): 601–631.

Ghatak, M. and Guinnane, T. (1999), 'The economics of lending with joint liability: theory and practice', *Journal of Development Economics*, **60** (1): 195–228.

Gill, A. (2003), 'Interlinked agrarian credit markets in a developing economy: a case study of Indian Punjab', Paper presented at the International Conference on Globalisation and Development, University of Strathclyde, Glasgow, 10–12 September.

Gill, A. (2014), 'Agricultural credit in Punjab: have policy initiatives made a dent in informal credit market?', Discussion Paper No. 7, retrieved from http://www.punjabiuniversity.

ac.in/cdeiswebsite/downloads/discussion_papers/7%20anita%20gill.pdf (accessed 30 April 2015).

Hoff, K. and Stiglitz, J. (1990), 'Imperfect information and rural credit markets: puzzles and policy perspectives', *World Bank Economic Review*, **4** (3): 235–250.

Howorth, C. (2001), 'Small firms' demand for finance', *International Small Business Journal*, **19** (4): 78–86.

Hussain, J. and Scott, J. (2006), *Access to Start-up Finance for Ethnic Minority Graduate Entrepreneurs*, unpublished Report prepared for the National Council for Graduate Entrepreneurship, Birmingham: University of Central England.

Lotka, A. (1956), *Elements of Mathematical Biology*, New York: Dover.

Madestam, A. (2014), 'Informal finance: a theory of moneylenders', *Journal of Development Economics*, **107** (C): 157–174.

Mascarenhas-Keyes, S. (2007), 'Ethnic minority enterprise in England: diversity and challenges', Paper presented at the 51st Conference of the International Council for Small Business, Melbourne, Australia, 18–21 June.

Mujumdar, N. (1988), 'Rapporteur's report on institutional credit', *Indian Journal of Agricultural Economics*, **41** (3): 538–543.

Mujumdar, N. (1999), 'Reviving rural credit' in R. Kapila and U. Kapila (eds), *Economics Development in India*, Monthly Update, **17**: 37–45.

Naidu, B. (1946), *Report of Economist for Enquiry into Rural Indebtedness*, Madras: Government of Madras.

Rajeev, M. Vani, B. and Bhattacharjee, M. (2012), 'Nature and dimensions of farmers' indebtedness in India', retrieved from http://mpra.ub.uni-muenchen.de/42358/1/MPRA_paper_42358.pdf (accessed 12 February 2013).

Ram, M. and Smallbone, D. (2001), *Ethnic Minority Enterprise: Policy in Practice*, Final Report prepared for Small Business Service, Sheffield: Small Business Service.

Ramachandran, V. and Swaminanthan, M. (2001), *Does Informal Credit Provide Security?: Rural Banking Policy in India*, Geneva, Switzerland: International Labour Organization.

Reserve Bank of India (1954), *All-India Rural Credit Survey Report 1951–52*, Mumbai: Reserve Bank of India.

Sandhu, N. (2007), *An Empirical Investigation of Financial Institutions' Lending Policies towards Agribusiness during the Post-green Revolution in Punjab, India*, Unpublished PhD Thesis, Birmingham: Birmingham City University.

Sandhu, N. Hussain, J. and Matlay, H. (2012a), 'Barriers to finance experienced by female owner/managers of marginal farms in India', *Journal of Small Business and Enterprise Development*, **19** (4): 640–655.

Sandhu, N. Hussain, J. and Matlay, H. (2012b), 'Entrepreneurship education and training needs of family businesses operating in the agricultural sector of India', *Education + Training*, **54** (8/9): 727–743.

Sangra, S. (2010), 'Population growth and agriculture in India', retrieved from http://indiamicrofinance.com/population-growth-agriculture-india.html (accessed 26 August 2011).

Sarap, K. (1991), 'Factors affecting small farmers: access to institutional credit in rural Orissa, India', *Development and Change*, **21** (2): 281–307.

Schreiner, M. (2000), 'Informal finance and the design of microfinance', *Development in Practice*, **11** (5): 637–640.

Shah, M., Rao, R. and Shankar, P. (2007), 'Rural credit in 20th century India: an overview of history and perspectives', *Economic and Political Weekly*, **42** (15): 1351–1364.

Shivamaggi, H. (1986), 'Rapporteur's report on institutional credit', *Indian Journal of Agricultural Economics*, **41** (3): 435–442.

Singh, M. and Joshi, A. (2008), 'Economic analysis of crop production and dairy farming on marginal and small farms in Punjab', *Agricultural Economics Research Review*, **21** (July–December): 251–257.

Sinha, S. and Martin, I. (1998), 'Imperfect substitutes: the local political economy of informal finance and microfinance in rural China and India', *World Development* **32** (9): 1487–1507.

Swaminathan, M. (1991), 'Segmentation, collateral under-valuation, and the rate of interest in agrarian credit markets: some evidence from two villages in South India', *Cambridge Journal of Economics*, **15** (2): 161–178.

Vani, B. and Rajeev, M. (2011), *Emerging from Shadow: New Dimensions of Household Indebtedness in India*, Germany: VDM Publishing.

Whitefield, P.J. (1979), *The Biology of Parasitism: an introduction to the study of associating organisms*, Aldershot, UK and Brookfield, VT, USA: Edward Elgar Publishing.

13. Unilateral microfinance? The commercial roots of entrepreneurial diversity
Madina Subalova, Haya Al-Dajani and Zografia Bika

INTRODUCTION

Entrepreneurship within transition economies is of fundamental importance because of its macro and micro effects; it is essential for the emergence of new ideas, the creation of new entities and jobs, and development as a whole (Bruyat and Julien, 2000). However, in transition economies small firms often emerge and survive 'in spite' of the political regulations and economic limitations (Chelariu et al., 2008). Indeed, both the number of bank loan applications and the number of successful loan approvals received by small businesses in developing countries are low (Bigsten et al., 2003), and local small firms here continue to be disadvantaged in receiving both short-term and long-term loans (Barth et al., 2011). Although the literature on the access of small firms to funding from commercial banks in transition economies is growing, it does not adequately address entrepreneurs' access to microfinance. The available literature that does so is embedded within developing economies and, therefore, will be drawn upon and discussed here. Hartarska and Gonzalez-Vega (2006) associate entrepreneurs' lack of access to external funding with the inability of formal finance providers to address the problems that arise from information asymmetries associated with small business lending. High information asymmetry is a result of entrepreneurs not maintaining records of their operations in books, mainly using cash, and in most cases combining their business and personal financial activities (Cook, 2001; Straub, 2005). Furthermore, Behr et al. (2011) argue that, in the context of a developing economy, small businesses are required by banks to provide a larger amount of collateral in order to reduce their own associated risks. Carpenter and Petersen (2002) further emphasize that the size of the collateral, as well as the nature of the assets, prevent access to external funding.

As a result, it can be argued that within transition economies the commercial banking sector mostly serves the entrepreneurs who have substantial assets and low information asymmetries. In fact, small businesses in developing economies tend to rely on sources of funding such

as overdrafts, trade loans and informal sources such as informal moneylenders, family members and friends, rather than bank financing (Bigsten
et al., 2003). Large firms generally have more opportunities to obtain
financial support from local and foreign banks, while small firms tend
to utilize internal funds and retained earnings, and informal sources of
finance (Nichter and Goldmark, 2009; Cull et al., 2006). However, usage
of personal wealth and informal funding results in higher risks of business failure (Goedhuys and Sleuwaegen, 2000). Although small businesses
prefer informal sources (for example, informal money lenders) of finance
to overcome financial constraints, when these sources are utilized, higher
interest rates are imposed (Nguyen et al., 2008).

Microfinance is thus an alternative to conventional sources of funding
and to informal sources of funding that can be utilized by entrepreneurs
(Morduch and Haley, 2002). However, existing studies are often focused
upon the role of microfinance as a poverty alleviator (Hoque and Chishty,
2011; Churchill, 2000) rather than an alternative source of funding for
entrepreneurs (Olivares-Polanco, 2005). In this context, this chapter aims
to explore the role of microfinance as an alternative source of funding for
entrepreneurs within transition economies.

MFOS AS AN ALTERNATIVE SOURCE OF ENTREPRENEURIAL FUNDING

Microfinance is viewed as a substitute for informal sources of finance and
a tool for reducing poverty in populations that are economically active
but socially unprotected with very limited access to funding (Morduch
and Haley, 2002). Microfinance funds enterprises that cannot use other
financial sources (Parker, 2009). As well as the promise of poverty reduction, microfinance is perceived as a vehicle for advancing the capacity of
financial institutions by enabling cost-effective loan distribution to the
poor (Morduch, 2000). It also eliminates the problem of mid-wage shortage of income; and, coupled with savings, allows a gradual transfer from
self-employment towards entrepreneurship (Ahlin and Jiang, 2008).

A unique characteristic of microfinance is the utilization of peer loans
without the requirement for collateral (Rahman, 1998). This feature
enables microfinance clients who do not have substantial personal assets
to access financial sources in groups, under the notion that social capital
will motivate full and timely repayment, as the group is liable as a unified
borrower (Rahman, 1998). That is, if one of the group's borrowers is
unable to repay, the rest of the group bears the arising costs. Parker (2009)
explained that this approach plays a crucially beneficial role as increased

loan repayment rates result from peer pressure among the group partici-pants. Indeed, previous studies have underlined the importance of social capital that is built through relationship lending in the microfinance sector (Baklouti and Baccar, 2013). Furthermore, Behr et al. (2011), in their research in Mozambique, found that the building of relationships allows MFOs to limit the information asymmetries and increases the likelihood of loan approval; and as the relationships progress, the time required for loan evaluation decreases, and less collateral is demanded. The borrowers recycle their improved loan records to negotiate lower interest rates and larger loans, as well as diminishing their asymmetric information over time (Parker, 2009). Hence, through utilization of group lending, micro-finance institutions are able to address the moral hazard associated with small business funding.

In fact, various entrepreneurs are excluded from loan distribution by commercial banks due to the imperfections of the financial market, high information asymmetry and limited or absent collateral (Beck et al., 2009). The academic consensus is that the asymmetric information between the commercial lenders and borrowers results in inefficient loan allocation (Jappelli and Pagano, 2002). Thus, the costs of monitoring and controlling are included in the debt agreements which increases the interest rates and is detrimental to the small firms' potential growth (Jappelli and Pagano, 2002).

The greater the risk of information asymmetry for the financial sup-plier, the higher the return on capital required from the small firms; as a result, small firms prefer internal financing to debt, short-term over long-term debt, and any debt rather than outside equity (Cassar and Holmes, 2003). Small firms tend to gain better access to short-term loans from commercial banks only when the information asymmetries decrease as a result of entrepreneurial growth and business maturity (Mac an Bhaird and Lucey, 2011). At initial stages of firm development, entrepreneurs rely upon their own wealth and, with time, retained earnings substitute for wealth, which in turn are gradually substituted by short-term debt (Mac an Bhaird and Lucey, 2011). It may be suggested, therefore, that at this point, microfinance becomes an alternative to commercial banks as a source of short-term loans. However, Gonzalez-Vega (1998) presented a more critical view of the microfinance model. He argues that the temporal nature of the microfinance agreements, the uncertainty of entrepreneurial activities faced by borrowers, and the moral hazard that alters the prob-ability of repayment, demonstrate how MFOs are only concerned with maintaining a high outreach rate to poor segments of the population. Instead Gonzalez-Veha (1998) calls MFOs to focus upon having both outreach and sustainable operations.

Much of the existing literature, in its recognition of the role of microfinance, is concerned with the question of trade-offs between outreach and sustainability (Bateman and Chang, 2012; Mair and Marti, 2009). Hence, the emerging debate asks if the commercialization of the microfinance sector is a social innovation or a 'wrong turn' (Hoque and Chishty, 2011). Morduch (2000, p. 67) argues that the existing perception within the field of microfinance draws its conclusion on a win-win proposition: 'microfinance institutions that follow the principles of good banking will also be those that alleviate the most poverty. By eventually eschewing subsidies and achieving financial sustainability, microfinance institutions will be able to grow without the constraints imposed by donor budgets'. However, Morduch (2000) further argued that this proposition does not hold up in practice, where MFO success stories are exceptions rather than the norm. The win–win proposition is thus based on rhetorical arguments rather than empirical results. There is also increasing concern that in its outreach attempts, microfinance does not reach the 'very poor' or the 'most needy'. In the example of Bangladesh, Mair and Marti (2009) revealed that the ultra-poor are neglected by development programmes as MFO staff discourage such applicants because any late repayments will negatively impact branch performance profiles. Furthermore, the loan distribution process model whereby larger amounts of funding are authorized following the repayment of initial smaller loans by the same client discriminates against the very poor and most needy, who are unable to repay their initial loans (Churchill, 2000). Thus McIntosh and Wydick (2005) argue that the establishment of a competitive market for microfinance results in the inability of MFOs to supply the very poor with financial resources, and that non-profitable customers become excluded rather than targeted by the profit-oriented microfinance organizations.

Hoque and Chishty (2011) extend this argument and proclaim that the commercialization of MFOs in developing countries is a 'wrong turn' as it results in increased costs of capital, when MFOs are not funded by non-governmental organizations (NGOs). Consequently, the higher cost of borrowing results in higher interest rates which in turn increase default and risk rates. Hence privately owned MFOs favour the profitability of their operations in the constant struggle to choose between outreach and sustainability (Fogel et al., 2011). However, it should be noted that, although MFOs charge high interest rates, they do not exceed the interest rates imposed by informal moneylenders who also provide small loans (Collins et al., 2009). Thus, given the significance of these small loans for the clients' day-to-day operations, MFO users maintain high repayment rates even when high degrees of competition and supply exist within the microfinance sector (Vogelgesang, 2003). In the case of MFOs being unable to simultaneously maintain their outreach to the poor and achieve full efficiency, they might also become a source of short-term loans for entrepreneurs. Taking these considerations into account, it becomes obvious that far too little attention has been paid to the role of MFOs other than that of poverty alleviation. The focus of microfinance scholars on outreach and sustainability limits our understanding of the potential impact that commercial MFOs may have upon entrepreneurs.

In practice, the increased investment into the microfinance sector has resulted in the creation of commercial MFOs which led to a further debate on microfinance as a viable development tool (Sonnekalb, 2014). Armendariz and Morduch (2010) revealed that commercialization of the microfinance sector influences which clients are served by the MFOs and how they are served. They also revealed that in recent years commercial MFOs experienced a flow of funding due to their high equity returns. Unlike the commercial MFOs, outreach oriented MFOs are empirically shown to be funded by development institutions which are focused upon outreach to the poor segments of the population. Therefore, commercial MFOs and outreach driven MFOs differ not only in terms of their sources of funding, but also in their orientation and customer profiles. These practical differences thus create a commercial and outreach driven dichotomy of MFOs representing some of the existing diversity within the microfinance sector.

However, in the literature the microfinance sector is still approached as a unilateral phenomenon where outreach and sustainability are the guiding factors and, therefore, the sector's diversity is largely ignored (Armendariz and Morduch, 2010; Morduch, 2000; Olivares-Polanco, 2005; Gonzalez-Vega, 1998). In this framework, the main contribution of this study is the recognition of the diversity of the microfinance sector in the case of Kazakhstan, and the classification of three different approaches to microlending. This study explores the heterogeneous and diverse nature of the microfinance sector by drawing on evidence from Almaty city and its surrounding district in Kazakhstan. The Kazakhstani context was chosen as it is a transition economy with a substantial microfinance sector where over 1,700 MFOs are operating, and the growth rate for the sector is about 10 per cent per annum. Kazakhstan is also currently undergoing significant political and economic change (Statistical Agency of Republic of Kazakhstan, 2010).

Undertaking the research in this under-researched transition economy context responds to calls made by Zahra (2007) and Welter (2010), among others, for contextualizing entrepreneurship research. Contextualizing entrepreneurship research enables theoretical expansion of existing American and Eurocentric views of entrepreneurship research, theory and practice (Bruton et al., 2008). Contextualization of entrepreneurial research provides opportunities for new approaches and interpretations of phenomena, theories and findings (Zahra et al., 2014). Welter (2010, p. 176) argues that the contextualization of research 'has to be combined with an individual perspective that takes into account the adaptability and learning behavior of entrepreneurs, thus drawing attention to the process dimension of entrepreneurship where individual action impacts context and contributes to changing a context'. Hence this study provides a unique opportunity to recognize the local entrepreneurial population's impact upon the arising diversity of the Kazakhstani microfinance sector.

The republic of Kazakhstan is situated in Central Asia and is the ninth largest country in the world. However, it remains an under-researched site and context for investigation (Low, 2006). One of Kazakhstan's main priorities is the development of the small business sector. Indeed, eliminating the barriers that prevent the development of the small business sector is a priority for all Central Asian states (Hubner, 2000). Within such transition economies, which are more dynamic and hostile than developed ones, entrepreneurs face several instabilities and uncertainties (Newman, 2000; Luthans and Ibrayeva, 2006) including:

- resistance to change within the governmental, cultural, business, and social institutions
- poorly developed legal and financial systems
- high interest rates for external funding and inflation of national currency.

METHODOLOGY

This chapter draws on two datasets from a wider study which adopted a mixed methodology approach. The qualitative dataset was obtained through in-depth interviews with key microfinance industry informants and the quantitative dataset was obtained through face-to-face structured interviews with clients of MFOs operating in Almaty and its surrounding district. More specifically, in order to trace the trends within the MFO sector, and to provide insights into the issues facing entrepreneurial actors in the industry, six key players within Kazakhstan's microfinance industry were interviewed, and these included employees and founding members of the Association of Micro Financial Organizations of Kazakhstan (AMFOK). The key informants provided information on the current stage of the sector's development with regards to the legislative environment and market situation, depth of outreach and sustainability. These in-depth

interviews facilitated the understanding of the social and financial preferences of MFOs' decision-making, as well as any shifts within the sector.
The data was analysed through thematic analysis with the utilization of a
conceptually clustered matrix as shown in Table 13.1.

The quantitative dataset was collected via a survey of 155 entrepreneurs who were clients of 14 different MFOs operating in Almaty city
and its surrounding district. The target population for this study was
both formal and informal Kazakhstani entrepreneurs using the services
of MFOs. A number of challenges in collecting data in Kazakhstan
have previously been documented by Erdener (2011) and include a low
response rate and withholding of personal information by respondents.
To overcome these potential limitations in our study, the snowballing
sampling technique was employed in order to improve the response rate
and obtain the respondents' full cooperation. Hence, the operating MFOs
in Almaty and its district were approached to provide contact details of
at least five of their clients, either former or current ones. These clients
were interviewed and then asked to refer other entrepreneurs who also
had experience of working with a MFO. As a result, the survey included
a diverse set of entrepreneurs who were clients of either outreach-
driven MFOs, profit-oriented MFOs, or unexpectedly, Kazakhstani state
MFOs. The survey data was analysed through descriptive statistics to
identify the target market of MFOs and their characteristics (Profiles can
be seen in Table 13.2). Based on these statistics (Table 13.2), three distinctive groups of MFOs were identified and the following section presents
these groups in detail.

RESULTS/FINDINGS

Previous studies emphasized the role of MFOs as providers of external
funding for poor segments of the population and as a policy vehicle to
enhance entrepreneurship (Morduch and Haley, 2002; Dasgupta, 2005;
Qayyum and Ahmad, 2008). However, a limited number of studies
(such as Gachet and Staehli, 2008; Armendariz and Morduch, 2010;
Vogelgesang, 2003) have examined the characteristics of MFOs' funding
beyond outreach and sustainability criteria. Hence, our study is focused
on revealing the entrepreneurial diversity that emerges from a varying
degree of MFOs' outreach and sustainability. The data analysis unveiled
the crucial finding that the Kazakhstan microfinance sector is heterogeneous and diverse with three main but different types of MFOs emerging:
Foreign, Private and State established MFOs. Further analysis revealed
that these three types of MFOs were different from each other in terms of

Table 13.1 Conceptually clustered matrix based on key industry informant interviews

RESPONDENT	OUTREACH AND SUSTAINABILITY OF MFOS' OPERATIONS		
	MFO sector	*Interest rates*	*Role of MFOs*
ALEXANDR	**Structure**: MFO sector has 4 categories, 2 of which work with entrepreneurs **Private MFOs**: Lack of external funding; utilize individual collateralized loans **Foreign MFOs**: Access to international funding institutions; utilize group loans **State MFOs**: focused on agricultural sector; funded by the state	**Flexibility**: are more flexible, no strict requirements, hence entrepreneurs are willing to pay more **Cost of borrowing**: receive funding by the commercial banks, which results in MFOs' higher interest rates	**Entrepreneurs' access to commercial banks**: MFOs become a substitute for commercial banks for entrepreneurs **External funder**: MFOs are competitive as the entrepreneurs who are unable to access commercial banks become clients of MFOs **Clients**: not able to prove income and operations, as they are informal and reluctant to register in fear of state agents
AINUR	**Structure**: sector is heterogeneous (large/small); many inactive MFOs **Private MFOs**: are not eligible for foreign and state investments due to their inability to comply with requirements; use their own internal capital; primarily provide collateralized loans; lack human resources **Foreign MFOs**: Have own networks to external funding; group loans mainly; still hard to collect a group loan, as people have a certain mindset	**Flexibility**: interest rates are higher due to flexible procedure and MFOs' case by case approach	**Entrepreneurs' access to commercial banks**: MFOs are more accessible; more able to analyse informal notes and are flexible in relation to collateral requirements; provide only collateralized loans as entrepreneurs' mind set tells them not to return uncollateralized loans **External funder**: MFOs are competitive as they serve entrepreneurs who are unable to secure loans from commercial banks; those who have previously been informal lenders often transform into MFOs; offer short-term small loans

Clients: are not able to provide suitable collateral for commercial banks; prefer to work informally, as this is often their start-up background

Entrepreneurs' access to commercial banks: MFOs have simplified procedures; a crisis often makes entrepreneurs unable to secure loans; clients have got used to not paying banks

External funder: MFOs are competitive as they mostly distribute small loans

Clients: small entrepreneurs in need of support mainly operate in the trade sector

Flexibility: results in higher interest rates; operational expenses due to client-oriented service are high; clients do not mind high interest rates because of the customer service they receive

Structure: ineffective for active MFOs that do not comprehend the sector

Foreign MFOs: do not face competition from other MFOs, as they work with lower layers of population

RAMONA

Entrepreneurs' access to commercial banks: MFOs fill the niche of small and micro firms overlooked by commercial banks; banks are not able to address the needs of entrepreneurs

External funder: MFOs provide small and micro loans

Clients: clients are very small entrepreneurs who are mainly traders and farmers; and are informal; clients who require small and micro loans

Flexibility: case by case evaluation; flexible towards requirements and collateral

Structure: the sector is flooded with inactive and unprofitable MFOs, as owners do not understand the MFO lending process

Private MFOs: are not able to access state funding, as this is corrupt; work on their internal resources; lack of qualified human resources; do not have a social mission; MFO owners aim to earn a living

Foreign MFOs: largest MFOs are supported by foreign funding

State MFOs: focused on state policy aims; extensively funded by state

SERGEY

Table 13.1 (continued)

RESPONDENT	OUTREACH AND SUSTAINABILITY OF MFOS' OPERATIONS		
	MFO sector	*Interest rates*	*Role of MFOs*
ABAI	**Private MFOs:** MFOs' development is stagnated by limited access to funding; primarily funded by internal resources or commercial banks; no access to state funded programmes; limited human resources; owners of private MFOs want to make a profit **Foreign MFOs:** large organizations; group loans distributed mainly by these MFOs, as these MFOs have resources to train their employees	**Cost of borrowing:** receive funding by the commercial banks, a fact which results in MFOs' higher interest rates	**Entrepreneurs' access to commercial banks:** MFOs can become not only financial providers but as well a consulting entity as to advance the business of the entrepreneurs **External funder:** MFOs are not able to attract good clients; thus they focus on only those clients who are overlooked by commercial banks; they may indirectly trigger formalization through initiating business growth **Clients:** informal entrepreneurs, with no proof of income and operations are a target market; clients who require very small amount of loans
ZHANAR	**Structure:** most MFO organizations are inactive, as these were created by people who do not understand microfinance **Private MFOs:** such MFO owners want to make money; no social mission; funding is a problem; not very transparent; do not use group loans, as they do not have knowledge of the lending process **Foreign MFOs:** major players; distribute group loans; their individual loans are always collateralized	**Flexibility:** flexible towards requirements and collateral; their case to case approach results in higher interest rates	**Entrepreneurs' access to commercial banks:** banks are not flexible **External funder:** MFOs are niche players **Clients:** depends on the organization's social mission and aims

238

Table 13.2   MFO clients' profiles based on the survey results

Variable	Private MFOs	Foreign MFOs	State MFOs
Entrepreneurs' Characteristics			
Clients' gender (male)	49.49 %	8.80%	80.00%
Clients' age mean	43.82	40.64	50.67
Clients have university degree	55.80%	28.90%	46.70%
Clients have college degree	21.10%	13.30%	33.30%
Clients have secondary education	23.10%	57.70%	20%
Clients have Professional working experience	42.10%	35.60%	66.7%
Clients have White collar working experience	14.70%	4.40%	0
Clients have Blue-collar working experience	27.30%	57.80%	33.30%
Clients own livestock	26.70%	17.80%	100.00%
Clients own vehicle	80.00%	47.7%	80.00%
Clients own property (apartment or house)	52.00%	48.9%	93.30%
Clients own land	41.00%	44.00%	93.30%
Business Characteristics			
Clients' years of business operation (mean)	9.95	6.9	10.07
Number of clients' employees (mean)	7.48	2.89	7.73
Clients registered as Private Entrepreneur	48.40%	26.70%	0
Clients registered as Legal Entity	20.00%	2.20%	13.30%
Clients registered as Agriculture entity	4.20%	0	73.30%
Clients operate as Informal entity	27.30%	71.00%	13.30%
Quarter turnover of clients business less than 3600 USD	35.80%	82.20%	40.00%
Quarter turnover of clients business 3600–7000 USD	58.90%	17.80%	60.00%
Quarter turnover of clients business above 7000 USD	5.20%	0	0
Quarter profits of clients business less than 2000 USD	29.50%	57.80%	33.30%
Quarter profits of clients business from 2000–6500 USD	35.80%	37.80%	47.70%
Quarter profits of clients business 6500 USD	34.70%	24.40%	20.00%
External Funding Usage			
Clients used commercial banks' funding	57.90%	51.10%	33.30%
Clients used loans from family and friends	20.00%	11.10%	6.25%
Clients used other sources of funding	9.50%	2.20%	0
Mean number of MFO loans obtained by clients	4.09	4.2	2.13
Avg. duration of MFOs' application process (days)	4.62	7.78	42.4
Group loan distributed by MFO	14.70%	64.40%	0
Individual collateralized loan distributed by MFO	77.90%	22.20%	93.30%

Table 13.2   (continued)

Variable	Private MFOs	Foreign MFOs	State MFOs
External Funding Usage			
MFO loan duration in months (mean)	13.28	8.87	37.07
Loans provided for less than 12 months	56.90%	71.10%	33.30%
Loan provided for 12–23 months	24.20%	24.40%	13.30%
Loan provided for longer than 24 months	18.90%	4.20%	53.30%
Loans provided for day-to-day expenditure	54.70%	77.80%	20.00%
Loans provided for business expenditure	26.30%	15.60%	20.00%
Loans provided for livestock purchase	2.10%	4.40%	33.30%
Loans provided for investment	8.40%	0	0

types of distributed loans and targeted clients, funding, and loan distribution processes. We now describe each of the three types of MFOs.

Foreign MFOs

The first type of MFOs that work with entrepreneurs in Kazakhstan includes the largest organizations, which are subsidized by foreign funding institutions. Key informants highlighted that this type of MFO tries to maintain its mission, while it is mainly funded, established, or controlled by international development organizations. According to the key industry informants, such organizations are few in number and do not face competition from private or state MFOs, as they largely operate in rural areas and target the poor segments of the population. Ramona* specified that: 'In an environment where MFOs operate with conventional methods of microfinance, they work in villages and with certain social layers of population. I think they do not face competition'. It became evident from the quantitative data analysis that 71 per cent of the entrepreneurs served by foreign MFOs are informal. Also 82.20 per cent of foreign MFOs' clients have low profits and 57.50 per cent have a low turnover. Interestingly, 91.20 per cent of these MFOs' clients are female, 57.70 per cent of the entrepreneurs have secondary education, and 57.80 per cent have blue-collar work experience. Furthermore, only 47.70 per cent of foreign MFOs' clients own a vehicle and 48.90 per cent own property, in contrast to what is the case with other entrepreneurs in the sample. 51.10 per cent of entrepreneurs served by foreign MFOs used commercial bank loans and only 13.40 per cent used other sources of funding. Hence, our results confirm that foreign MFOs focus on the poor segments of the population who do not have access to sources of funding other than microfinance due to their low profits and turnover and absence of assets that can be used as collateral.

Interestingly, 64.40 per cent of loans distributed by foreign MFOs in our sample were group loans. As group lending is designed to serve individuals who not only lack access to external funding, but also collateral, foreign MFOs appear to attract micro entrepreneurs. In contrast, private MFOs and state MFOs do not use group lending as extensively as the foreign MFOs. The key industry informants associated this phenomenon with the fact that unlike private or state MFOs, foreign MFOs are able to provide training to their employees to operate the group loans, and have developed procedures to maintain these loan processes. More than 70 per cent of foreign MFOs' clients obtained loans with a duration of less than 12 months, and 77.80 per cent loans provided by foreign MFOs in the sample were used by clients for day-to-day purposes. Hence foreign MFOs provide entrepreneurs with short-term loans that facilitate working capital issues, or mid-wage shortage of income (Ahlin and Jiang, 2008). Foreign MFOs with access to funding from international institutions are, therefore, able to maintain a high level of outreach without experiencing high competition, with almost an exclusive focus upon micro entrepreneurs with low income and turnover, via the utilization of group lending.

Private MFOs

The second type of MFOs that work with entrepreneurs in Kazakhstan are privately owned, underfunded and focused on sustaining their own operations. According to the key informants, the majority of Kazakhstani MFOs are established to generate profit rather than to perform a social mission. This finding verifies the argument made by Fogel et al. (2011) that commercial organizations prefer profitability to outreach. Private MFOs, according to all key informants in our study, are focused on generating profit and prefer to work with individual collateralized loans in order to minimize their own risks. According to key industry informants, the concentration by these private MFOs on individual collateralized loans is due to the high costs of obtaining funding from commercial banks. In fact, the entrepreneur survey results revealed that 77.90 per cent of loans distributed by private MFOs are collateralized. As a result, their interest rates are higher and they are focused upon ensuring the repayment of loans. Hence these private MFOs are facing high risks when distributing their funds to entrepreneurs, and they try to minimize such risks by obtaining collateral.

In contrast to foreign MFOs, private MFOs tend to provide loans for more diverse purposes. For example, 8.40 per cent of loans by private

MFOs are for investment purposes while 56.90 per cent of loans are for less than 12 months, and 43.10 per cent of loans are distributed for more than one year. Moreover, 57.90 per cent of private MFOs' clients in the sample use commercial bank loans and 29.50 per cent use other sources of finance; which is more than what clients of foreign and state MFOs do. In fact, the key industry informants revealed that private MFOs try to maintain a flexible loan distribution process to attract clients who are overlooked by commercial banks, but at the same time with better entrepreneurial profiles than the clients of foreign MFOs. Results of the entrepreneur survey indicated that private MFOs tend to provide loans to formal entrepreneurs with a higher mean number of employees (7.48), of which 55.80 per cent have a university degree. Furthermore, 42.10 per cent of private MFOs' clients have professional working experience and another 14.70 per cent have white-collar experience. Interestingly, 80 per cent of private MFOs' clients own a vehicle and 52 per cent own property, which indicates a high level of accumulated assets. Moreover, the turnover and profits of private MFOs' clients tended to be higher than those of foreign MFOs' clients. Thus, the private MFOs are able to provide loans to established entrepreneurs, who are often overlooked by commercial banks. According to the key industry informants, this is because the entrepreneurs do not declare their income, and do not maintain financial records. This goes hand-in-hand with the tendency of commercial banks in Kazakhstan to have a long loan application process taking up to two months to complete in some instances. In contrast, private MFOs tend to provide loans on average within 4.62 days. According to the key industry informants, MFOs' fast loan distribution is essential for entrepreneurs, as it allows them to grab existing opportunities and address their working capital issues with immediate effect. Sergey stated: 'no one is interested in lending a 500,000 or 300,000 KZT loan to a small business or a person working in the bazaar who needs money to replenish his turnover'.

As a result, the features of private MFOs, such as flexibility and fast distribution processes, allow these MFOs to compete effectively with commercial banks in order to attract established entrepreneurs, who are able to provide collateral and maintain profitable businesses.

State MFOs

The state MFOs appeared as an outlier within both the qualitative and quantitative analyses. Only two key industry informants mentioned this group of MFOs, according to whom the latter are extensively funded by the state and focus upon governmental policy to develop the agricultural sector. According to key industry informant Alexander: 'In Kazakhstan there are many state policies implemented, which are aimed to develop agricultural sector, through MFO financing'. This claim was also supported by the entrepreneur survey results. All state MFOs' clients own livestock and 73.30 per cent are agricultural entities. Furthermore, state MFOs work with entrepreneurs who have substantially different profiles when compared with the clients of the private and foreign MFOs. Just over 93 per cent of state MFOs' clients own a property, which is a clear indicator of a high level of accumulated assets, 80 per cent are male, and own a vehicle. Moreover, 47.70 per cent of state MFOs' clients earn over 2,000 USD per quarter and 60 per cent have a turnover over 3,600 USD. However, state MFOs take on average 43 days to distribute collateralized loans, with an average duration of 37.07 months. Interestingly, 33.30 per cent of state MFOs' clients used loans from commercial banks, and only 6.25 per cent used loans from friends and family. Also state MFO's clients have a lower mean number of previous loans with MFOs (only two in contrast to four of both private and foreign MFOs). Thus, in comparison with foreign and private MFOs, state MFOs have a bureaucratic loan distribution process, which attracts entrepreneurs with substantial assets used as collateral and transparent financial records. Hence state MFOs are targeting entrepreneurs in the agricultural sector with established businesses, a high amount of accumulated assets, and low information asymmetries.

DISCUSSION AND CONCLUSIONS

The results of this study provide new insights into the microfinance funding of entrepreneurs in transition economies. In contrast to the extant literature which sees commercialization as undermining the development role of microfinance (Hoque and Chishty, 2011; Sonnekalb, 2014), this study demonstrates that microfinance offers an alternative to conventional external funding by providing entrepreneurs with short-term loans. Commercial banks overlook the entrepreneurs (Beck et al., 2009; Bigsten et al., 2003), who are in need of short-term loans due to their information asymmetries (Mac an Bhaird and Lucey, 2011). As a result private MFOs, which are commercialized MFOs, fill the niche that arises, and are able to attract established entrepreneurs who are in immediate need of working capital. Moreover, as private MFOs are focused upon flexibility and fast distribution in their processes, entrepreneurs are able to obtain the required working capital without any delays or excessive bureaucratic procedures. This aspect highlights the role of MFOs as an additional and alternative financial source for entrepreneurs. In fact, it appears that clients of both private and foreign MFOs tend to obtain short-term MFO loans for day-to-day purposes, and at the same time use longer-term loans from commercial banks. Hence the role of the MFOs goes beyond poverty alleviation, and becomes a provider of working capital for entrepreneurs. This argument is supported by the Vogelgesang (2003) who previously suggested that, despite high interest rates, MFOs are able to maintain their client base, as entrepreneurs recognize the value of short-term loans. The problem of high interest rates arises for private MFOs as a result of the flexibility of their evaluation process and inability to secure funding other than from commercial banks. Nevertheless, such funding sources do indeed contribute to the evident diversity of Kazakhstan's microfinance sector.

Private MFOs utilize commercial bank loans and their owners' personal wealth. As a result, they are oriented toward profit generation and distribute mainly collateralized loans to ensure high repayment rates and decrease their own risks. On the other hand, foreign MFOs are funded by international organizations that are mostly concerned with outreach, which results in their focus on fulfillment of their social mission and work with poor segments of the population. Finally, state MFOs are guided by governmental policy to develop the agricultural sector. As such, the three different types of MFOs emerge as being complementary rather than competitive, as their target markets have different MFO funding needs and requirements.

Still, private and foreign MFOs in Kazakhstan are targeting entrepreneurs with limited access to external funding due to their inability to prove their income or because they lack collateral and cannot comply with the formal requirements of the commercial banks. State MFOs target entrepreneurs who are registered and maintain established agricultural entities. This finding demonstrates that within the Kazakhstani microfinance sector, the diversity goes beyond the debate of outreach and sustainability. In fact, Morduch (2000) argued that the existing perception within microfinance research which promotes the idea of self-sustainable MFOs serving the poor, is an illusion rather than a depiction of reality. This theme was also evident within the results of this study. The foreign MFOs were able to focus upon their social mission, because they had the support of international institutions. The private MFOs however, could only survive and maintain their sustainability by targeting established entrepreneurs with collateral. This study detected a new type of MFO, that is, the state MFO, which is not focused on providing loans for the poor segments of the population or short-term loans for the working capital needs of entrepreneurs to ensure profitability. Instead, state MFOs only provided loans to well-established agricultural entities. Hence it remains unclear whether state MFOs represent a viable business model that fulfils long-term policy targets, since such entrepreneurs with substantial assets and profits are also targeted by commercial banks.

Taking into consideration this study's findings of the diversity within the microfinance industry, several important research and policy implications arise. First, the commercialization of MFOs provides a new alternative for entrepreneurs overlooked by commercial banks to fulfil their need for working capital. Second, microfinance is multilateral and heterogeneous with three different target markets and thus, microfinance research must go beyond the dichotomy of outreach and sustainability. Third, the funding sources of MFOs influence the procedures and objectives of their role as funding institutions.

Future research is required and recommended to further identify and evaluate the diversity within the MFO sector beyond the geographical boundaries of Kazakhstan. Future studies can focus upon the performance of each type of MFO globally, and their influence upon entrepreneurs' potential business growth and entrepreneurial development. Such future research could also explore in detail the state MFOs' operations to identify their viability within modern developing and/or transition economies. According to Sergey, a key informant who has worked in the Kazakhstani microfinance sector for more than 15 years: 'microfinance will always have its own niche, because banks are not able or do not want to occupy this niche . . . that is exactly small business'. From a policy perspective, our findings thus recommend a review of existing programme targets in Kazakhstan and other transition economies, focusing on outreach-oriented rather than sustainability-driven MFOs. Entrepreneurial evidence from Kazakhstan shows that it is necessary to review the policy approach to microfinance commercialization and more generally, acknowledge its wide, ongoing and diverse impact on the poor and entrepreneurs across the Global South. Moreover, it is probable that the diversity within the microfinance sector extends beyond the three types of MFOs identified in our study, and can vary from one context to another. Hence, future research can expand in this direction by further conceptualizing the diverse nature of MFOs in both transition and developing economies.

NOTE

*   To protect the identities of our participants, only pseudonyms are used in this chapter.

REFERENCES

Ahlin, C. and Jiang, N. (2008), 'Can micro-credit bring development?', *Journal of Development Economics*, **86** (1): 1–21.

Armendariz, B. and Morduch, J. (2010), *The Economics of Microfinance*, Cambridge, MA: The MIT Press.

Baklouti, I. and Baccar, A. (2013), 'Evaluating the predictive accuracy of microloan officers' subjective judgment', *International Journal of Research Studies in Management*, **2** (2): 21–34.

Barth, J.R., Lin, D. and Yost, K. (2011), 'Small and medium enterprise financing in transition economies', *Atlantic Economic Journal*, **39** (1): 19–38.

Bateman, M. and Chang, H.J. (2012), 'Microfinance and the illusion of development: from hubris to nemesis in thirty years', *World Economic Review*, **1**: 13–36.

Beck, T., Demirgüç-Kunt, A. and Honohan, P. (2009), 'Access to financial services: measurement, impact, and policies', *The World Bank Research Observer*, **24**: 119–145.

Behr, P., Entzian, A. and Güttler, A. (2011), 'How do lending relationships affect access to credit and loan conditions in microlending?', *Journal of Banking and Finance*, **35** (8): 2169–2178.

Bigsten, A., Collier, P., Dercon, S., Fafchamps, M., Gauthier, B., Gunning, J.W. and Al, E. (2003), 'Credit constraints in manufacturing enterprises in Africa', *Journal of African Economies*, **12** (1): 104–125.

Bruton, G.D., Ahlstrom, D. and Obloj, K. (2008), 'Entrepreneurship in emerging economies: where are we today and where should the research go in the future', *Entrepreneurship Theory and Practice*, **32** (1): 1–14.

Bruyat, C. and Julien, P.A. (2000), 'Defining the field of research in entrepreneurship', *Journal of Business Venturing*, **16** (2): 165–180.

Carpenter, R.E. and Peterson, B.C. (2002), 'Is the growth of small firms constrained by internal finance?', *The Review of Economics and Statistics*, **84** (2): 298–309.

Cassar, G. and Holmes, S. (2003), 'Capital structure and financing of SMEs: Australian evidence', *Accounting and Finance*, **43** (2): 123–147.

Chelariu, C., Brashear, T.G., Osmonbekov, T. and Zait, A. (2008), 'Entrepreneurial propensity in a transition economy: exploring micro-level and meso-level cultural antecedents', *Journal of Business and Industrial Marketing*, **23** (6): 405–415.

Churchill, C. (2000), 'Banking on customer loyalty', *Journal of Microfinance*, **2** (2): 1–22.

Collins, D., Morduch, J., Rutherford, S. and Ruthven, O. (2009), *Portfolios of the Poor: How the World's Poor Live on Two Dollars a Day*, Princeton, NJ: Princeton University Press.

Cook, P. (2001), 'Finance and small and medium-sized enterprise in developing countries', *Journal of Developmental Entrepreneurship*, **6** (1): 17–24.

Cull, R., Davis, L.E., Lamoreaux, N.R. and Rosenthal, J.L. (2006), 'Historical financing of small- and medium-size enterprises', *Journal of Banking and Finance*, **30** (11): 3017–3042.

Dasgupta, R. (2005), 'Micro finance in India: empirical evidence, alternate models, and policy imperatives', *Economic and Political Weekly*, **40** (12): 1229–1237.

Erdener, C. (2011), 'Business ethics as a field of teaching, training, and research in central Asia', *Journal of Business Ethics*, **104** (1): 7–18.

Fogel, K., Lee, K. and Mccumber, W. (2011), 'Institutional impact on the outreach and profitability of microfinance organizations', in Audretsch, D.B., Falck, O. and Heblich, S. (eds), *Handbook of Research and Innovation and Entrepreneurship*, Cheltenham, UK and Northampton, MA, USA: Edward Elgar Publishing, Chapter 10.

Gachet, N. and Staehli, V. (2008), 'Formalisation through micro-finance: an empirical study in Egypt', Working Paper No. 52. Social Finance Program.

Goedhuys, M. and Sleuwaegen, L. (2000), 'Entrepreneurship and growth of entrepreneurial firms in Cote D'Ivoire', *Journal od Development Studies*, **36** (3): 122–145.

Gonzalez-Vega, C. (1998), 'Microfinance: broader achievements and new challenges, economics and sociology', Occasional Paper No. 2518, Ohio State University. Department of Agricultural, Environmental, and Development Economics, retrieved from http://kb.osu.edu/dspace/handle/1811/66761 (accessed 11 August 2015).

Hartarska, V. and Gonzalez-Vega, C. (2006), 'What affects new and established firms' expansion? Evidence from small firms in Russia', *Small Business Economics*, **27** (2–3): 195–206.

Hoque, M. and Chishty, M. (2011), 'Commercialization and changes in capital structure in microfinance institutions an innovation or wrong turn?', *Managerial Finance*, **37** (5): 414–425.

Hubner, W. (2000), 'SME development in countries of central Asia (Kazakhstan, Kyrgyzstan and Uzbekistan): constraints, cultural aspects and role of international assistance', Austria: United Nations Industrial Development Organization (UNIDO).

Jappelli, T. and Pagano, M. (2002), 'Information sharing, lending and defaults: cross-country evidence', *Journal of Banking and Finance*, **26** (10): 2017–2045.

Low, P.K.C. (2006), 'Father leadership and small business management: the Kazakhstan perspective', *Journal of Management Development*, **26** (8): 723–736.

Luthans, F. and Ibrayeva, E.S. (2006), 'Entrepreneurial self-efficacy in Central Asian transition economies: quantitative and qualitative analyses', *Journal of International Business Studies*, **37** (1): 92–110.

Mac An Bhaird, C. and Lucey, B. (2011), 'An empirical investigation for the financial growth lifecycle', *Journal of Small Business and Enterprise Development*, **18** (4): 715–731.

Mair, J. and Marti, I. (2009), 'Entrepreneurship in and around institutional voids: a case study from Bangladesh', *Journal of Business Venturing*, **24** (5): 419–435.

McIntosh, C. and Wydick, B. (2005), 'Competition and microfinance', *Journal of Development Economics*, **78** (2): 271–298.

Morduch, J. (2000), 'The microfinance schism', *World Development*, **28** (4): 617–629.

Morduch, J. and Haley, B. (2002), 'Analysis of the effects of microfinance on poverty', Working Paper No. 1014. New York: Wagner Graduate School of Public Service, New York University.

Newman, K.L. (2000), 'Organizational transformation during institutional upheaval', *Academy of Management Review*, **25** (3): 602–619.

Nguyen, T.H., Alam, Q. and Prajogo, P. (2008), 'State and market relationships: public financial policy support for SMEs growth in Vietnam', *International Review of Business Research Papers*, **4** (2): 203–216.

Nichter, S. and Goldmark, L. (2009), 'Small Firm growth in developing countries', *World Development*, **37** (9): 1453–1464.

Olivares-Polanco, F. (2005), 'Commercializing microfinance and deepening outreach? Empirical evidence from Latin America', *Journal of Microfinance*, **7** (2): 47–69.

Parker, S.C. (2009), *Economics of Entrepreneurship*, New York: Cambridge University Press.

Qayyum, A. and Ahmad, M. (2008), 'Efficiency and sustainability of micro finance institutions in South Asia', Working Paper No.11647, Munich Personal RePEc Archive.

Rahman, A. (1998), 'Micro-credit initiatives for equitable and sustainable development: Who pays?', *World Development*, **27** (1): 67–82.

Sonnekalb, S. (2014), 'Microcredit market structure and financing obstacles for micro firms', *Economics of Transition*, **22** (3): 497–538.

Statistical Agency of Republic of Kazakhstan. (2010), *Small and medium entrepreneurs* [Online]. Astana: Statistical Agency of Republic of Kazakhstan, retrieved from http://www.stat.kz/digital/mal_pred/Pages/default.aspx (accessed 30 July 2015).

Straub, S. (2005), 'Informal sector: the credit market channel', *Journal of Development Economics*, **78** (2): 299–321.

Vogelgesang, U. (2003), 'Microfinance in times of crisis: the effects of competition, rising indebtedness, and economic crisis on repayment behavior', *World Development*, **31** (12): 2085–2114.

Welter, F. (2010), 'Contextualizing entrepreneurship-conceptual challenges and ways forward', *Entrepreneruship Theory and Practice*, **35** (1): 165–184.

Zahra, S.A. (2007), 'Contextualizing theory building in entrepreneurship research', *Journal of Business Venturing*, **22** (3): 433–452.

Zahra, S.A., Wright, M. and Abdelgawad, S.G. (2014), 'Contextualization and the advancement of entrepreneurship research', *International Small Business Journal*, **32** (5): 479–500.

14. Entrepreneurial finance, poverty reduction and gender: the case of women entrepreneurs' microloans in Pakistan
Javed G. Hussain, Samia Mahmood and Jonathan M. Scott

INTRODUCTION

While financial exclusion is a challenge for developed economies irrespective of gender, it is more acute in developing economies where the financial environment is often underdeveloped and challenging. The problems are further exacerbated where illiteracy, inadequate health facilities and poor infrastructure cause acute poverty and the exit route is often via entrepreneurship or skills acquisition through education. Researchers have established a link between entrepreneurship, economic growth, employment, better health and educational achievement (Wennekers and Thurik, 1999). In the case of microenterprises (MEs) and women entrepreneurs (WEs) in developing economies, entrepreneurial initiatives are hampered by a lack of business networks, social networks and access to finance. Among many constraints faced by WEs, finance appears to be the dominant barrier resulting in negative impacts on the welfare of individuals, as well as their families, community and country.

A low propensity to save – coupled with information asymmetry, lack of financial education and collateral among the poor – becomes a challenge for lenders. To make the unbankable bankable, it is essential to provide an enabling environment and access to credit for enterprise development (Morrison et al., 2007). Formal financial institutions are reluctant to provide credit to MEs due to loan sizes, credit histories, moral hazard and asymmetric information that increase the risk of adverse selection for the banks (Armendariz de Aghion and Morduch, 2005). Financially excluded people, therefore, prefer to borrow from informal sources, rely on their own savings and finance from family and friends, and as a last resort approach external finance providers, in line with the pecking order hypothesis (POH) (Berger and Udell, 1998). However, informal sources neither have the capacity nor appetite to meet the needs of MEs (Bhatt and Tang, 2001), who often live at the fringes of society and are dispossessed.

To meet the needs of financially excluded people, governmental development programmes and non-governmental organizations (NGOs) intervene through the provision of subsidized loans to reduce poverty and to increase community well-being. However, these interventions, as Goheer (1999) suggests, though well intended, benefit richer landlords rather than the poor in the past. This empirical finding suggests the need for targeted and inclusive programmes not only to overcome the problems of formal and informal credit networks, but also to bridge the gap in the provision of credit facilities for MEs.

Microfinance has been hailed as one of the most successful development programmes in the developing world (Bhatt and Tang, 2001) to support the disenfranchised and non-collateralized section of the population in both urban and rural areas. Though microfinance is provided irrespective of gender, evidence suggests that its core focus is on WEs. Women are relatively immobile, poorer than men and have lower default rates compared with men (Lucy et al., 2008). Moreover, women are effective at reducing poverty and increasing the welfare of their families and, in turn, the development of their local and national economies. In developing countries, women's economic contribution, though in many cases unaccounted for, is significant.

Yet, women tend to work within a household, are often not remunerated, hence have limited choices and inability to accumulate capital to enable them to start up. Globally, microfinance institutions (MFIs) continue to remain popular among development economists. Indeed, Brière and Szafarz (2015) reported that microfinance loans have become less risky and MFIs more closely correlated with the financial sector and, further, that microfinance has changed dramatically during the last decade: which itself requires a close examination of the role MFIs play in empowering women. Such findings suggest that microfinance provision remains something of an enigma in enabling women to access finance for their MEs.

In summary, microfinance has a significant role to play in poverty reduction, empowering women and enhancing the well-being of the family through engagement with entrepreneurial start up. There are large numbers of ME start-ups supported by MFIs, of which some have a significant impact on the well-being of families in enabling them to exit poverty – but there are failures too. This chapter examines theoretical and practical issues leading to the development of a contextualized conceptual framework that guides this study. A set of hypotheses has been formulated, tested and the findings discussed before providing conclusions and suggestions for future research.

MICROFINANCE: AN OVERVIEW OF THEORY AND PRACTICE

Poverty reduction propels the economic development of a country and results in political and socio-economic well-being (Gurses, 2009), and financial, institutional and market reforms. Financial institutions (particularly in developing economies) that exclude marginalized sections of society, for example low-income people and women, from accessing financial services such as credit, savings and insurance (Haq, 2008) can hinder country-level economic development. There is evidence that the sheer presence of financial institutions does not equally benefit all sections of the population, specifically the poor. To overcome this shortcoming, microfinance has gained greater acceptance. Microfinance, indeed, originated in the early fifteenth century in the form of pawnshops and the seventeenth century Irish loan fund system for uncollateralized poor farmers (Helms, 2006). Over the last several decades, microfinance has emerged as a tool of policy and practice to alleviate poverty. In particular, its success in several districts of Bangladesh in 1972 (Sengupta and Aubuchon, 2008) has evoked a resurgence of interest within this field. Microfinance is now considered to be a practical solution for poverty alleviation and reducing social inequalities (Kanak and Iiguni, 2007). It has been suggested that there exists a need for microfinance in developed economies too (Schreiner and Woller, 2003), but that topic is beyond the scope of this chapter.

Microfinance serves the financially excluded who have no collateral for loans to engage in an income-generating activity (Islam, 2009). The unique features of microfinance include other financial services such as savings, insurance and money transfer (Sengupta and Aubuchon, 2008). The loans offered have other distinctive characteristics that comprise innovative lending techniques, such as group lending, progressive lending, accepting informal collateral, small instalments with frequent repayments and repayment in public. These facilities are not offered by large financial institutions, partly because loan sizes are simply not economical and, in part, they do not wish to take on high risks. However, it is now acknowledged that group and community lending both lower default rates and community reference is a substitute for credit history and reduces the risk of moral hazard and adverse selection (Armendariz de Aghion and Morduch, 2005; Rallen and Ghazanfar, 2006).

The role played by microfinance has, though, been performed for centuries by informal savings and credit groups who supported low-income people (Helms, 2006). Other groups exist, such as the Rotating Saving and Credit Association (ROSCA) and the Credit Cooperative or Credit Union. However, these organizations lack capacity to meet the needs of the poor due to limited capital, flexibility in loan sizes and their time-consuming administration (Rallen and Ghazanfar, 2006). Microfinance is related to two Millennium Development Goals (MDGs) that aim to mitigate extreme poverty and gender inequality (Mawa, 2008). Poverty is complex and cannot be measured only in monetary terms, such as lack of income, assets and resources; it is a comprehensive term including lack of non-monetary resources such as health, education, self-respect and independence (Cagatay, 1998). Human poverty influences financial or income poverty (Ravalion, 1996). The United Nations Development Programme (UNDP) (2008) considers poverty not only in terms of income or expenditure but includes non-quantifiable items, such as access to health services, basic education, security and independence, a definition that is consistent with that offered by Cagatay (1998). Weiss et al. (2003) argued that, in order to reduce poverty, it is necessary to appreciate its causes, consequences and reasons. The concept of poverty is non-static and, therefore, a definition needs to take into account the duration of poverty, the ownership of assets, its transitory or permanent nature, whether it is due to external shock or is health-related. The chronically poor can be destitute due to their physical or social disadvantage and remain poor without support, living below the poverty line. Microfinance thus serves different groups of the poor differently.

Morrison et al. (2007) suggest that developing countries with gender equality have lower levels of poverty; hence the third MDG aims to persuade MFIs to promote gender equality, as gender inequality has a negative impact on economic growth and poverty reduction. This assertion is supported by Francisco's (2007) study in South East Asian countries that reported that gender inequalities obstruct socio-economic growth and development. Based on the evidence from these countries, it is rational to develop bespoke gender equality policies and programmes for different groups experiencing differential levels of poverty.

Gender disparities are due to cultural, religious and legal inequalities that have affected the distribution of income, access to credit, control over property, the labour market and politico-economic institutions (Cagatay, 1998). Similarly, Lucy et al. (2008) found that Bangladeshi women and children bear the brunt of the poverty burden in comparison to men. Therefore, there is a need to formulate macroeconomic policies to reduce poverty and gender inequalities (Cagatay, 1998). Jones et al. (2006) showed that women's status in the household increases due to their contribution to such economic activity; it also leads to broader empowerment at individual, household, community and societal levels. Therefore, access to credit for women is essential (Cagatay, 1998) for their welfare and that of their families.

With the issues of poverty and gender inequality in mind, the most important challenges faced by most of the developing world and in some cases in pockets of developed countries too require strategies and development programmes, such as microfinance, which promote self-reliance (Mawa, 2008). A number of studies have been conducted on the issue of poverty reduction by microfinance; however, there are a few empirical studies but these have contradictory results (Hermes and Lensink, 2007). Various studies (Morris and Barnes, 2005; Khandker et al., 1998; Chemin, 2008; Chowdhury et al., 2005; Khandker, 2005; Pitt and Khandker, 1998; Pitt, 1999) found a positive impact of microfinance upon poverty reduction. Nevertheless, other studies show no evidence of an impact of microfinance upon poverty reduction (Coleman, 1999, 2006). The above literature suggests a gap in knowledge about the effects of microfinance upon poverty alleviation through entrepreneurial activity. Furthermore, this study extends the countries studied and attempts to identify the real impact microloans had on poverty reduction among women and their families. This study is based on a conceptual framework related to poverty reduction as a three-phased process through entrepreneurship (Mahmood et al., 2014). The authors focused on the first two phases of *Failure* and *Improvement*. The first phase is when women face poverty that limits their role as an entrepreneur. However, with the access to microloans, they engaged in enterprise and exited poverty. In view of the above discussion and gap in the literature, the research question for this study is: 'Do microloans help to reduce the levels of poverty of women in developing countries through entrepreneurship?'

The research question leads to two hypotheses. The proposed hypotheses are:

H1: *The increase in microloan size decreases the financial poverty of women borrowers.*

H2: *The increase in microloan size decreases the human poverty of women borrowers*

METHODOLOGY

The data utilized in this chapter have been collected from 116 self-administered semi-structured questionnaires from women who borrowed from three MFIs in order to support their income-generating activities. These WEs had household incomes of no more than Rs.[1] 180,000[2] (£1,133.98)[3] per annum before taking microloans into consideration.

Hence the sample is aligned with the first phase of the conceptual framework of 'Failure' where women are poor and have no access to credit before they obtained microfinance (Mahmood et al., 2014). Data were collected in 2011 in Pakistan's Punjab province, in which a growing number of MFIs have been established in the last decade. Pakistan's microfinance sector has received substantial government attention in recent years due to its potential to assist with poverty alleviation and the support of start-ups by women (World Bank, 2007). Although serving both men and women, due to women's higher repayment rates many MFIs prefer women borrowers. To achieve geographical variety, the three selected organizations are located in the urban districts of Lahore and Gujranwala and the rural districts of Vehari and Kasur of Punjab province. Indeed, Punjab province has the highest percentage (70 per cent)[4] of active borrowers of microfinance in Pakistan, while the Lahore and Gujranwala districts have the highest percentage of active borrowers in the region (Khalid, 2010). Purposive sampling was employed to select women borrowers who were having their bi-monthly meetings during the fieldwork period and they were given questionnaires to collect data[5] that was later subjected to rigorous quantitative analysis. A total of 116 completed questionnaires were returned, which is judged by Saunders et al. (2003) to be an acceptable number on which to conduct statistical analysis. The study was designed so that a roughly equal number of questionnaires would be completed from each of the MFIs with a mix of data from rural and urban areas in order to achieve consistency and rigour of both sampling and subsequent analysis.

The questionnaire comprised questions on poverty, including relevant financial indicators (such as income, expenditures on necessity goods and savings after microfinance) and non-financial indicators of human poverty (for example, basic health and education after microfinance), both of which were collected qualitatively as dichotomous variables and were thus perceptual variables. Such perceptual concepts of poverty, therefore, imply the second phase of 'Improvement', which involves the reduction of poverty through microfinance interventions. Hence these are the foundations of both hypotheses and they have been analysed using binary logistic regression in order to infer a relationship between poverty reduction – represented by the aforementioned financial poverty reduction (FPR) and human poverty reduction (HPR) – indicators and microfinance.

The independent variable used is the size of the microloan, a categorical variable with 'Rs. 5,000–15,000 (£31–£95)'[6] coded as 1, 'Rs. 15,000–25,000 (£95–£158)' as 2, and 'more than Rs. 25,000 (> £158)' as 3. Some other categorical variables that were used, which have been assumed to affect the relationship, have been presented descriptively in Table 14.1.

Table 14.1   Independent variables statistics

Variables	Percentage	Variables	Percentage
Age of Women (in years)		*Entrepreneurship Training*	
18–39	67%	*Provided by MFI*	
40–more than 40	33%	Yes	53%
		No	47%
Education of Women		*Applied for Bank Loan*	
No education,	53%	Yes	7%
School/College/University/	47%	No	93%
Professional education			
Number of Children		*Increase in Business Profit*	
No children	12%	*after Microfinance*	
1–4 children	53%	Yes	84%
5 and more	35%	No	16%
Family System		*Membership Years in MFIs*	
Nuclear	59%	0–1 year	22%
Joint	41%	1–3 years	36%
		3–5 years	42%
Household Head		*Business Sector*	
Woman	27%	Manufacturing	27%
Husband	45%	Services	35%
Both	28%	Retail and Livestock	38%
Business Experience of Women		*Microloan Size (amount in*	
Less than 1 year – 2 years	23%	*Rupees)*	
3–5 years	26%	5000–15,000 – low	47%
6–10 and more years	51%	15,001–25,000 – medium	35%
		25,001–35,000 and more	18%
		– high	
Enterprise Developed by Women			
Existing enterprise	86%		
Newly established enterprise	14%		

A multicollinearity test has been run to check the collinearity between independent variables; and shows that the predictor variables are not correlated as the values of tolerance are not less than 0.1 and the variance inflation factor (VIF) is not greater than ten.

In order to run logistic regression, we needed to use one dependent variable of FPR and HPR each – both of which had three discrete indicators that were combined into one dependent variable. Hence FPR had three indicators ('increase in household income', 'increase in expenditure on necessity goods' and 'increase in savings') as did HPR ('increase in women's health', 'increase in family health' and 'increase in children's education'). Principal Component Analysis (PCA) has not been used to composite the variables as it would have caused the loss of information from the indicators' categories. There are many ways to composite the indicators, but mean or average has been selected as it can help to retain correctly the information on the categories of the indicators of 'No' coded as 0 and 'Yes' coded as 1.

According to Ravalion (1996), the aggregate of multiple indicators into a single variable should not be without any justification. Therefore, the Spearmen's rho correlation has been measured to find the strength of the indicators before compositing. The indicators for each variable of FPR and HPR were checked for correlation and all of the indicators for each variable have been correlated at the 1 per cent significance level. The reliability of indicators of each variable has been checked by Cronbach's Alpha for which the value is .637 for FPR and .655 for HPR. Therefore, the indicators for each variable of FPR and HPR were correlated as reliable and can be composited to represent those variables.

RESULTS

Binary logistic regression has been used to measure the impact of the size of microloans on the likelihood that financial poverty was reduced after a microloan was obtained. The model contained one variable of interest; that is, 'microloan size'. The other variables used are displayed in Table 14.1. The full model containing all predictors is statistically significant, $\chi2$ (13, N = 116) = 54.279, p < .01, indicating that the model is able to distinguish between the WEs that have or have not experienced financial poverty reduction after obtaining microfinance. The model, as a whole, explained between 40.4 per cent (Cox–Snell R square) and 59.3 per cent (Nagelkerke R square) of the variance in the reduction of financial poverty, and correctly classified these in 84.8 per cent of cases. Moreover, Table 14.2 shows that only three of the variables (*viz* 'microloan size', 'increase in business profit after microfinance', and 'household head') made a statistically significant contribution to the model. The loan size predictor indicated that women obtaining a medium-sized loan were over seven times (odd ratio of 7.769) more likely to report a reduction of their financial poverty than those who obtained a smaller loan, controlling for all other factors in the model. Similarly, the women obtaining a larger loan were over 36 times more likely to report a reduction of their financial poverty than those who obtained low and medium-sized loans, with all other variables remaining constant. This result shows that H1 is supported by the logistic regression model.

Table 14.2   Logistic regression estimation of financial and human poverty reduction

	Financial poverty reduction (FPR) after microfinance			Human poverty reduction (HPR) after microfinance		
	Coef. B	Sig. P	Odds ratio Exp B	Coef. B	Sig. P	Odds ratio Exp B
Constant	0.936	.375	2.550	−1.702	.032	.182
Microloan Size						
Low	−			−		
Medium	2.050*	.028	7.769	−.254	.708	.776
High	3.610*	.012	36.950	−.891	.299	.410
Membership Years in MFIs						
0–1 year	−			−		
1–3 years	−1.459	.185	.232	−.100	.896	.905
3–5 years	−1.549	.231	.213	−1.699	.076	5.470
Age						
18–39 years	−			−		
More than 40	−.943	.318	.389	−.385	.586	1.470
Education						
No education	−			−		
School/College/Uni.	.062	.945	1.064	.082	.902	1.086
Children						
No children	−			−		
1–4 children	1.804	.203	6.074	2.745**	.010	15.570
5 and more	1.473	.329	4.362	2.601*	.031	13.475
Household Head						
Woman	−			−		
Husband	.898	.260	2.456	.581	.393	1.788
Both	2.559*	.029	12.917	.992	.219	2.697
Family System						
Nuclear	−			−		
Joint	1.423	.120	4.150	1.022	.111	2.779
Applied for Bank loan						
Yes	−			−		
No	−1.427	.303	.240	.573	.553	1.774
Entrepreneurship Training Provided by MFI						
Yes	−			−		
No	.712	.386	2.038	.615	.301	1.850

	Financial poverty reduction (FPR) after microfinance			Human poverty reduction (HPR) after microfinance		
	Coef. B	Sig. P	Odds ratio Exp B	Coef. B	Sig. P	Odds ratio Exp B
Enterprise Developed by Women						
Existing enterprise	–			–		
Newly established enterprise	.318	.828	1.375	−.391	.662	.676
Business Sector						
Manufacturing	–			–		
Services	−.460	.659	.631	.312	.677	1.365
Retail and Livestock	−1.700	.092	.183	−.070	.925	.925
Business Experience of Women						
Less than 1 year – 2 years	–			–		
3–5 years	−1.020	.408	.361	.004	.997	1.004
6–10 and more years	−1.403	.226	.246	−.456	.545	.634
Increase in Business Profit after Microfinance						
Yes	–			–		
No	−5.625**	.002	.004	−3.612**	.000	.027

Notes:
FP Notes: – indicates the reference category; number of obs. = 116; R^2 = .565 (Hosmer–Lemeshow), .404 (Cox–Snell), .593 (Nagelkerke); Model χ^2 = 54.279, p < .01; * p < .05, **p < .01.
HP Notes: – indicates the reference category; number of obs. = 116, R^2 = .526 (Hosmer–Lemeshow), .338 (Cox–Snell), .459 (Nagelkerke); Model χ^2 = 43.248, p < .01; * p < .05, **p < .01.

Two additional variables, 'household head' and 'increase in business profit', were also significant. The former demonstrated that women were more likely to report a reduction of poverty if both spouses were joint heads of the family, as compared with only one spouse. However, if the head of the family was the woman's husband, then this relationship was not significant. The odd ratio of .002 for increase in business profit is less than 1, indicating that women with increased business profit after obtaining a microloan were .002 times less likely to report reduced financial poverty in comparison with women with decreased business profit, controlling for all the factors in the model (Pallant, 2007, pp. 177–178).

Binary logistic regression has been run to assess the impact of microloan size on the likelihood of a reduction of their human poverty. The model contained thirteen variables. The full model containing all predictors is statistically significant χ^2 (13, N = 116) = 43.248, p < .01, indicating that the model is able to distinguish between the women with or without a reduction of their human poverty. The model as a whole explained between 33.8 per cent (Cox–Snell R square) and 45.9 per cent (Nagelkerke R square) of the variance in human poverty reduction, and correctly classified 75.2 per cent of cases. Table 14.2 shows that only two independent variables – the number of children and an increase in business profit after microfinance – made a statistically significant contribution to the model. The number of children predictor indicates that women having 1–4 children were 15 times (odd ratio of 15.570, p < .01) and women having 5 or more children were 13 times (odd ratio 13.475, p < .05) more likely to report a reduction of their human poverty than if they were childless, while controlling for all other factors in the model.

There was less probability of a reduction of their human poverty if there was an increase in business profit after obtaining a microloan in comparison with cases where there was no profit increase. The odd ratio of .032 for the increase in business profit is less than 1, indicating that women with increased business profit after obtaining microfinance are .032 times less likely to report a reduction of their human poverty in comparison with women with decreased business profit, controlling for all the factors in the model. The variable of interest 'loan size' is not significant and thus H2 is not supported. The models used in binary logistic regression were run with linear regression to check the robustness of the results and they showed overall that our results for financial and human poverty remain robust under the linear regression model.

DISCUSSION

The reported empirical results suggested that microfinance helped WEs to overcome financial poverty but did not contribute significantly to reducing human poverty. A closer examination of the results suggested that reduced financial poverty was positively correlated with loans of medium or large size, rather than small loans. This result showed that women taking higher amounts of loans were more likely to escape from the vicious circle of poverty that they faced after they increased their income, expenditures and savings. Therefore, we accept H1 at p < .05 for medium and large loans, thus supporting prior evidence of the positive outcome of microfinance on income and expenditure (Chemin, 2008). The 'household head' variable gives further insight that, when both spouses are joint heads of the household, financial poverty was further reduced. It shows that the equal position of a woman in a household can reduce financial poverty, which is an important implication for policymakers. Accordingly, the women in our sample moved from the 'Failure' phase to the 'Improvement' phase after accessing microloans.

The second hypothesis is not supported as there is no probability of a reduction of their human poverty as the loan size increases. Women borrowers are generally not the main decision-makers in the household and less involvement of women in the decision-making process can impact the decisions relating to the health and education of their children and family (Banerjee et al., 2015). Therefore, loans did not impact on the reduction of human poverty by increasing health and children's education. A number of studies provided evidence of a positive impact of microfinance upon family well-being (for example, Copestake et al., 2001; Ghalib et al., 2015; Mamun et al., 2011; Montgomery, 2006). However, the extent to which microfinance reduces their human poverty depends upon the proper and appropriate use of the loan to support income-generating projects. Given that Banerjee et al. (2015) show that expenditure on durable goods by the recipient increased after obtaining a microloan, proper use of microloans on entrepreneurial activities can help to reduce human poverty and financial poverty. Moreover, it is possible that financial poverty reduction is more visible in the short run in comparison with human poverty reduction which may require longer term germination. Observation of human poverty indicators in a short time period does not provide rich results because of changes in household poverty levels over time (Ravalion, 1996) and it is beyond the scope of this study to differentiate the impact of microfinance upon the chronic and transient poor.

Further, the significant variable 'number of children' interestingly indicated that households that have larger numbers of children have greater chances of increasing the welfare of women and their family. To some extent, this result runs counter to the presuppositions and assumptions of development specialists who seek, through healthcare interventions (such as birth control) to reduce the size of families because they correlate large family sizes and poverty, whereas larger family sizes may, in fact, be an outcome of poverty[7] and not vice versa. This significant variable, though not the variable of interest, has key implications for policymakers for poverty reduction through the use of microfinance.

Both of our binary logistic models demonstrate that the variable of 'increase in business profit after microfinance' is significant and has a negative relationship in relation to the reduction of their human and financial poverty. This result shows that the income earned from entrepreneurship may be reinvested in the microenterprise to generate more profit in the future and hence may also not help to reduce their human poverty in the short or even medium term. The cross-sectional nature of the data and the small sample size (although large enough for statistical analysis (Saunders et al., 2003)) is not able to capture the long-term benefit achieved by women borrowers from microfinance which might be feasible in the case of larger-scale, longitudinal datasets.

Ravalion (1996) has also recommended the use of repeated cross-sectional surveys to capture the dynamic properties of poverty. Therefore, further investigation is required to find the long-term impact of the usage of microloans by WEs. Mosley and Rock (2004) view the advantage of microfinance from a larger and long-term perspective in six African MFIs. Their study establishes that microfinance in an area benefits the whole community indirectly due to the enhancement of the labour market, human and social capital in the long run (ibid). However, the success of the loan depends on the proper utilization of the microfinance services for development purposes, which also minimizes pilferage (ibid). A study of this kind would be of value if conducted in other developing countries, such as in South Asia, specifically in Pakistan.

Overall, microloans help women borrowers to escape from financial poverty when they use their fledgling entrepreneurial skills, although the reduction of their human poverty is negligible in the shorter term.

CONCLUDING COMMENTS

The overarching aim of this chapter was to examine the impact of microfinance, specifically microloans, and the related extent to which poverty is reduced for entrepreneurial women in a developing country, namely rural and urban districts of Punjab Province, Pakistan. We found that microloans provided finance and thus opportunities by which women could grow their business, generate income and achieve empowerment that eventually impacted positively on their families. The chapter, building on the underpinning theoretical foundations of extant microfinance studies, provided the reported empirical results that show that the size of a microloan impacted on women's poverty reduction when they were engaged in entrepreneurial activity. We examined both 'hard' quantitative financial poverty indicators and softer, perceptual qualitative-based indicators of human poverty or the welfare of women and their families. We used latent variables of poverty that have been measured, on the one hand, as financial poverty by indicators of income, savings and expenditure; and, on the other hand, as human poverty by women's health, family health and children's education. Furthermore, we explored poverty reduction by applying the conceptual model of Mahmood et al. (2014) with a focus on the first two phases of 'Failure' and 'Improvement' in the context of financial and human poverty. This model shows that access to finance can extract women borrowers from the vicious circle of poverty by using it appropriately for their entrepreneurial activities.

Results reported using binary logistic regression suggested a relationship between microfinance and the reduction of poverty. The perceptual variables of financial and human poverty have been collected by three indicators for each variable that were dichotomous in nature. Before compositing the indicators for financial and human poverty, Spearman's correlation and reliability tests were conducted which provided results of reliably correlated indicators of each variable.

This empirical study showed that large microloans were positively related to a reduction of women's financial poverty. Moreover, spouses both acting jointly as household heads also had a positive relationship with the reduction of their financial poverty. On the other hand, the loan size was not a significant variable in the case of human poverty. The more interesting results were that families with many children experienced higher human poverty reduction compared with those with fewer children. This result showed that variables other than loan size could impact on the reduction of poverty. For example, increase in business profit has a negative association with financial and human poverty and hence we may infer that women entrepreneurs required retained profits in their business venture in order to achieve growth and development. Thus human poverty reduction is a longer term process that may be achieved with the reinvestment of business profits and ultimately growth of the venture which, in turn, helped to alleviate household poverty.

The limitations of this research study is that its data is cross-sectional, collected at one point in time, that may not capture the full longitudinal and temporally contextualized impact of microfinance. This feature may explain the contradictory findings of prior studies of microfinance and poverty reduction. Moreover, the increase in the sample size with WEs at different stages of their enterprise life cycle would help us not only to understand the relationship between microfinance and human poverty reduction but also would illuminate the association between women's enterprise growth and their household welfare. The conundrum of this study, the negative association between the increase in business profit and the reduction of human poverty, needs further in-depth longitudinal or panel-based study to examine the causes and consequences of such a relationship. For this purpose, panel data or longitudinal analysis may provide better explanations for microloan-driven poverty reduction.

For practitioners and policymakers, our results suggest that different microloan sizes are helpful to reduce the financial poverty of women borrowers' households through engagement with income-generating activity. Therefore, simplified rules and procedures adopted by MFIs would be effective in comparison with more demanding commercial bank loans. In summary, the chapter augments the controversial literature on microfinance and poverty reduction in general and contributes in particular to the growing literature on women entrepreneurs and access to entrepreneurial finance.

NOTES

1. Rs.-Rupee is the currency of Pakistan.
2. It is almost $5 per day for a family with an average household size of four.
3. Mid-market rate on 4 September 2015: http://www.xe.com/currencyconverter/convert/?Amount=180000&From=PKR&To=GBP.
4. Calculated: Active borrowers in Punjab / Total Active Borrowers (Khalid, 2010).
5. Data were collected between February and April 2011.
6. 1 GBP (£) = 158.645 PKR (Rs.) on 4 September 2015, retrieved from http://www.xe.com/currencyconverter/convert/?Amount=1&From=GBP&To=PKR.
7. Or, indeed, geography: that is, traditionally larger families in rural areas due to the need to work the land.

REFERENCES

Armendariz de Aghion, B. and Morduch, J. (2005), *The Economics of Microfinance.* Cambridge, MA and London: The MIT Press.

Banerjee, A., Duflo, E., Glennerster, R. and Kinnan, C. (2015), 'The miracle of microfinance? Evidence from a randomized evaluation', *American Economic Journal: Applied Economics*, **7** (1): 22–53.

Berger, A. and Udell, G. (1998), 'The economics of small business finance: the roles of private equity and debt markets in the financial growth cycle', *Journal of Banking and Finance*, **22** (6–8): 613–673.

Bhatt, N. and Tang, S.Y. (2001), 'Designing group-based microfinance programs: some theoretical and policy considerations', *International Journal of Public Administration*, **24** (10): 1103–1125.

Brière, M. and Szafarz, A. (2015), 'Does commercial microfinance belong to the financial sector? Lessons from the stock market', *World Development*, **67** (C): 110–125.

Cagatay, N. (1998), 'Gender and poverty', Working Paper No. 5, New York: Social development and poverty elimination division, UN Development Programme.

Chemin, M. (2008), 'The benefits and costs of microfinance: evidence from Bangladesh', *Journal of Development Studies*, **44** (4): 463–484.

Chowdhury, M.J.A., Ghosh, D. and Wright, R.E. (2005), 'The impact of microcredit on poverty: evidence from Bangladesh', *Progress in Development Studies*, **5** (4): 298–309.

Coleman, B.E. (1999), 'The impact of group lending in Northeast Thailand', *Journal of Development Economics*, **60** (1): 105–141.

Coleman, B.E. (2006), 'Microfinance in Northeast Thailand: who benefits and how much?', *World Development*, **34** (9): 1612–1638.

Copestake, J., Bhalotra, S. and Johnson, S. (2001), 'Assessing the impact of microcredit: a Zambian case study', *Journal of Development Studies*, **37** (4): 81–100.

Francisco, J.S. (2007), 'Gender inequality, poverty and human development in South East Asia', *Development*, **50** (2): 103–114.

Ghalib, A., Malki, I. and Imai, K.S. (2015), 'Microfinance and household poverty reduction: empirical evidence from rural Pakistan', *Oxford Development Studies*, **43** (1): 84–104.

Goheer, N. (1999), 'Micro finance: a prescription for poverty and plight of women in rural Pakistan', *Periscope*, **2** (1), retrieved from http://www.gdrc.org/icm/country/pak-microfinance.pdf (accessed 29 April 2015).

Gurses, D. (2009), 'Microfinance and poverty reduction in Turkey', *Perspectives on Global Development and Technology*, **8** (1): 90–110.

Haq, A. (2008), *Microfinance Industry assessment: A report on Pakistan.* Islamabad: Pakistan Microfinance Network and SEE Network, retrieved from www.pmn.org.pk/assets/articles/MF%20Industry%20Assessment.pdf (accessed 29 April 2015).

Helms, B. (2006), *Access for All: Building Inclusive Financial Systems*, Washington: The World Bank, retrieved from http://www.cgap.org/sites/default/files/CGAP-Access-for-All-Jan-2006.pdf (accessed 29 April 2015).

Hermes, N. and Lensink, R. (2007), 'Impact of microfinance: a critical survey', *Economic and Political Weekly*, 10 February, pp. 462–465, retrieved from http://citeseerx.ist.psu.edu/viewdoc/download?doi=10.1.1.182.2949&rep=rep1&type=pdf (accessed 29 April 2015).

Islam, N. (2009), 'Can microfinance reduce economic insecurity and poverty? By how much and how?' DESA Working Paper No. 82, United Nations Department of Economic and Social Affairs, retrieved from http://www.un.org/esa/desa/papers/2009/wp82_2009.pdf (accessed 29 April 2015).

Jones, L., Snelgrove, A. and Muckosy, P. (2006), 'The double-X factor: harnessing female human capital for economic growth', *International Journal of Emerging Markets*, **1** (4): 291–304.

Kanak, S. and Iiguni, Y. (2007), 'Microfinance programs and social capital formation: the present scenario in a rural village of Bangladesh', *The International Journal of Applied Economics and Finance*, **1** (2): 97–104.

Khalid, Z. (2010), *MicroWatch* **18** (4), Islamabad: Pakistan Microfinance Network.

Khandker, S.R. (2005), 'Microfinance and poverty: evidence using panel data from Bangladesh', *The World Bank Economic Review*, **19** (2): 263–286.

Khandker, S.R., Samad, H.A. and Khan, Z.H. (1998), 'Income employment effects of micro-credit evidence from Bangladesh', *The Journal of Development Studies*, **35** (2): 96–124.

Lucy, D.M., Ghosh, J. and Kujawa, E. (2008), 'Empowering women's leadership: a case study of Bangladeshi microcredit business', *S.A.M. Advanced Management Journal Cincinnati*, **73** (4): 31–50.

Mahmood, S., Hussain, J. and Matlay, H. (2014), 'Optimal microloan size and poverty reduction amongst female entrepreneurs in Pakistan', *Journal of Small Business and Enterprise Development*, **21** (2): 231–249.

Mamun, A., Malarvizhi, C.A., Hossain, S. and Abdul Wahab, S. (2011), 'Examining the effect of participation in microcredit programs on assets owned by hardcore poor households in Malaysia', *African Journal of Business Management*, **5** (22): 9286–9296.

Mawa, B. (2008), 'Impact of microfinance: towards achieving poverty alleviation?', *Pakistan Journal of Social Sciences*, **5** (9): 876–882.

Montgomery, H. (2006), 'Serving the poorest of the poor: the poverty impact of the Khushhali Bank's microfinance lending in Pakistan', in J. Weiss and H. A. Khan (eds), *Poverty Strategies in Asia: A Growth Plus Approach*, Cheltenham, UK and Northampton, MA, USA: Edward Elgar Publishing, pp. 222–244.

Morris, G. and Barnes, C. (2005), 'An assessment of the impact of microfinance: a case study from Uganda', *Journal of Microfinance*, **7** (1): 39–54.

Morrison, A., Raju, D. and Sinha, N. (2007), Gender equality, poverty and economic growth. Gender and development group, poverty reduction and economic management network. WPS4339. The World Bank, retrieved from http://www.worldbank.org (accessed 6 June 2009).

Mosley, P. and Rock, J. (2004), 'Microfinance, labour markets and poverty in Africa: a study of six institutions', *Journal of International Development*, **16** (3): 467–500.

Pallant, J. (2007), *SPSS Survival Manual: A Step By Step Guide to Data Analysis Using SPSS Version 15*, Maidenhead: Open University Press.

Pitt, M. (1999), 'Reply to Jonathan Morduch's "Does microfinance really help the poor?" New evidence from flagship programs in Bangladesh'. Department of Economics. Brown University, retrieved from http://www.brown.edu/research/projects/pitt/sites/brown.edu.research.projects.pitt/files/uploads/reply_0.pdf (accessed 29 April 2015).

Pitt, M.M. and Khandker, S.R. (1998), 'The impact of group-based credit programs on poor households in Bangladesh: does the gender of participants matter?', *Journal of Political Economy*, **106** (5): 958–996.

Rallen, T. and Ghazanfar, S.M. (2006), 'Microfinance recent experience, future possibilities', *The Journal of Social, Political and Economic Studies*, **31** (2): 197–212.

Ravalion, M. (1996), Issues in measuring and modelling poverty, Policy Research Working Paper no. 1615, New York: The World Bank, retrieved from http://elibrary.worldbank.org/doi/pdf/10.1596/1813-9450-1615 (accessed 29 April 2015).

Saunders, M., Lewis, P. and Thornhill, A. (2003), *Research Methods for Business Students* (3rd edition), London: Pearson Education.

Schreiner, M. and Woller, G. (2003), 'Microenterprise development programs in the United States and in the developing world', *World Development*, **31** (9): 1567–1580.

Sengupta, R. and Aubuchon, C. (2008), 'The microfinance revolution: an overview', *Federal Reserve Bank of St. Louis Review*, January 2008: 9–30.

United Nations Development Program (2008), *Strong Institutions, Inclusive Growth: Poverty Reduction and Achievement of the MDGs*, UNDP Annual Report 2008, retrieved from http://www.undp.org/content/dam/undp/library/corporate/UNDP-in-action/2008/English/UNDP-in-action-2008-PovRed-en.pdf (accessed 29 April 2015).

Weiss, J., Montgomery, H. and Kurmanalieva, E. (2003), 'Microfinance and poverty reduction in Asia', in J. Weiss (ed.), *Poverty Targeting in Asia*, Cheltenham, UK and Northampton, MA, USA: Edward Elgar Publishing, pp. 247–268.

Wennekers, S. and Thurik, R. (1999), 'Linking entrepreneurship and economic growth', *Small Business Economics*, **13** (1): 27–55.

World Bank (2007), *Microfinance in South Asia – Towards the Financial Inclusion for the Poor*, New York: World Bank.

Index

Acaravcı, S. 72
access to finance 20
 minority entrepreneurs 169, 174–6, 180
 New Zealand 31
 opportunity exploitation 82
 small firms, transition economies 229–30
 small/marginal farmers, India 215–17
 Turkish SMEs 74–6
accreditation 53, 61–2
administrative review stage, angel investment 152, 156–9, 161
adverse selection 19, 23, 248, 250
affective trust 85
age of firm, bank manager/entrepreneur relationships 31
agri-business sector, New Zealand 38, 41, 46
Agricultural Indebtedness Report (1935) 207
alignment question, angel exit discussions 111
All India Debt and Investment Survey (1951) 208
Allinson, G. 19
Alpkan, L. 74
Amit, R. 52
Angel Co-investment Fund 142
angel investment 147
 administrative review stage 152, 156–9, 161
 due diligence stage 104, 106, 110–12, 152
 exits *see* business angel exits
 fund management 119
 legal documentation 110
 New Zealand 40–41
 post-investment stage 110
 readiness for *see* readiness for funding (study)
 returns to 104–6

screening stage 109–11, 150, 152
 successful 104–5, 117
 term sheets 112–13
 women and 147–8
 see also business angels
ANZ 39
applications funnel 131
Archangels 106
Armendariz, B. 233
arthiyas 211–12, 215, 217–21, 224
ASB 39
Ascendant Corporate Finance 114, 119
Aspire Fund 126–8, 133–4, 137, 139, 141
asset tangibility 71–2

Banerjee, A. 259
Bangladesh 232, 250–51
bank credit 28, 130, 169
bank finance
 economic growth 70
 New Zealand 31–3
 Sri Lanka 92
 unreliability of 75
 use of, Indian moneylenders 222
bank loans
 MFO clients, Kazakhstan 241–2, 244
 minority entrepreneurs, Israel 174, 176–80
 SMEs, New Zealand 32–3, 37
 SMEs, Turkey 75–7
banking sector, New Zealand 30–31, 39–40, 46
Bayraktaroğlu, A. 72–3
Beck, T. 70
behaviour (entrepreneurial) 27
Behr, P. 229, 231
Bell, C. 211
Bhaduri, A. 211
Bhalla, S. 211
Binks, M. 52
Birchall, J. 12–13
black entrepreneurs 169